Key Management Ratios

FT Prentice Hall

FINANCIAL TIMES

In an increasingly competitive world, we believe it's
quality of thinking that will give you the edge – an idea
that opens new doors, a technique that solves a
problem, or an insight that simply makes sense of it all.
The more you know, the smarter and faster you can go.

That's why we work with the best minds in business
and finance to bring cutting-edge thinking and best
learning practice to a global market.

Under a range of leading imprints, including
Financial Times Prentice Hall, we create world-class print
publications and electronic products bringing our
readers knowledge, skills and understanding which can be
applied whether studying or at work.

To find out more about our business publications, or tell us
about the books you'd like to find, you can visit us at
www.business-minds.com

For other Pearson Education publications, visit
www.pearsoned-ema.com

Key management ratios

Master the management metrics that drive and control your business

Ciaran Walsh

FT Prentice Hall
FINANCIAL TIMES

An imprint of Pearson Education

London ■ New York ■ Sydney ■ Singapore ■ Tokyo ■ Singapore ■ Hong Kong ■ Cape Town
New Delhi ■ Madrid ■ Paris ■ Amsterdam ■ Munich ■ Milan ■ Stockholm

PEARSON EDUCATION LIMITED

Head Office
Edinburgh Gate
Harlow CM20 2JE
Tel: +44 (0)1279 623623
Fax: +44 (0)1279 431059

London Office:
128 Long Acre
London WC2E 9AN
Tel: +44 (0)20 7447 2000
Fax: +44 (0)20 7447 2170
Website: www.business-minds.com

First published in Great Britain in 1996
Second edition published in Great Britain 2003

© Ciaran Walsh 2003

British Library Cataloguing in Publication Data
A CIP catalogue record for this book can be obtained from the British Library.

ISBN: 0 273 66345 3

10 9 8 7 6 5 4 3 2 1

Typeset by Pantek Arts Ltd, Maidstone, Kent
Printed and bound in Great Britain by Bell and Bain Ltd, Glasgow

The Publishers' policy is to use paper manufactured from sustainable forests.

About the Author

Ciaran Walsh is Senior Specialist Finance at the Irish Management Institute, Dublin.

He is trained both as an economist and an accountant (BSc (Econ) London, CIMA) and had 15 years' industrial experience before joining the academic world.

His work with senior managers over many years has enabled him to develop his own unique approach to training in corporate finance. As a consequence, he has lectured in most European countries, the Middle East and Eastern Europe.

His main research interest is to identify and computerize the links that tie corporate growth, and capital structure into stockmarket valuation.

He lives in Dublin and is married with six children.

He can be contacted at ciaranwalsh@eircom.net or at ciaran-walsh.com

To our grandchildren

Rebecca
Isobel
Benjamin
Eleanor
Sophie
Eve
Hanna
Holly
Grace
Aaron

Contents

Acknowledgments

I wish to express my deep gratitude to those who helped to bring about this publication. To Richard Stagg of Financial Times Prentice Hall, who originated the concept and carried it through. To my friends and colleagues: the late John O'Sullivan, who was an unequaled source of reference on even the most esoteric subjects, and John Dinan, who restarted the motor after a blow-out.

I am grateful to the staff of the Irish Management Institute Library and Dublin Central Library for their unstinted provision of all the financial data that I sought, including data from the *Financial Times* and Extel Financial Ltd, and to Geraldine McDonnell and Carol Fitzpatrick, who cheerfully coped with all the work of the section while the author was in seclusion.

Finally, I acknowledge the debt I owe to my fellow travellers: Tom Cullen; the late Des Hally; Diarmuid Moore; Martin Rafferty. They ploughed the first furrows and sowed the seed.

Foreword

The subject of corporate finance is explored in a hundred books, most of which have a formidable and forbidding aspect to them. They contain page after page of dense text interspersed with complex equations and obscure terminology.

The sheer volume of material and its method of presentation suggests that this is a subject that can be conquered only by the most hardy of adventurers. However, the truth is that the sum and substance of this area of knowledge consists of a relatively small number of essential financial measures by means of which we can appraise the success of any commericial enterprise.

These measures are derived from relationships that exist between various financial parameters in the business. While each measure in itself is simple to calculate, comprehension lies not in how to do the calculations but in understanding what these results mean and how the results of different measures mesh together to give a picture of the health of a company.

The first edition of this book set out to remove the obscurity and complexity so as to make the subject accessible to all business managers. It turned out to be very successful.

In this third edition, the same basic structure and approach is used. However, the examples and the benchmark data have been updated and expanded to make the book more relevant to a wider audience.

Data has been drawn from approximately 160 companies worldwide so the results have very wide usage.

A new chapter has been added to illustrate how the techniques used throughout the book can be used for the analysis of a proposed acquisition. It shows first how to value the two companies in relative terms and then how to value them in absolute terms using an SVA approach.

SVA is an exciting new area of analysis that all managers will want to become familiar with because it is one that will have most impact on their responsibilities over the coming years.

Key for symbols

The following icons and the concepts they represent have been used throughout this book.

 **Thinkers**

 **Checklist/summary**

 **Example**

 **Key idea**

 **Definition**

 **Action/taking note**

Part I Foundations

Background

Why do we need this book?
· The form and logic · Method
· The philosophy · Excitement
· Data that makes sense

And all I ask is a tall ship
And a star to steer her by.
JOHN MASEFIELD

Why do you need this book?

Business ratios are the guiding stars for the management of enterprises; they provide their targets and standards. They are helpful to managers in directing them towards the most beneficial long-term strategies as well as towards effective short-term decision-making.

Conditions in any business operation change day by day and, in this dynamic situation, the ratios inform management about the most important issues requiring their immediate attention. By definition the ratios show the connections that exist between different parts of the business. They highlight the important interrelationships and the need for a proper balance between departments. A knowledge of the main ratios, therefore, will enable managers of different functions to work more easily together towards overall business objectives.

The common language of business is finance. Therefore, the most important ratios are those that are financially based. The manager will, of course, understand that the financial numbers are only a *reflection* of what is actually happening and that it is the *reality* not the ratios that must be managed.

The form and logic

This book is different from the majority of business books. You will see where the difference lies if you flip through the pages. It is not so much a text as a series of lectures captured in print – a major advantage of a good lecture being the visual supports.

It is difficult and tedious to try to absorb a complex subject by reading straight text only. Too much concentration is required and too great a load is placed on the memory. Indeed, it takes great perseverance to continue on to the end of a substantial text. It also takes a lot of time, and spare time is the one thing that busy managers do not have in quantity.

 Diagrams and illustrations, on the other hand, add great power, enhancing both understanding and retention. They lighten the load and speed up progress. Furthermore, there is an elegance and form to this subject that can only be revealed by using powerful illustrations.

Managers operating in today's ever more complex world have to assimilate more and more of its rules. They must absorb a lot of information quickly. They need effective methods of communication. This is the logic behind the layout of this book.

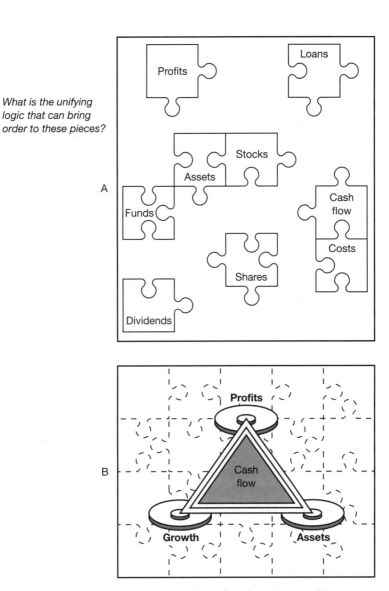

What is the unifying logic that can bring order to these pieces?

Fig. 1.1 Fitting data together for decision-making

Financial statements

*Business is really a profession often
requiring for its practice quite as much
knowledge, and quite as much skill, as
law and medicine; and requiring also the
possession of money.*
WALTER BAGEHOT (1826–1877)

Introduction

To have a coherent view of how a business performs, it is necessary, first, to have an understanding of its component parts. This job is not as formidable as it appears at first sight, because:

- much of the subject is already known to managers, who will have come in contact with many aspects of it in their work,
- while there are, in all, hundreds of components, there are a relatively small number of vital ones;
- even though the subject is complicated, it is based on common sense and can, therefore, be reasoned out once the ground rules have been established.

This last factor is often obscured by the language used. A lot of jargon is spoken and, while jargon has the advantage of providing a useful short-hand way of expressing ideas, it also has the effect of building an almost impenetrable wall around the subject that excludes or puts off the non-specialist. I will leave it to the reader to decide for which purpose financial jargon is usually used, but one of the main aims here will be to show the common sense and logic that underlies all the apparent complexity.

 Fundamental to this level of understanding is the recognition that, in finance, there are three – and only three – documents from which we obtain the raw data for our analysis. These are:

- the balance sheet
- the profit and loss account
- the cash flow statement.

A description of each of these, together with their underlying logic, follows.

The balance sheet (B/S)

The balance sheet can be looked on as an engine with a certain mass/weight that generates power output in the form of profit. You will probably remember from school the power/weight concept. It is a useful analogy here that demonstrates how a balance sheet of a given mass of assets must produce a minimum level of profit to be efficient.

But what is a balance sheet? It is simply an instant 'snapshot' of the assets used by the company and of the funds that are related to those assets. It is a static document relating to one point in time. We therefore take repeated 'snapshots' at fixed intervals – months, quarters, years – to see how the assets and funds change with the passage of time.

The profit and loss (P/L) account

The profit and loss account measures the gains or losses from both normal and abnormal operations over a period of time. It measures total income and deducts total cost. Both income and cost are calculated according to strict accounting rules. The majority of these rules are obvious and indisputable, but a small number are less so. Even though founded on solid theory, they can sometimes, in practice, produce results that appear ridiculous. While these accounting rules have always been subject to review, recent events have precipitated a much closer examination of them. Major changes are under way in the definition of such items as cash flow, subsidiary companies and so on.

Cash flow (C/F) statement

The statement of cash flow is a very powerful document. Cash flows into the company when cheques are received and it flows out when cheques are issued, but an understanding of the factors that cause these flows is fundamental.

Summary

These three statements are not independent of each other, but are linked in the system, as shown in figure 2.1. Together they give a full picture of the financial affairs of a business. Now let us look at each of these in greater detail.

The complete set of accounts consists of:

(a) opening balance sheet
(b) closing balance sheet
(c) profit and loss account
(d) cash flow statement

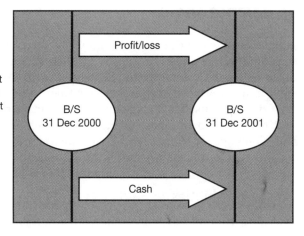

Balance sheet

The balance sheet gives a snapshot of the company assets at an instant in time, e.g.,12 o'clock midnight on 31 December 2000.
Further snapshots will be taken at fixed intervals. After each interval the sums recorded against the various components of the balance sheet will have changed.
An analysis of these changes gives crucial information about the company's activities over the period in question.

Profit and loss account

The profit and loss account quantifies and explains the gains or losses of the company over the period of time bounded by the two balance sheets.
It derives some values from both balance sheets. Therefore it is not independent of them. It is not possible to alter a value in the profit and loss account without some corresponding adjustment to the balance sheet. In this way the profit and loss account and balance sheet support one another.

Cash flow statement

The cash flow statement depends on the two balance sheets and the profit and loss account.
It links together the significant elements of all three, so that even though its inclusion in the set of accounts is the most recent in time, it is now regarded in some quarters as the most important.

Fig. 2.1 Three basic financial statements

The balance sheet

The balance sheet is the basic document of account. Traditionally it was always laid out as shown in figure 2.2, i.e., it consisted of two columns that were headed, respectively, 'Liabilities' and 'Assets.' (Note that the word 'Funds' was often used together with or in place of 'Liabilities.')

The style now used is a single-column layout (see figure 5.3). This new layout has some advantages, but it does not help the newcomer to understand the logic or structure of the document. For this reason, the two-column layout is mainly used in this publication.

Assets and liabilities

The 'Assets' column contains, simply, a list of items of value owned by the business.

The 'Liabilities' column lists amounts due to parties external to the company, including the owners.

(The company is a legal entity separate from its owners, therefore, the term 'liability' can be used in respect of amounts due from the company to its owners.)

Assets are mainly shown in the accounts at their cost (or unexpired cost). Therefore the 'Assets' column is a list of items of value at their present cost to the company. It can be looked on as a list of items of continuing value on which money has been used or spent.

The 'Liabilities' column simply lists the various sources of this same sum of money.

The amounts in these columns of course add up to the same total, because the company must identify exactly where funds were obtained from to acquire the assets.

All cash brought into the business is a source of funds, while all cash paid out is a use of funds. A balance sheet can, therefore, be looked on from this angle – as a statement of sources and uses of funds (see figure 2.3). You will find it very helpful to bear this view of the balance sheet in mind as the theme is further developed (see chapter 11 for hidden items that qualify this statement to some extent).

Assets   **Liabilities/Funds**

Assets	Liabilities/Funds
Things owned by the business	**Amounts owed** by the business
$1,000	$1,000

Traditional form of balance sheet in two columns.

This form is now superseded, but will be used here for illustrative purposes.

Fig. 2.2 The balance sheet – traditional layout

Assets	Liabilities/Funds
Uses Where money spent	**Sources** Where money obtained
$1,000	$1,000

A most useful way of looking at the financial affairs of a business is to consider its liabilities as **sources** and assets as **uses** of funds.

The two sides are merely two different aspects of the same sum of money, i.e., where the money came from and where it went to.

Fig. 2.3 The balance sheet – sources and uses of funds approach

Balance sheet structure

Figure 2.4 shows the balance sheet divided into five major blocks or boxes. These five subsections can accommodate practically all the items that make up the total document. Two of these blocks are on the assets side and three go to make up the liabilities side. We will continually come back to this five-box structure, so it is worthwhile becoming comfortable with it, as we go through each box in turn.

Let us look first at the two asset blocks. These are respectively called:

- fixed assets (FA)
- current assets (CA).

These can also be considered as 'long' and 'short' types of assets. We will see that while this distinction is important in the case of assets, it is even more significant in the case of funds.

Current assets (CA)

This box in the south-west corner contains all the short-term assets in the company. By short-term we mean that they will normally convert back into cash quickly, i.e. in a period of less than 12 months.

The various items that find their home in this box can be gathered together under four headings:

- inventories (stocks)
- accounts receivable (trade debtors)
- cash
- miscellaneous current assets.

These items (see figure 2.5) are in constant movement. Inventories of raw materials are converted into finished goods. These when sold are transformed into accounts receivable which in due course are paid in cash to the company.

The 'miscellaneous' heading covers any short-term assets not included elsewhere and is usually not significant. The amount of cash held is often small also, because it is not the function of a company to hold cash. Indeed, where there are large cash balances, there is usually a very specific reason for this, such as a planned acquisition.

The two significant items in current assets therefore are the inventories and accounts receivable. They are very important assets that often amount to 50 percent of the total balance sheet of the company.

Assets	Liabilities
Fixed assets (FA)	**OF**
	$450
$600	**LTL**
	$250
Current assets (CA)	**CL**
$400	$300
$1,000	$1,000

The basic five-box layout of the balance sheet

There are five basic sections to a balance sheet, as shown. This is a most effective format for explaining even the most difficult aspects of business finance.

Almost every item that can appear on a balance sheet will fit into one of these boxes. Each box can then be totalled and we now have a balance sheet that consists of five numbers only. These five numbers will tell us much about the company's structure.

Fig. 2.4 The balance sheet – basic five box layout

Valuation

The question of the valuation of assets is a most important one. It can also be the most controversial.

Assets	Liabilities/Funds
Fixed assets (FA)	**OF**
	$450
(Long) $600	**LTL**
	$250
Current assets (CA)	**CL**
(Short) $400	$300
$1,000	$1,000

All short-term assets
(1) Inventories (stocks)
Raw materials, work-in-progress, finished goods, maintenance spares.
(2) Accounts receivable
Trade debtors – amounts due from customers arising from normal business.
(3) Cash
Includes all cash equivalents, for example bank short-term deposits and other liquid securities.
(4) Miscellaneous
All other short-term assets, e.g. pre-payments to suppliers, amounts due to the company of a short-term non-trading nature.

Fig. 2.5 The balance sheet – current assets box

Balance sheet structure – fixed assets

Fixed assets comprise the second major block of assets. They, occupy the north-west corner of the balance sheet (see figure 2.6).

We use the term 'fixed assets' even though the block contains items that do not strictly fall under this heading. A more accurate description would be 'long investment,' but the term 'fixed assets' is more commonly used.

The items that fall into this block are grouped under three headings:

1 Intangibles

Included under the heading intangibles are all assets that do not have a physical presence. The main item is goodwill. This is a component that gives rise to some controversy and is dealt with in appendix 1.

2 Net fixed assets

Large, expensive, long-lasting, physical items required for in the operations of the business are included here. Land, buildings, machinery, and office and transport equipment are the common entries. The standard method of valuation is to take original cost and deduct accumulated depreciation. In the case of property, adjustments may be made to reflect current values (see overleaf).

3 Investments

'Investments/other assets' include long-term holdings of shares in other companies for trading purposes. Not all such investments are shown in this way. Where the holding company has dominant influence – either by virtue of a majority shareholding or other means – then the accounts of the subsidiary company are totally consolidated. This means that the separate assets and liabilities of the subsidiary are aggregated with corresponding items in parent company's balance sheet. It is only investments in non-consolidated companies that are shown here.

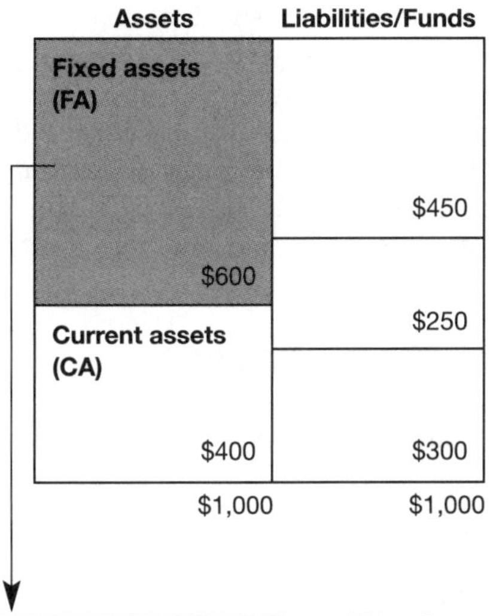

	Assets	Liabilities/Funds
Fixed assets (FA)		$450
	$600	
		$250
Current assets (CA)		
	$400	$300
	$1,000	$1,000

All long-term assets

(1) **Intangibles**
  Goodwill, patents, licenses, etc.

(2) **Net fixed assets**
  Land and buildings, plant and equipment, transport, computers, office equipment etc.

(3) **Long-term investments**
  Often shares in associated companies.

Valuation

The question of the valuation of both fixed and current assets is a most important one.

It can also be the most controversial. The accounting rules are detailed and thorough. They rely heavily on cost, but will permit other forms of valuation. However we must insist that the balance sheet does not pretend to reflect the market value of the company or the individual assets.

Fig. 2.6 The balance sheet – the fixed assets box

The question as to whether the balance sheet values should be adjusted to reflect current market values has, for years, been a contentious question. In times of high inflation, property values get out of line – often considerably so – and it is recommended that they be revalued. However, it is important to note that the balance sheet does not attempt to reflect the market value of either the separate assets or the total company. Prospective buyers or sellers of course examine these matters closely.

Balance sheet structure – liabilities

Figure 2.7 shows three subdivisions of the liabilities column:

- owners' funds (OF)
- long-term loans (LTL)
- current liabilities (CL).

(There are certain types of funds that do not fit comfortably into any one of the above listed classes. At this stage we will ignore them. Usually the amounts are insignificant and they are dealt with in appendix 1).

Current liabilities (CL)

Current liabilities (see figure 2.7) have a strong parallel relationship with current assets. 'Accounts payable' counterbalance 'accounts receivable,' 'cash' and 'short-term loans' reflect the day-to-day operating cash position at different stages. We will return to the relationship between current assets and current liabilities again.

Long-term loans (LTL)

These include mortgages, debentures, term loans, bonds, etc., that have repayment terms longer than one year.

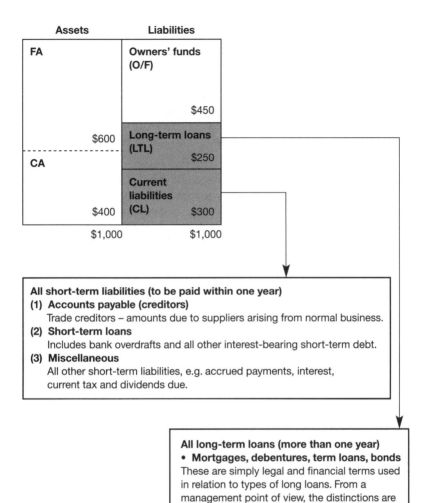

Assets   **Liabilities**

FA	Owners' funds (O/F)
	$450
$600	**Long-term loans (LTL)** $250
CA	
$400	**Current liabilities (CL)** $300
$1,000	$1,000

All short-term liabilities (to be paid within one year)
(1) **Accounts payable (creditors)**
   Trade creditors – amounts due to suppliers arising from normal business.
(2) **Short-term loans**
   Includes bank overdrafts and all other interest-bearing short-term debt.
(3) **Miscellaneous**
   All other short-term liabilities, e.g. accrued payments, interest, current tax and dividends due.

All long-term loans (more than one year)
• **Mortgages, debentures, term loans, bonds**
These are simply legal and financial terms used in relation to types of long loans. From a management point of view, the distinctions are not important. However, a distinction is often made between:
• Medium: 3-5 years and
• Long: more than 5 and up to 20 years.

Fig. 2.7 The balance sheet – the three subdivisions of the liabilities column

Owners' funds (OF)

This is the most exciting section of the balance sheet. Included here are all claims by the owners on the business. Here is where fortunes are made and lost. It is where entrepreneurs can exercise their greatest skills and where takeover battles are fought to the finish. Likewise it is the place where 'financial engineers' regularly come up with new schemes designed to bring ever-increasing returns to the brave. Unfortunately, it is also the area where most confusing entries appear in the balance sheet.

For the newcomer to the subject the most important thing to remember is that the total in the box is the figure that matters, not the breakdown between many different entries. We will discuss this section at length in chapter 12. It is important to note that while our discussions center on publicly quoted companies, everything said applies equally strongly to non-quoted companies. The rules of the game are the same for both.

 Note the three major subdivisions illustrated in figure 2.8:

- issued common stock
- capital reserves
- revenue reserves.

1 Issued common stock

The issuing of common stock for a cash consideration is the main mechanism for bringing owners' capital into the business. Three different values are associated with issued common stock:

- nominal value
- book value
- market value.

These will be covered in detail in chapter 12.

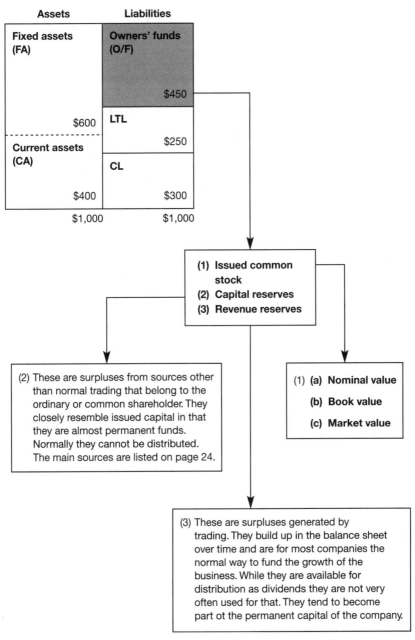

Fig. 2.8 The balance sheet – owners' funds in more detail

In the diagram:

Assets | Liabilities

Fixed assets (FA)
Owners' funds (O/F) $450
$600
LTL $250
Current assets (CA)
CL
$400 $300
$1,000 $1,000

(1) Issued common stock
(2) Capital reserves
(3) Revenue reserves

(2) These are surpluses from sources other than normal trading that belong to the ordinary or common shareholder. They closely resemble issued capital in that they are almost permanent funds. Normally they cannot be distributed. The main sources are listed on page 24.

(1) (a) Nominal value
(b) Book value
(c) Market value

(3) These are surpluses generated by trading. They build up in the balance sheet over time and are for most companies the normal way to fund the growth of the business. While they are available for distribution as dividends they are not very often used for that. They tend to become part ot the permanent capital of the company.

2 Capital reserves

The heading 'capital reserves' is used to cover all surpluses accruing to the common stockholders that have not arisen from trading. The main sources of such funds are :

- revaluation of fixed assets
- premiums on shares issued at a price in excess of nominal value
- currency gains on balance sheet items, some non-trading profits, etc.

A significant feature of these reserves is that they cannot easily be paid out as dividends. In many countries there are also statutory reserves where companies are obliged by law to set aside a certain portion of trading profit for specified purposes – generally to do with the health of the firm. These are also treated as capital reserves.

3 Revenue reserves

These are amounts retained in the company from normal trading profit. Many different terms, names, descriptions can be attached to them:

- revenue reserves
- general reserve
- retained earnings, etc.

This breakdown of revenue reserves into separate categories is unimportant and the terms used are also unimportant. All the above items belong to the common stockholders. They have all come from the same source and they can be distributed as dividends to the shareholders at the will of the directors.

Summary

We use this five-box balance sheet for its clarity and simplicity. It will be seen later how powerful a tool it is for cutting through the complexities of corporate finance and explaining what business ratios really mean.

Balance sheet terms

Introduction · The terms used

It sounds extraordinary but it's a fact that balance sheets can make fascinating reading.
MARY ARCHER (1989)

Introduction

In order to understand and use business ratios we must be clear about what it is that is being measured. Definitions and terms used must be precise and robust. We will define four terms each from the balance sheet and the profit and loss account. These are critical values in the accounts that we come across all the time. In any discussion of company affairs, these terms turn up again and again, under many different guises and often with different names. The five-box balance sheet layout will assist us greatly in this section.

The terms used

The four terms used in the balance sheet are very simple but important:

- total assets
- capital employed
- net worth
- working capital.

Each of these terms will be defined and illustrated in turn, with a further one introduced in Chapter 17 (invested capital).

Total assets (TA)

You will see from figure 3.1 that the definition is straightforward:

TA	=	FA	+	CA		
$1,000	=	$600	+	$400		

However, very often we use the term 'total assets' when we are really more interested in the right-hand side of the balance sheet where the definition more properly is:

TA	=	OF	+	LTL	+	CL
$1,000	=	$450	+	$250	+	$300

We must be able to see in our mind's eye the relationship that exists between this and other balance sheet definitions.

NB: Sometimes we come across the term 'total tangible assets' (the matter of intangibles is discussed further in appendix 1).

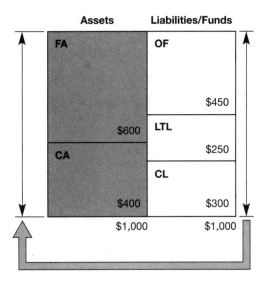

Total assets (TA)

	Assets	Liabilities/Funds	
	FA	OF	
			$450
	$600	LTL	
			$250
	CA	CL	
	$400		$300
	$1,000	$1,000	

Total assets (TA)

The value of total assets of $1,000 can be arrived at in two ways:

(1) FA + CA   = $600 + $400   = $1,000
(2) OF + LTL + CL = $450 + $250 + $300 = $1,000

"Total assets" is a value we will use often. As can be seen, it is simply the sum of everything in the balance sheet from top to bottom. This is the same number whether we use the right-hand or left-hand side.

Sometimes it will make more sense to look at this value from the point of view of the assets, and sometimes from the point of view of the funds.
We may use the same expression "total assets" in both situations.

Fig. 3.1 Defining total assets

Capital employed (CE)

This is the second important balance sheet term and it is one that is used very widely. Most books on finance give the definition of capital employed as being:

> Fixed assets + investments + inventory + accounts receivable + cash, less accounts payable and short-term loans.

To disentangle this definition, look at figure 3.2 and you will see that it means:

CE	=	FA	+	CA	–	CL
$700	=	$600	+	$400	–	$300

From figure 3.2, we can see that it also comprises the two upper right-hand boxes of the balance sheet, which gives the definition:

CE	=	OF	+	LTL
$700	=	$450	+	$250

These definitions are identical.

In the first case, we start off at the top left-hand side, work down through fixed assets and current assets to the very bottom and then come back up through current liabilities to end up at the long-term loans line.

In the second case, we start at the top right-hand side and work our way down through owners' funds and long-term loans.

Either way, we can see that the distinction between total assets and capital employed is that all the *short-term liabilities* in the current liabilities box are omitted from capital employed. Capital employed, therefore, includes only the *long-term funds* sections of the balance sheet.

Many analysts place great emphasis on capital employed. They say, with justification, that it represents the long-term foundation funds of the company. In looking at company performance they are concerned to ensure that profits are sufficient to keep this foundation intact. However, others will argue that in the current liabilities category we have, normally, bank borrowings that are, in theory, very short-term but are, in reality, permanent funds. They should therefore be included in the funding base when calculating rates of return. We will deal with this matter in chapter 17.

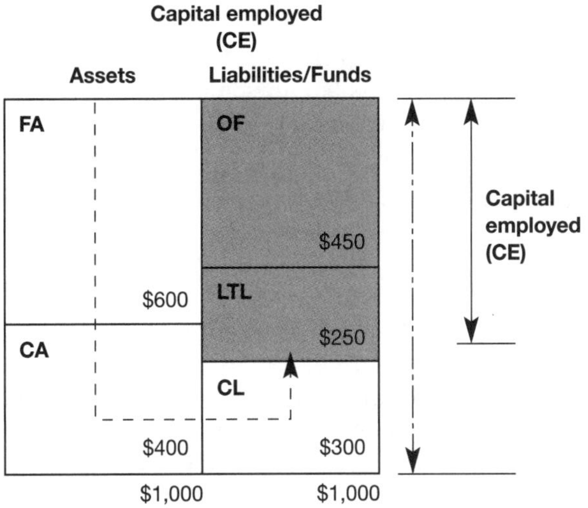
Capital employed
(CE)
Assets
Liabilities/Funds
FA
$600
CA
$400
$1,000
OF
$450
LTL
$250
CL
$300
$1,000
Capital
employed
(CE)

Capital employed

Capital employed can be arrived at in two ways:

FA + CA – CL	= $600 + $400 – $300	= $700
OF + LTL	= $450 + $250	= $700

Capital employed is a widely used term. It defines the long-term funds in the balance sheet. We will often see a rate of return expressed as a percentage of this value.

The common definition is total assets less current liabilities. We can see that this is equivalent to owner's funds plus long loans (see appendix 1 for special items).

Fig. 3.2 Defining capital employed

Net worth (NW)

This third term includes the top right-hand box only of the balance sheet. We have already looked at this box in some detail (see chapter 2), but it emerges here again with a new name – net worth. We know from the previous pages that the following values are included here:

- issued common stock
- capital reserves
- revenue reserves.

Accordingly, the first definition of net worth is the sum of the above three items, amounting to $450 (see figure 3.3).

For the second definition we can use the same method that we used for capital employed. That is, we work our way down through the assets and back up through the liabilities to arrive at the same value:

NW	=	FA	+	CA	–	CL	–	LTL
$450	=	$600	+	$400	–	$300	–	$250

This latter definition conveys more accurately the significance of the value in this box. It says to us that the value attributable to the owners in a company is determined by the value of all the assets less all external liabilities, both short and long. This is simple common sense. The shareholders' stake in the company is simply the sum of the assets less loans outstanding to third parties.

The first way of looking at this box is by means of the accounting definition, where shares are issued and reserves are accumulated over time using various accounting rules and conventions. The latter is a more pragmatic approach: simply take all the values on the assets side of the balance sheet and deduct outstanding loans – anything left is shareholders' money, no matter what name we give it. If recorded book values for assets are close to actual values, both approaches will give almost the same answer.

The amount of realism in the net worth figure, then, depends entirely on the validity of the asset values.

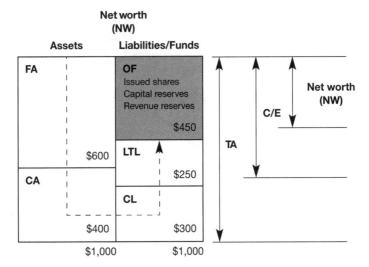

Fig. 3.3 caption region:

Net worth
(NW)

Assets	Liabilities/Funds

FA

OF
Issued shares
Capital reserves
Revenue reserves

$450

$600

LTL

$250

TA

CA

CL

$400

$300

$1,000

$1,000

C/E

Net worth
(NW)

Net worth (NW)

The value of net worth is:

TA – CL – LTL = $1,000 – $300 – $250 = $450
OF (issued + c/reserves + r/reserves) = $450

Net worth
This is another term often used to refer to the top
right-hand box in the balance sheet.
This box is such a significant section of the balance sheet
that it has many names attached to it.
The term "net worth" has the advantage that it expresses
the fact that the value in this section is derived from:
the total assets less the total external liabilities.

Fig. 3.3 Defining net worth

Working capital (WC)

This fourth and final balance sheet term is illustrated in figure 3.4. It is an important term that we will come back to again and again in our business ratios.

The widely used definition of working capital is:

WC	=	CA	–	CL
$100	=	$400	–	$300

This figure is a measure of liquidity. We can consider liquidity as an indicator of cash availability. It is clearly not the same thing as wealth: many people and companies who are very wealthy do not have a high degree of liquidity. This happens if the wealth is tied up in assets that are not easily converted into cash. For instance, large farm and plantation owners have lots of assets, but may have difficulty in meeting day-to-day cash demands – they have much wealth but they are not liquid. This can be true for companies also. It is not sufficient to have assets; it is necessary to ensure that there is sufficient liquidity to meet ongoing cash needs.

We have an alternative definition in figure 3.5, that looks at working capital from the right-hand side of the balance sheet. This definition gives perhaps a more significant insight. Here, we see that it can be calculated as:

WC	=	OF	+	LTL	–	FA
$100	=	$450	+	$250	–	$600

This definition is not often used in the literature but it is a very important way of looking at the structure of a company.

The amount of working capital available to a company is determined by the long-term funds that are not tied up in long-term assets. When a business is being set up, long-term funds are injected from the owners and other long sources. A considerable amount of these will be spent to acquire fixed long-term assets. However a sufficient amount must remain to take care of short-term day-to-day working capital requirements. Normally as time goes on this need grows with the development of the company. This need can be met only from additional long-term funds e.g., retained earnings, or long loans, or from the disposal of fixed assets.

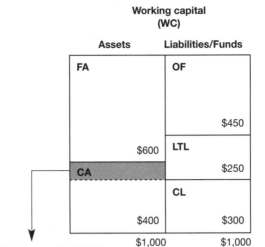

Working capital (WC)

The definition of W/C is current assets less current liabilities. A most important value, it represents the amount of day-to-day operating liquidity available to a business.

Operating liquidity is a term used to describe cash and near-cash assets available to meet ongoing cash needs.

A company can be very rich in assets, but short of liquidity if these assets cannot readily be converted into cash.

Fig. 3.4 Defining working capital

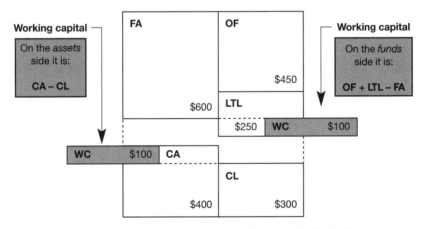

Like other balance sheet terms, working capital can be looked at from the side of either the assets side or liabilities.
The different approaches give separate insights into the company affairs.

Fig. 3.5 Alternative definition of working capital

Profit and loss account

Introduction · Working data

A large income is the best recipe for happiness I ever heard of.
JANE AUSTEN (1775–1817)

Introduction

Figure 4.1 identifies where the profit and loss account fits into the set of accounts. It is a link or bridge between the opening and closing balance sheets of an accounting period. Its function is to identify the total revenue earned and the total costs incurred over that period. The difference between these two values is the operating profit. It is, therefore, a document that relates to a very precise time period. There are many accounting rules to do with the identification of revenue and costs.

Total revenue earned

Total revenue earned is generally the amount invoiced and, in most situations, there is no problem with its accurate identification. However, if we receive cash today for a contract to supply a service over the next three years, when should we take that into our accounts as revenue?

Also, there could be more than one view on the subject of what constitutes total revenue in the second year of, say, a large, three-year civil works project. Finally, if we are an engineering company and we sell a warehouse, is that part of revenue?

Total costs incurred

The figure for total costs can give rise to even more intractable problems.

Two rules will help to identify costs that must be included:

- those costs that relate directly to the revenue, for example the direct cost of the goods sold; and
- those costs that relate to the time period covered by the accounts, such as staff salaries for the period.

Even with these rules, however, there are still many areas where the decision could go either way. Should research and development costs be charged in the year in which they were incurred? If we replace the factory roof in a period, is that correctly chargeable as a cost? We could question whether a particular depreciation charge is correct. The list can go on.

The statement of accounting policies attached to all published accounts will give some information regarding this aspect and it is wise to examine it before attempting an analysis of the financial statements.

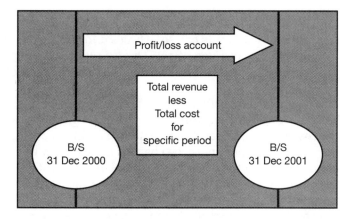

The profit and loss account relates very specifically to the time period 31 December 2000 to 31 December 2001.

Total costs are set against total revenue for this period to yield operating profit.

Relevant costs are:
(a) those that relate directly to the revenue
(b) those that relate directly to the time period.

There are many accounting rules to do with the identification of cost and revenue. Particularly in the cost area, some items can be interpreted in different ways using different assumptions, e.g. we can ask what amounts have been included for depreciation, and how have research and development costs been handled.

Therefore in the analysis of a company's accounts, it is well to ask what important assumptions or accounting policies have had an effect on the final profit.

Fig. 4.1 Place of the profit and loss account in company

Profit and loss – general observations

In a situation where accountants can sometimes differ, it is not surprising that non-accounting managers go astray. One or two basic signposts will eliminate many problems that arise for the non-specialist in understanding this account.

The distinction between profit and cash flow is a common cause of confusion. The profit and loss account as such is not concerned with cash flow. This is covered by a separate statement. For instance, employees' pay incurred but not yet paid must be charged as cost even though there has been no cash flow. On the other hand, payments to suppliers for goods received are not costs, simply cash flow. Costs are incurred when goods are consumed, not when they are purchased or paid for.

Cash spent on the purchase of assets is not a cost, but the corresponding depreciation over the following years is.

A loan repayment is not a cost because an asset (cash) and a liability (loan) are both reduced by the same amount, so there is no loss in value by this transaction.

In recent years, the question of extraordinary items has been much discussed. The issue here is whether large, one-off gains or losses should be included with normal trading activities. We can readily accept for analysis purposes the argument that these should be set to one side and not allowed to distort the normal operating results. This was the approach used in producing accounts for many years. However, in some companies, the rule was used selectively. Items became extraordinary or otherwise in order to present the desired picture. The rule has now been changed to avoid the possibility of distortion.

Finally the question of timing is vital. Having established what the true costs and revenue are, we must locate them in the correct time period. The issue mainly arises just before and just after the cut-off date between accounting periods. As shown in figure 4.2, we may have to move revenue or costs forwards or backwards to get them into their correct time periods.

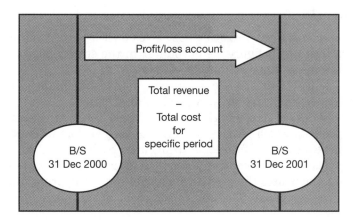

Timing adjustments

Revenue and costs occurring in a period must be adjusted with adjoining periods to ensure that each period is credited and charged only with what is appropriate (see below).

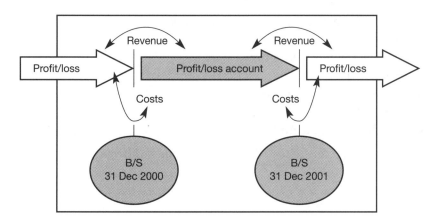

Fig. 4.2 The profit and loss account – timing adjustments

Profit/loss – terms

Total revenue less total operating cost gives operating or trading profit. This is the first profit figure we encounter in the statements of account but there are many other definitions of profit.

We will identify four specific definitions and assign financial terms to them. These are related to the way profit is distributed.

All the assets used in the business have played a part in generating the operating profit to which we give the term 'earnings before interest and tax (EBIT)'. Therefore this profit belongs to and must be distributed among those who have provided the assets. This is done according to well defined rules.

Figure 4.3 illustrates the process of distribution or 'appropriation' as it is called in the textbooks. There is a fixed order in the queue for distribution as follows:

- to the lenders (interest)
- to the taxation authorities (tax)
- to the shareholders (dividends/retentions).

At each of the stages of appropriation the profit remaining is given a precise identification tag. Stripped of non-essentials, the following is a layout of a standard profit and loss appropriation account. When looking at a set of accounts for the first time it may be difficult to see this structure because the form of layout is not as regular as we see in the balance sheet. However if one starts at the EBT figure, it is usually possible to work up and down to the other items shown:

- EBIT – Earnings before interest and tax
  Deduct interest
- EBT – Earnings before tax
  Deduct tax
- EAT – Earnings after tax
  Deduct dividend
- RE – Retained earnings

(See appendix 1 for further discussion of unusual items.)

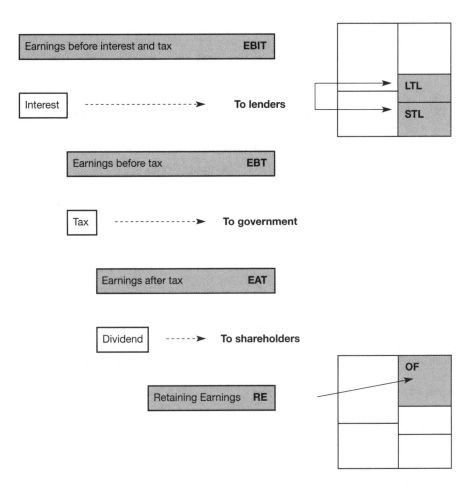

Fig. 4.3 The profit and loss account – distribution or appropriation of profits

Working data

Throughout the various stages of the book we will work with three sets of data:

- The **Example Co. plc** has been devised with simple numbers to highlight various aspects of accounts and show the calculation of ratios (see figure 4.4).
- The **US Consolidated Company Inc.** (see figure 4.5).
- **Sectoral/geographical data** (see appendix 3).

The Example Company plc

Figure 4.4 shows for the Example Company plc:

- the balance
- the profit/loss account
- share data.

It is worth while spending a moment looking over the now familiar five-box balance sheet and the structured profit/loss account to become familiar with the figures. They will be used a lot in the following chapters.

Please review the following items:

Balance Sheet

- Fixed assets
- Current assets
- Current liabilities
- Long-term loans
- Owners' funds

Profit/Loss Account

- EBIT
  Interest
- EBT
  Tax
- EAT
  Dividend
- RE

Example Co. plc

Balance sheet ($000,000s)

Fixed assets	$	$	Owners' funds	$	$
Intangibles	0		Issued capital	80	
Net fixed assets	440		Capital reserves	60	
Long-term investments	40		Revenue reserves	220	
					360
		480	**Long-term loans**		
Current assets					200
Inventory	128				
Accounts receivable	160		**Current liabilities**		
Cash	20		Short loans	60	
Miscellaneous	12		Accounts payable	140	
			Miscellaneous	40	
		320			240
		800			800

Profit/loss account ($000,000s)

	$	$
Sales		1,120
Operating costs		1,008
EBIT (Earnings before interest and tax)		112
Interest	20	
EBT (Earnings before tax)		92
Tax	32	
EAT (Earnings after tax)		60
Dividends	24	
RE (Retained earnings)		36

Share data

Number of ordinary shares	= 32,000,000
Share market price	= $22.5

Fig. 4.4 Working data – the Example Co. plc

The US Consolidated Company

This company is made up of an aggregate of the accounts of approximately 40 large successful US public companies drawn from different business sectors. These companies are flagships of US industry and they have been selected to provide aggregate data for the calculation of ratios that can be used as standards or norms for good industrial performance.

The balance sheet and profit/loss account for the year 2000 are laid out according to our agreed structure in figure 4.5. We will use these for setting targets of performance (see appendix 2).

The aggregate stockmarket value of these companies in mid-2001 was $1,876bn.

Sectoral/geographical data

In addition to the above, almost 160 high-profit companies from different business sectors and four geographic areas have been selected to indicate the types of variation that arise in different types of operation in different locations. These business sectors are:

- health care
- food
- machinery and equipment
- retail.

The locations are:

- US
- UK
- EU
- Japan.

This produces 16 subgroups for which results are compared and reported in graphical form throughout the book.

Balance sheet

$bn

Long investment	$	$	Owners' funds	$	$
Intangibles	66.2		Issued capital	22.8	
Net fixed assets	185.0		Reserves	186.1	
Other long assets	49.0				
					208.9
		300.2	Misc. long funds	52.3	
			Long-term loans	90.9	
Current assets					143.2
Inventories	86.6				
Accounts receivable	68.2		Current liabilities		
Cash	40.4		Short-term loans	42.4	
Miscellaneous	21.4		Accounts payable	56.1	
			Miscellaneous	66.2	
		216.6			164.7
		516.8			516.8

Profit and loss account

$bn

	$	$
Sales		**725.9**
EBIT (Earnings before interest and tax)		**92.8**
Interest	8.5	
EBT (Earnings before tax)		**89.3**
Tax	26.7	
EAT (Earnings after tax)		**57.6**
Dividends	21.6	
RE (Retained earnings)		**360**

Aggregate stockmarket value in mid-2001 was $1,876.5 bn.

Fig. 4.5 Working data – the US Consoldated Company Inc.

Part II Operating performance

Measures of performance

Relationships between the balance sheet and profit and loss account · The ratios 'return on total assets' and 'return on equity' · Balance sheet layouts

I often wonder what the vintners buy one half so precious as the goods they sell.
RUBAIYAT OF OMER KHAYYAM (1859)

Relationships between the balance sheet and profit and loss account

When we wish to examine a company's profitability performance, we look at its absolute profit in relation to the assets tied up in the business. But the question arises: which figure should we take from the profit/loss account, and which figure from the balance sheet?

Figure 5.1 shows the accounts for the Example Company plc with values extracted for:

- **Profit/Loss account**
  - EBIT
  - EBT
  - EAT
- **Balance sheet**
  - TA
  - CE
  - NW

Performance is measured by establishing relationships between these two sets of values.

However, we have a choice as to which value we use from each statement. Earnings before interest and tax could be measured against total assets or capital employed or net worth. We could do likewise, with earnings before tax and earnings after tax. This gives us nine possible measures of performance. In practice, we meet with all of these measures and even with some other variations.

Various names are given to these linkages or ratios between the balance sheet and the profit and loss account values. The names come and go, becoming popular for a while and then maybe disappearing according to fashion. A selection of these could be:

- return on assets   – ROA
- return on net assets   – RONA
- return on capital employed – ROCE
- return of invested capital   – ROIC

This multiplicity of terms causes difficulty to the non-specialist, but the point to remember is that these are not different ratios. They all simply measure in one way or another the return on assets. The name used does not greatly matter. What is important, however, is that we know which profit and loss figure is being related to which balance sheet figure.

Example Co. plc

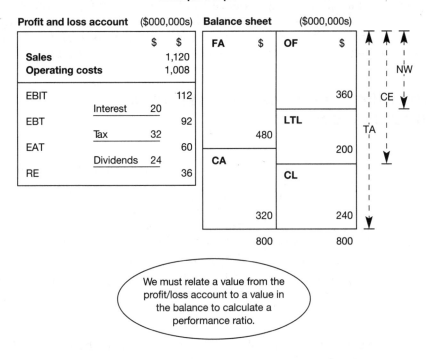

Profit and loss account   ($000,000s)   Balance sheet   ($000,000s)

	$	$
Sales		1,120
Operating costs		1,008
EBIT		112
Interest	20	
EBT		92
Tax	32	
EAT		60
Dividends	24	
RE		36

Balance sheet:
FA $ OF $
                  360   NW CE
            LTL   TA
      480   200
CA
      CL
      320   240
      800   800

We must relate a value from the profit/loss account to a value in the balance to calculate a performance ratio.

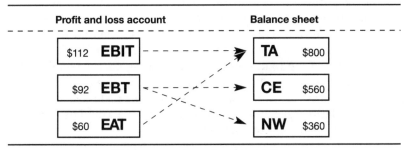

Profit and loss account   Balance sheet

$112 **EBIT** -----> **TA** $800

$92 **EBT** -----> **CE** $560

$60 **EAT** -----> **NW** $360

Which measure is most appropriate?
In practice almost all combinations
are used.

Fig. 5.1 Important terms from the profit and loss account and balance sheet using data from the Example Co. plc

This book will initially use two measures only. They have been carefully selected and are illustrated in figure 5.2. We do not imply that these are the only correct ones or that all others are deficient in some way. However, they are two of the better measures. There is sound logic for choosing them in preference to others as we will see in due course.

The ratios 'return on total assets' and 'return on equity'

The two ratios chosen here for the measurement of company performance are illustrated in figure 5.2. These are:

- 'return on total assets' (ROTA) which gives a measure of the operating efficiency of the total business. The method of calculation is EBIT/TA expressed as a percentage. For the Example Company plc the answer arrived at is 14 percent.
- 'return on equity' (ROE) which assesses the return made to the equity shareholder. The method of calculation is EAT/OF as a percentage. In our example the answer is 16.6 percent.

The significance of these numbers will be examined in chapter 6. In the opinion of the author these are the two fundamental performance ratios.

This said, there are many possible variations to them and some may well be more suitable for particular types of businesses. One that is widely used is 'return on capital employed' (ROCE). As we saw earlier in chapter 3, capital employed is the figure we get by deducting current liabilities from total assets. The corresponding profit and loss value used is EBIT with the deduction of interest on short-term loans. Because a smaller denominator is used in calculating return on capital employed, we would expect a higher answer than for return on total assets.

When new expressions for these ratios are encountered it is often not clear which profit and loss value is being measured against which balance sheet value. Then the question to ask is 'How is it calculated?' When you know what the calculation method is, it is as easy to work with one combination as another. However, there is a certain logic that should be followed in deciding on any particular ratio – if the value from the balance sheet includes loans, then the profit and loss value should include the corresponding interest charge and vice versa. This rule is not always adhered to and the resulting answers can be suspect.

Example Co. plc.

Profit and loss account ($000,000s)

	$	$
Sales		1,120
Operating costs		1,008
EBIT		112
Interest	20	
EBT		92
Tax	32	
EAT		60
Dividends	24	
RE		36

Balance sheet ($000,000s)

FA	$	OF	$
			360
		LTL	
	480		200
CA		CL	
	320		240
	800		800

Of all the possible combinations of values
from the P/L and the B/S which measures
are most appropriate?
The following two are selected.

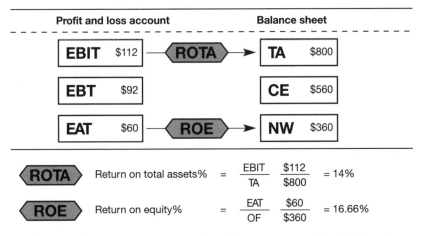

| ROTA | Return on total assets% | = | $\dfrac{\text{EBIT}}{\text{TA}}$ | $\dfrac{\$112}{\$800}$ | = 14% |
| ROE | Return on equity% | = | $\dfrac{\text{EAT}}{\text{OF}}$ | $\dfrac{\$60}{\$360}$ | = 16.66% |

**Fig. 5.2 The two measures of performance used in this book:
return on total assets and return of equity applied to data
from the Example Co. plc**

Balance sheet layouts

A number of alternative forms of layout, particularly in the case of the balance sheet, are used in presenting accounts. While the layout itself does not affect any of the numbers, it can be difficult when faced with an unfamiliar format to find where items are located and what are values for 'total assets,' 'capital employed,' etc.

The first point to remember is that the items within each of the five boxes will always appear grouped together – they are never scattered around among other items. Sometimes, however, the total only of a sub-section will appear in the balance sheet proper while the detail is to be found in the notes to accounts.

Vertical balance sheet – version 1

Given the five-box grouping, it follows that there is only a limited number of ways in which the boxes can be arranged. In figure 5.3, one such re-arrangement is shown. It is easy to see how the items in the two-column format have been re-ordered into a single vertical column. This type of layout has the advantage that corresponding values for successive years can be laid out side by side for ease of comparison. In this format, values for 'total assets' and 'total funds' are also emphasized.

Balance sheet ($000,000s)

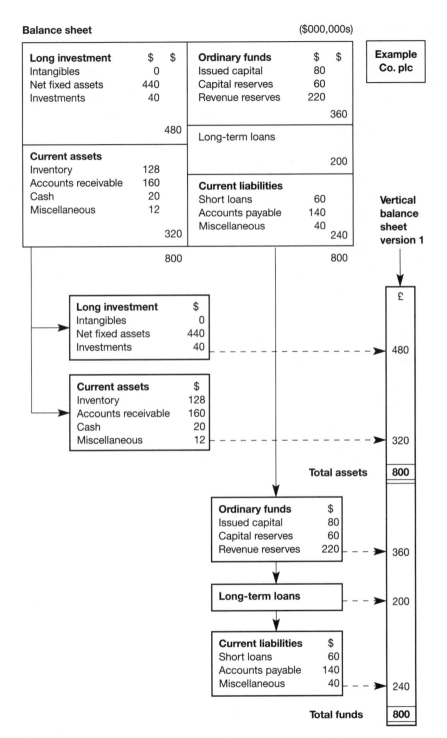

Fig. 5.3 *Vertical sheet version 1 using data from the Example Co. plc*

Vertical balance sheet – version 2

The second layout, as shown in figure 5.4, is a slightly more sophisticated version, but it is the one most often seen in published accounts. The difference here is that current liabilities have been moved out of the liabilities section and are instead shown as a negative value side by side with current assets. The totals of these two sections are netted off to give the figure for 'working capital.'

Both sides of the balance sheet are, accordingly, reduced by the amount of the current liabilities – $240. The original totals amounted to $800, so the new balancing figure is $560. This figure, as seen earlier, is 'capital employed.'

The advantage of this layout is that both working capital (current assets less current liabilities) and capital employed values are identified. The disadvantage is that the figure for total assets does not appear anywhere on the balance sheet.

It is largely a matter of personal preference as to which format is adopted. In the three types of layouts illustrated (the five-box format and vertical versions 1 and 2), practically all possible situations have been covered, so most balance sheets should now make sense. It is a good idea to take whatever form is used and transfer the figures into the familiar five-box format as the significant features will then quickly become evident.

Appendix 1 lists a number of items that we have deliberately omitted here because we can do most of our analysis without taking them into account. Two of these items are (1) preference shares and (2) minority interests. These will not be present at all in many accounts you encounter and where they exist they are likely to be insignificant.

Note: The headings 'Creditors: amounts falling due within one year,' and 'Creditors: amounts falling due after more than one year,' are widely used to refer to current liabilities and long-term loans respectively.

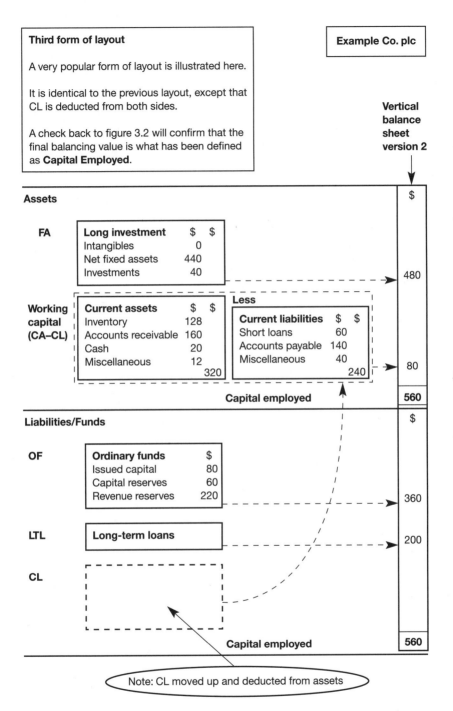

Third form of layout

A very popular form of layout is illustrated here.

It is identical to the previous layout, except that CL is deducted from both sides.

A check back to figure 3.2 will confirm that the final balancing value is what has been defined as **Capital Employed**.

Example Co. plc

Vertical balance sheet version 2

Assets

		$
FA	**Long investment** $ $	
	Intangibles 0	
	Net fixed assets 440	
	Investments 40	480

Working capital (CA–CL)

Current assets $ $	**Less**	
Inventory 128	**Current liabilities** $ $	
Accounts receivable 160	Short loans 60	
Cash 20	Accounts payable 140	
Miscellaneous 12	Miscellaneous 40	
320	240	80

Capital employed — 560

Liabilities/Funds $

		$
OF	**Ordinary funds** $	
	Issued capital 80	
	Capital reserves 60	
	Revenue reserves 220	360
LTL	**Long-term loans**	200
CL		

Capital employed — 560

Note: CL moved up and deducted from assets

Fig. 5.4 Vertical sheet version 2 using data from the Example Co. plc

6

Operating performance

Return on investment (ROI)

· Return on equity (ROE)

· Return on total assets (ROTA)

· Standards of operating performance

But the age of chivalry is gone. That of sophisters, economists, and calculators, has succeeded; and the glory of Europe is extinguished for ever.
EDMUND BURKE (1729–1797)

Return on investment (ROI)

The generic phrase 'return on investment' relates to one of the most important concepts in business finance.

Each dollar of assets has to be matched by a dollar of funds drawn from the financial markets. These funds have to be paid for at the market rate. Payment can come only from the operating surplus derived from the efficient use of the assets. It is by relating this surplus to the value of the underlying assets/funds that we find a measure of return on investment.

If this return on investment is equal to or greater than the cost of funds, then the business is currently viable. However, if the long-term rate is less than the cost of funds, the business has no long-term future. In any particular instance, this generic term 'ROI' will be expressed by one of the more specific terms, ROTA, ROE, etc.

From the balance sheet we get asset figures and from the profit/loss account we get operating surplus. We relate these two to establish the rate of return.

We have already seen the beginnings of this concept in chapters 4 and 5, but in this chapter we examine it more deeply. The concept of return on investment is universal, but the methods of measurement vary widely.

This lack of consistency causes confusion in the minds of many financial and non-financial people alike.

Two measures of return on investment

The two complementary approaches to return on investment that we have already met with will be developed in depth. When these are fully locked into place, variations on the basic themes can be examined and understood without difficulty.

The two measures we will concentrate on are:

- return on total assets (ROTA)
- return on equity (ROE).

The two separate measures are necessary because they throw light on different aspects of the business, both of which are important. Return on total assets looks at the operating efficiency of the total enterprise, while return on equity considers how that operating efficiency is translated into benefit to the owners. This chapter will concentrate on these two areas. First we will look at methods of calculation, using the Example Co. plc accounts to explore them. Then we will use the aggregated accounts of the US Consolidated Company Inc. to establish what values can be expected from successful businesses.

Return on equity (ROE)

Figure 6.1 shows how return on equity is calculated. The figure for EAT from the profit and loss account is expressed as a percentage of OF (owners' funds /net worth) in the balance sheet.

This ratio is arguably the most important in business finance. It measures the absolute return delivered to the shareholders. A good figure brings success to the business – it results in a high share price and makes it easy to attract new funds. These will enable the company to grow, given suitable market conditions, and this in turn leads to greater profits and so on. All this leads to high value and continued growth in the wealth of its owners.

At the level of the individual business, a good return on equity will keep in place the financial framework for a thriving, growing enterprise. At the level of the total economy, return on equity drives industrial investment, growth in gross national product, employment, government tax receipts and so on.

It is, therefore, a critical feature of the overall modern market economy as well as of individual companies.

Measures of performance
Example Co.

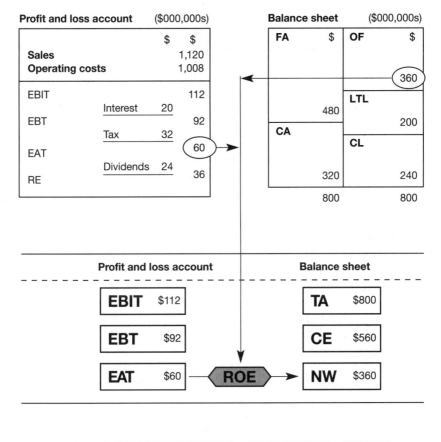

Profit and loss account		($000,000s)
	$	$
Sales		1,120
Operating costs		1,008
EBIT		112
	Interest 20	
EBT		92
	Tax 32	
EAT		60
	Dividends 24	
RE		36

Balance sheet		($000,000s)
FA $	OF	$
		360
480	LTL	
		200
CA	CL	
320		240
800		800

Profit and loss account   **Balance sheet**

EBIT $112   **TA** $800

EBT $92   **CE** $560

EAT $60 — ROE → **NW** $360

$$\text{ROE} = \frac{\text{EAT}}{\text{Owners Funds}} \times 100 = \frac{\$60}{\$360} \times 100 = 16.6\%$$

ROE is possibly the single most important business ratio there is!

Fig. 6.1 Return on equity ratio applied to data from the Example Co. plc

Return on total assets (ROTA)

Return on total assets provides the foundation necessary for a company to deliver a good return on equity. A company without a good ROTA finds it almost impossibe to generate a satisfactory ROE. Figure 6.2 shows how ROTA is calculated, i.e. EBIT/TA.

EBIT is the amount remaining when total operating cost is deducted from total revenue, but before either interest or tax have been paid. Total operating cost includes direct factory cost, plus administration, selling and distribution overheads.

This operating profit figure is set against the total assets figure in the balance sheet. The percentage relationship between the two values gives the rate of return being earned by the total assets. Therefore this ratio measures how well management uses all the assets in the business to generate an operating surplus.

Some practitioners contend that the figure taken from the balance sheet should include the long-term funds and only those short-term funds for which a charge is made, i.e. STL (short-term loans). Their position is that assets funded by 'free' creditors should not be included in the rate of return calculation. There is considerable merit in this argument, but a counter argument is that the rate of return issue is separate from the funding issue and that assets should produce a return irrespective of the method of funding. For example, some companies choose to fund by suppliers' credit, others from a bank loan. The author's view is that, for most companies, the balance of advantage lies with the latter school of thought.

Whichever method of calculation is adopted, return on total assets uses the three main operating variables of the business.

- total revenue
- total cost
- assets utilized (some definition of).

It is therefore the most comprehensive measure of total management performance available to us.

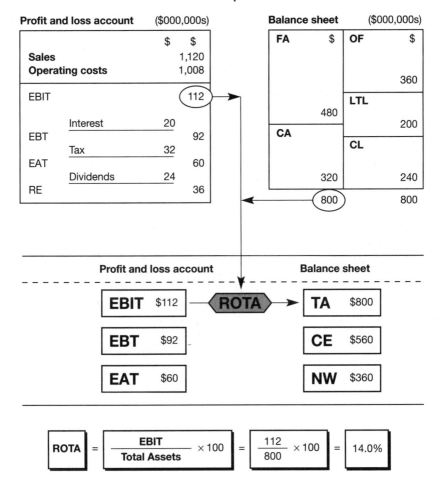

Fig. 6.2 **Return on total assets ratio applied to data from the Example Co. plc**

Standards of operating performance

Figure 6.3 shows a summary balance sheet and profit and loss account for the US Consolidated Company Inc. in 2000. The ratio values extracted from these accounts are:

■ return on total assets – 17.9 percent
■ return on equity – 27.5 percent.*

We should remember that the return on total assets is pre-tax and return on equity is calculated using an after-tax profit figure.

These are the rates of return that were achieved by high-level US companies in that year. They are obviously all very good performers and are the gold medallists, as it were, of US industry.

This is not to say that, because they are the largest, they are the most profitable. Indeed better results are often produced by smaller businesses. However, to reach their pre-eminent position, these companies have consistently produced good results, they have survived and grown over many years.

Their continued success is justification for using an average of their combined results as a good target for other firms to aim for.

The rates of return derived from these combined accounts are very high indeed. Levels of inflation have a considerable impact on required rates of return, but allowing for the levels of inflation experienced in recent years, a return on equity of 27 percent (after corporation tax) is exceptional. It is likely that these returns will not be maintained over the coming years.

---

* These values are very high, but they have been derived from the results of the most successful US corporations (see appendix 2). Also, ROE values have been boosted by the fact that many of these companies have reduced their equity amount through considerable buy back of shares. For a broader view of ROE, see figures 6.4 and 6.5.

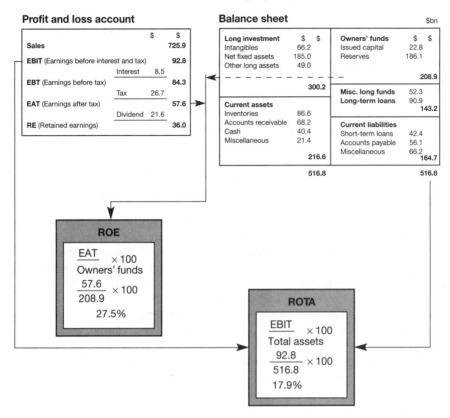

Standards of performance
US Consolidated Company Inc. 2000

Profit and loss account

	$	$
Sales		725.9
EBIT (Earnings before interest and tax)		92.8
	Interest 8.5	
EBT (Earnings before tax)		84.3
	Tax 26.7	
EAT (Earnings after tax)		57.6
	Dividend 21.6	
RE (Retained earnings)		36.0

Balance sheet $bn

Long investment	$	$	**Owners' funds**	$	$
Intangibles	66.2		Issued capital	22.8	
Net fixed assets	185.0		Reserves	186.1	
Other long assets	49.0				
					208.9
		300.2	**Misc. long funds**	52.3	
Current assets			**Long-term loans**	90.9	
Inventories	86.6				143.2
Accounts receivable	68.2				
Cash	40.4		**Current liabilities**		
Miscellaneous	21.4		Short-term loans	42.4	
		216.6	Accounts payable	56.1	
			Miscellaneous	66.2	164.7
		516.8			516.8

ROE

$$\frac{EAT}{\text{Owners' funds}} \times 100$$

$$\frac{57.6}{208.9} \times 100$$

27.5%

ROTA

$$\frac{EBIT}{\text{Total assets}} \times 100$$

$$\frac{92.8}{516.8} \times 100$$

17.9%

Fig. 6.3 Summary balance sheet and profit and loss account for the US Consolidated Company Inc. 2000

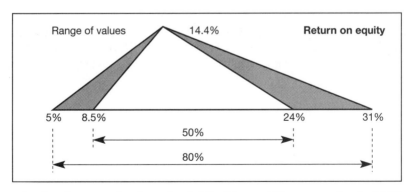

Range of values   14.4%   **Return on equity**

5%   8.5%   24%   31%

50%

80%

Fig. 6.4 Range of values for ROE of large UK companies in 2000

Return on equity – geographic and sectoral analysis

We have described return on equity as being, probably, the single most important financial ratio we have. It is the great driver of company value. Therefore it is important to know what is happening in the world in terms of this ratio.

 From very profitable companies in the US and the UK we get very high values of 26 percent to 27 percent. Figure 6.4 reflects results of research on simply the largest UK companies in 2000.

The results of current research into approximately 160 worldwide companies are shown in figure 6.5.

In Chart A, we see that there is a wide spread between the US and UK on the one hand and the EU and Japan on the other. In the former countries, we see returns in the high 20s; in the latter we see rates just above and below 10 percent.

Some of these variations can be explained by the differences in methods of accounting. For instance, in an environment that has experienced heavy takeover activity, followed by high goodwill write-offs, equity values in the balance sheet no longer give us a true value for shareholders' investment, and ROE values would be overstated accordingly. It is the author's opinion that an ROE of 15 percent is a very satisfactory return.

Across the industrial sectors there is no regular pattern between countries. The low overall return for Japan is consistent across all sectors. The food sector is the worst offender. It yields only 5 percent. It has shown a dramatic decline over the previous four years, indicating perhaps that the strong yen has caused the greatest damage here.

Outstanding at the other end of the scale are the very high returns being delivered by the US food sector. Included in this category are world-famous names such as Kellogg, Campbell's Soup, Quaker Oats, H.J. Heinz, etc. These companies with powerful brand identification deliver extraordinary levels of profit.

It is interesting that this is the sector where companies have bought back a considerable amount of their own shares, a fact that suggests that they have difficulty in finding outlets for their enormous cash flow that will not dilute their very high returns.

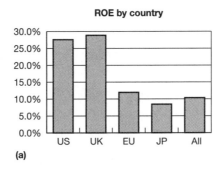

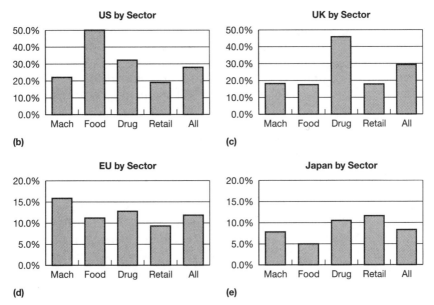

Fig. 6.5 Return on equity by country and by sector

Return on total assets – geographical and sectoral analysis

We know that this is the second great performance measure and its importance cannot be over-stated. It is:

■ the greatest single driver of return on equity*.

■ the prime measure of operating efficiency

■ the ratio over which operations management has most control.

Figures 6.6 and 6.7 will help to set targets for good performance.

When we look at standard values for ROTA and ROE, the effects of leverage are clearly seen. Even though ROTA is a pre-tax measure it consistently comes out 3 percent to 6 percent less than after-tax ROE values. In the US and UK economies we find results of 15 percent to 17 percent. Figure 6.6 shows that 50 percent of companies clustered within a range of 8.5 percent plus or minus 3 percent.

However figure 6.7 shows that these values again far exceed the rest of the world. Japanese companies and EU companies produce about 7 percent.

The drug sector in the US again shows outstanding results. All sectors in Japan except drugs produce results we would consider to be very low.

A company in the western world would currently need to set its sights on attaining a value of 8 percent to 12 percent as a 'return to total assets' ratio. This is quite a difficult value to achieve and it may have to fall in the coming years.

*The links between these two ratios are discussed in chapter 13.

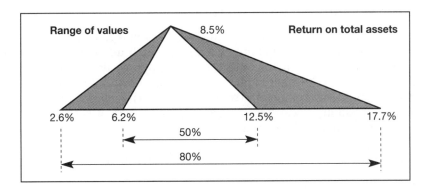

Fig. 6.6 Range of values for ROTA of large UK companies in 2000

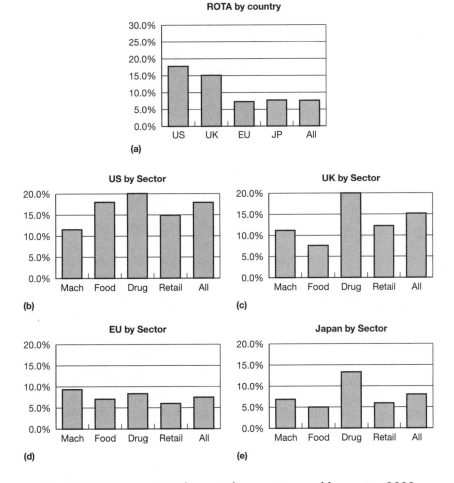

Fig. 6.7 Return on total assets by country and by sector 2000

The components of return on total assets

Return on total assets is a key tool in directing management's day-to-day activities. It provides a benchmark against which all operations can be measured. However as a single figure it simply provides a target. To be useful in decision making it must first be broken down into its component parts. This will now be done in two stages. First the main ratio is divided into two subsidiary ratios (see figure 6.8), then each of these is further divided into its detailed constituents.

In Stage 1 the two prime subsidiary ratios are identified:

- margin on sales percentage
- sales to total assets ratio (asset turn).

ROTA is calculated by the fraction : EBIT/TA. We introduce the figure for 'Sales' and link it to each variable to give us two fractions instead of one. We get the ratios (a)EBIT/sales (profit margin) and (b)sales/TA (asset turn). It is simple mathematics to show that the product of these will always combine to the value of ROTA. This first split is so important that we will take the risk of over-emphasizing it here. The formula is:

$$\textbf{ROTA} = \frac{\textbf{Profit}}{\textbf{Margin}} \times \frac{\textbf{Asset}}{\textbf{Turn}}$$

$$\frac{\text{EBIT}}{\text{TA}} = \frac{\text{EBIT}}{\text{Sales*}} \times \frac{\text{Sales*}}{\text{TA}}$$

* Note that 'Sales' cancel out above and below the line.

$$\frac{\$14}{\$100} = \frac{\$14}{\$200} \times \frac{\$200}{\$100}$$

$$14\% = 7\% \times 2 \text{ times}$$

We have now derived two most important ratios, 'profit margin' and 'asset turn.' The former identifies profit as a percentage of sales and is often described as the net profit margin. It is a well-known measure and almost universally used in the monitoring of a company's profitability.

The latter ratio looks at the total sales achieved by the company in relation to its total assets, a measure that is less often emphasized in the assessment of company performance. However its contribution to ROTA is just as powerful and important as the profit margin.

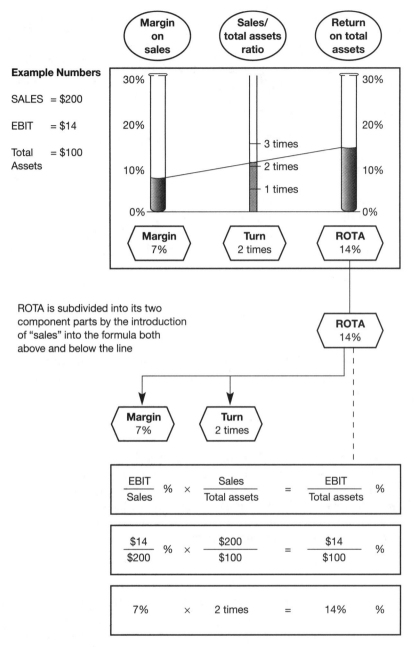

Example Numbers

SALES = $200

EBIT = $14

Total Assets = $100

ROTA is subdivided into its two component parts by the introduction of "sales" into the formula both above and below the line

Fig. 6.8 The return on total assets ratio and its two subsidiary ratios

> The importance of this interrelationship of ratios is difficult to exaggerate. To repeat our logic so far:
>
> - ROE is the most important driver of company value.
> - ROTA is the most important driver of ROE
>
> The ratios that drive ROTA are:
>
> - margin on sales percentage
> - sales to total assets ratio.

We have seen that average return on total assets values for companies from many different industrial sectors tend to fall within a fairly narrow band, e.g. 12.5 percent, plus or minus 5 percent. However, the subsidiary ratios that deliver this standardized final result vary widely across different sectors.

Figure 6.9 shows some typical values for companies with vastly different profiles.

Example A

Here we see typical figures for a distribution-type company, where low margins, e.g. 5 percent to 7 percent combine with a high asset turn, e.g. 2 times.

Example B

Here the opposite applies. Very high margins and low asset turns are typical of companies that require large quantities of fixed assets. The telecommunications sector generates sales margins in the region of 25 percent. However, their enormous investment in fixed assets with correspondingly low asset turns means that this margin is only just adequate to make a reasonable return on total assets.

Example C

Here we see fairly average figures, with margins at 10 percent or more, and asset turn values somewhat greater than 1. Quite a number of medium-sized manufacturing companies have this kind of pattern. The difference between success and mediocrity in this type of business is often less than 2 percent on margin and a small improvement in asset turn.

Example A
This company has a relatively low margin, combined with a high sales/total assets ratio.

This may indicate a distribution-type company.

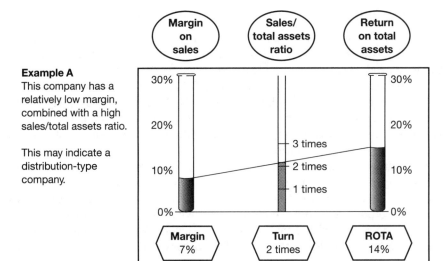

Example B
This company has a very high margin, combined with a very low sales/total assets ratio.

Such a company has very heavy assets . Telecommunication operations have this type of profile.

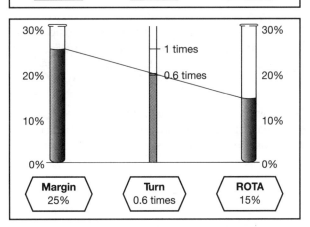

Example C
This company shows average values under both headings.

Many manufacturing companies would be similar.

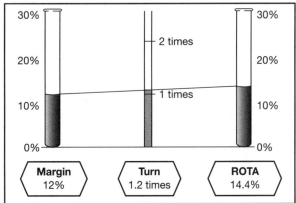

Fig. 6.9 Indicative margin on sales and sales to total asset ratios for different types of business

'Margin' and 'Sales to Total Assets' standards

Figure 6.10 illustrates the calculations and results for the US Consolidated Company Inc. An average sales margin of 12.8 percent is delivered 1.4 times to produce a 'return on total assets' value of 17.9 percent.

A comparison by country (see figure 6.11) shows a strong similarity between companies in the US and the UK. In the US a slightly lower margin is accompanied by a somewhat higher 'sales to total assets.' However the size of the sample would not allow us to give great statistical significance to these variations.

Companies in the EU seem to operate on lower margins and their asset utilization is also low. Companies in Japan operate on low margins but appear to have a somewhat better assets utilization. This latest finding runs contrary to popular belief. Much has been written about Japanese achievements in operating with very low inventory levels. While this may be true in specific industries it does not seem to hold across a wide range of companies.

A rule of thumb would be that a margin of approximately 10 percent, combined with an asset turn of between 1.3 and 1.5 would be where many western companies would find a comfortable and profitable position.

It rests with the skill of each management team to discover for itself the unique combination of margin and asset turn that will give their company its own particular, and successful, market niche.

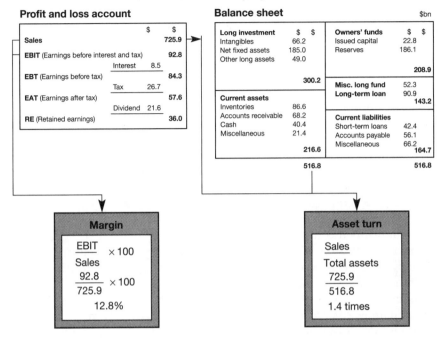

Fig. 6.10 Margin on sales and sales to total asset ratios applied to data from the US Consolidated Company Inc.

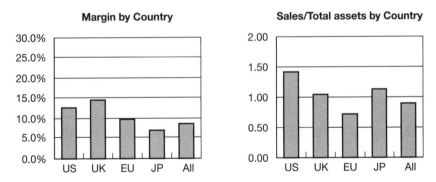

Fig. 6.11 Margin on sales and sales to total asset ratios by country

Sector parameters – return on total assets

In figure 6.12, results of research into top UK companies in 1992 are still used here because they give a dramatic illustration of the interrelationship that exists between the two key variables that determine what a company will achieve in terms of return on total assets.

Chart A shows values for 'Sales to total assets' and chart B 'Margin' values for six industrial sectors ranging from 'food' to 'health care.' The two charts are almost minor images of one another. High sales to assets ratios are generally offset by low margins and vice versa. It is where the minor images do not exactly match where the high and low performers are located.

The values shown in Chart A of figure 6.12 point to a question concerning business performance that is absolutely critical. What level of investment is required to support any given level of sales? The results displayed here help us to understand why some sectors of industry seem to have a built-in advantage over others.

Chart A shows the high sales to total assets ratios inherent in the food industry. While this ratio is high in both retailing and manufacturing sectors, it is more pronounced in retailing.

Chemicals and stores both have 'sales to total asset' ratios that are approximately 20 percent above the average, but this advantage is mostly offset by their lower margins – particularly in the case of chemicals. The two sectors are still quite good overall.

When we look to the two final sectors, we see a dramatic contrast. The brewing value is very low, with a sales to total assets ratio of 0.6 times. It may be more informative to turn this ratio upside down and say that it requires $1.60 of assets to carry $1.00 of sales. For any given level of sales, the investment in assets is enormous. In contrast, in the food retailing sector it takes only $0.45 to support $1.00 of sales. The brewing/distilling sector requires almost four times this investment to produce this result.

In the health sector, we note that the 'sales to total assets' ratio is also below average but this sector has a margin on sales that compensates by almost 200 percent for these somewhat high assets. The high margins in brewing are still not sufficient to pay for the very high investment in assets in this sector.

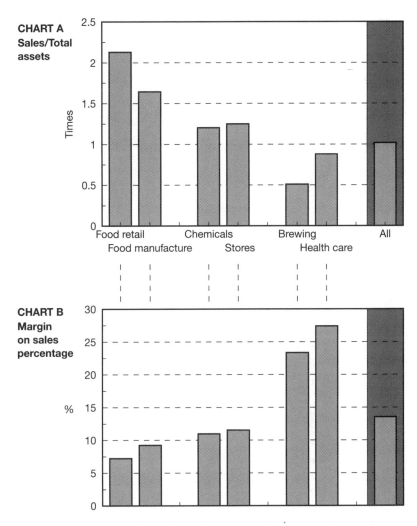

Fig. 6.12 Sector values for sales to total assets and margin on sales ratios for data from top UK companies in 1992

Performance drivers

Operating performance

· Operating profit model

Everything, then, must be assessed in money; for this enables men always to exchange their services, and so makes society possible.
ARISTOTLE (384–322 BC)

Operating performance

The two prime ratios that drive return on total assets have been identified:

- margin on sales percentage
- sales to total assets ratio

and these are laid out again for the Example Co. plc in figure 7.1.

It is on these two drivers that managers must concentrate in order to improve performance: However, these ratios cannot be operated on directly. Each is dependent on a whole series of detailed results from widely separated parts of the operation. These in turn can be expressed in ratio form and all that managers need is a system that will enable them to identify and quantify these subsidiary values so that they can:

- set the target value for each ratio that, if achieved, will deliver the required overall performance level
- delegate the achievement of these targets to specific individuals.

The system outlined in the following pages achieves this end. It will be seen that it incorporates all the main elements in both the profit and loss account and balance sheet. Each of the elements is a performance driver and must be managed accordingly.

Drivers of margin on sales

At its simplest, we can say that the margin is what is left when the total operating cost is deducted.

If the margin were 10 percent, the total cost would be 90 percent. The margin can be improved only if this 90 percent can be reduced. To reduce the figure, we must know its component parts. So, the next stage is identify the separate cost elements and see what percentage each of the main cost elements bears to sales (see figure 7.2).

Drivers of the sales to total assets ratio

This ratio is also broken down into its component parts. We identify the main groups of assets straight from the balance sheet and we then express the ratio between each group and the sales figure as shown in figure 7.3.

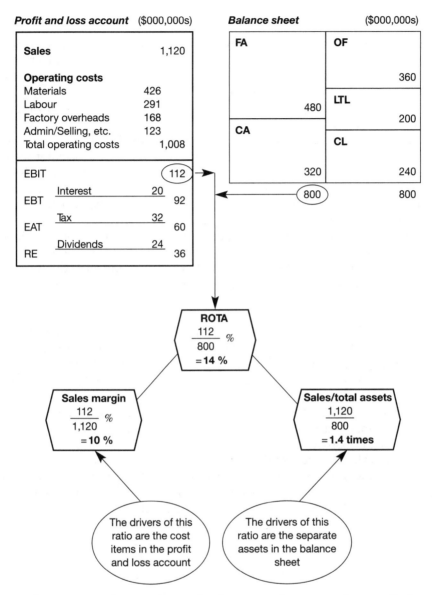

Fig. 7.1 Margin on sales and sales to total assets ratios applied to data from the Example Co. plc

Margin on sales – drivers

Figure 7.2 shows the development of the left-hand side of the model, which is concerned with profit and loss values. The four main cost elements that accumulate to total operating costs are identified as materials, labor, factory overheads and admin/selling. These large cost groups are used for example purposes: in practice they would be broken down into much more detail.

In the lower part of the diagram, each cost element is shown expressed as a percentage of sales. For instance, the first box shows that materials is 38 percent (material cost of $426 over sales of $1,120 multiplied by 100). The sum total of all the costs is 90 percent, giving a margin of 10 percent.

If management wishes to improve this margin, then one or more of the cost percentages must fall. For instance, if the material cost percentage could be reduced by two points, from 38 to 36 percent, then, other things being equal, the margin percentage would improve by two points to 12 percent. This margin of 12 percent would then combine with the sales to total assets ratio of 1.4 times to give an improved return on total assets of 16.8 percent (that is, 12 percent multiplied by 1.4).

These cost ratios allow managers to plan, budget, delegate responsibility and monitor the performance of the various functional areas under their control. They can quantify targets for all areas, and calculate the effect of a variation in any one of the subsidiary ratios on the overall performance.

The results achieved by different managers, products and divisions can also be compared and the experiences of the best passed on to the others to help them improve. We must recognize, however, that there are operating factors that the model does not cope with. The variables of selling price, volume and product mix, which have such a powerful impact on profit, are not easily distinguished from other factors in the model. In later chapters these factors will be discussed further.

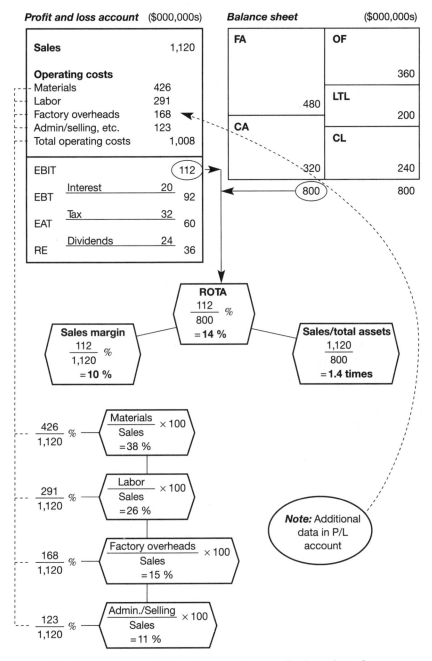

Fig. 7.2 Drivers of margin on sales applied to data from the Example Co. plc

Sales/total assets – drivers

In figure 7.3 it will be seen that just as the subsidiary values of the left-hand side were derived from the profit and loss account, so these right-hand elements are taken from the balance sheet. Each of the main asset categories is related to sales.

The three major asset blocks in most enterprises are:

- fixed assets
- inventories (stocks)
- accounts receivable (debtors).

The value of each in relation to sales is shown in the subsidiary boxes. For instance, the ratio for fixed assets is 2.5 times (from sales of $1,120 divided by fixed assets of $440). Note that the sum of these separate values does not agree with the sales to total assets ratio as did the sales margin on the other side with the operating costs. This is because they are expressed differently. If the reciprocals of the values are taken, the link will become clear.

To managers, this display shows the importance of managing the balance sheet as well as the profit and loss account. For instance, if the total assets could be reduced from $800 to $700, then the sales to total assets ratio would move up from 1.4 to 1.6 times. The effect on the return on total assets would be to increase it from 14 to 16 percent. If, in addition, the margin were increased by 1 percent to 11 percent, then the new return on total assets would be almost 18 percent (11 percent × 1.6 times). The original value of 14 percent for ROTA is an average value whereas a return on total assets of 18 percent represents an excellent performance.

In these areas, production managers can work with finance and market-ing departments to quantify targets for stock holdings and accounts receivable. The impact of an increase in fixed assets caused by a major capital investment project can also be assessed in profitability terms.

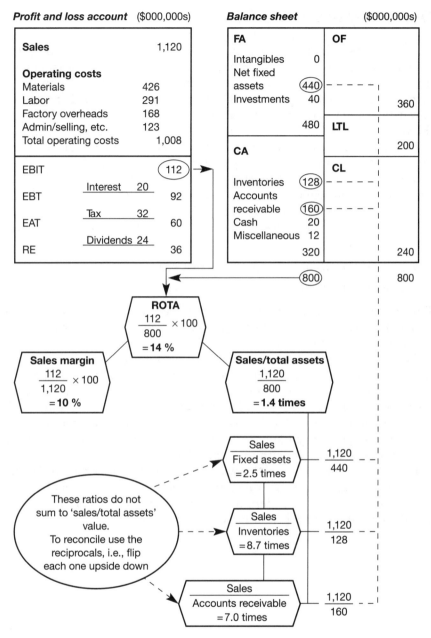

Fig. 7.3 Drivers of sales to total assets ratio applied to data from the Example Co. plc

Operating profit model

The complete model is shown in figure 7.4. It gives a very powerful insight into the drivers of good performance. It enables managers and functions to work better together as a team. It helps with the definition of responsibilities, delegation of authority and target setting. It provides a powerful framework for a management information system. However, there are a number of issues the model does not highlight.

First, a business normally deals not just in one product, but in a broad range. Cost percentages are averages of the cost elements of the individual products. For management control, it is not satisfactory to work with averages because favorable movements in one product will mask adverse movements in another (these issues are dealt with further in chapter 15).

Second, a cost percentage, such as materials, can vary for two totally different reasons :

- a change in the absolute material cost per unit.
- a change in the unit selling price of the product

The model, however, cannot distinguish between these two causes, despite the fact that one of the most effective ways to reduce the cost percentages is a price increase.

Third, the model does not cope very well with changes in volume, which can be one of the most powerful ways open to a company to improve performance. A volume increase will certainly be picked up by the sales to total assets ratio – a 10 percent improvement in volume would move this ratio up from 1.4 to 1.54 times – but, because of fixed costs, the volume change is very likely to have an effect on the sales margin too (this subject is also dealt with in chapter 15).

Fourth, the perceptive reader will have noted that this ratio is dependent on the valuation of the assets in the balance sheet. Difficulties can arise when we compare different businesses or divisions because of the age of plant, different depreciation policies and so on.

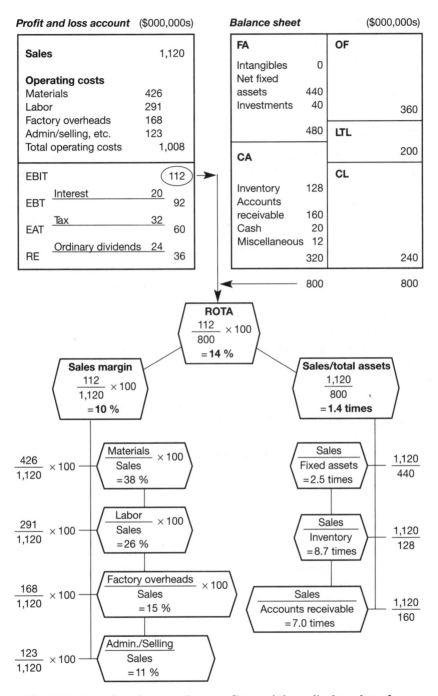

Profit and loss account ($000,000s)

Sales		1,120
Operating costs		
Materials	426	
Labor	291	
Factory overheads	168	
Admin/selling, etc.	123	
Total operating costs	1,008	
EBIT		112
Interest	20	
EBT		92
Tax	32	
EAT		60
Ordinary dividends	24	
RE		36

Balance sheet ($000,000s)

FA		OF	
Intangibles	0		
Net fixed			
assets	440		
Investments	40		360
	480	**LTL**	
CA			200
Inventory	128	**CL**	
Accounts			
receivable	160		
Cash	20		
Miscellaneous	12		
	320		240
		800	800

ROTA
$$\frac{112}{800} \times 100 = 14\%$$

Sales margin
$$\frac{112}{1,120} \times 100 = 10\%$$

Sales/total assets
$$\frac{1,120}{800} = 1.4 \text{ times}$$

$\frac{426}{1,120} \times 100$ — $\frac{\text{Materials}}{\text{Sales}} \times 100 = 38\%$

$\frac{291}{1,120} \times 100$ — $\frac{\text{Labor}}{\text{Sales}} \times 100 = 26\%$

$\frac{168}{1,120} \times 100$ — $\frac{\text{Factory overheads}}{\text{Sales}} \times 100 = 15\%$

$\frac{123}{1,120} \times 100$ — $\frac{\text{Admin./Selling}}{\text{Sales}} = 11\%$

$\frac{\text{Sales}}{\text{Fixed assets}} = 2.5 \text{ times}$ — $\frac{1,120}{440}$

$\frac{\text{Sales}}{\text{Inventory}} = 8.7 \text{ times}$ — $\frac{1,120}{128}$

$\frac{\text{Sales}}{\text{Accounts receivable}} = 7.0 \text{ times}$ — $\frac{1,120}{160}$

Fig. 7.4 Completed operating profit model applied to data from the Example Co. plc

Model variations

Many business ratios appear under different names, or are calculated differently, and this can cause some confusion. In the set of ratios we are looking at here, there are two that appear under a number of different guises.

Sales to accounts receivable

This ratio is commonly expressed in terms of day's sales and the method of calculation is shown in figure 7.5. Instead of the formula we have been using here of sales over accounts receivable, the alternative is to show accounts receivable over sales and multiply the result by 365. The answer represents the average number of days' credit customers take before paying off their accounts.

This ratio is often referred to as 'debtor days' or the 'collection period'. The concept of the number of days outstanding is easy to understand. The number is very precise, which means that a slippage of even a few days is instantly identified. Also, figures can be compared with the company's normal terms of trade and the effectiveness or otherwise of the credit control department can, therefore, be monitored.

Companies will vary their methods of calculation to reflect their own business circumstances and to provide answers that make sense to them in particular. For instance:

- VAT may be included in the debtors but not the sales figure and this distortion will have to be removed
- When there is a heavy seasonal variation, the monthly figures calculated in the normal way may not be very helpful and so the company may work, not on an annual sales basis, but on quarterly sales figures that are annualised.

Sales to inventories

This calculation is similar to the one above and is also known as inventory days. The link of inventories with sales is not so close as that of sales with accounts receivable. It may, therefore, be linked to purchases or material usage, whichever gives the most useful guidance.

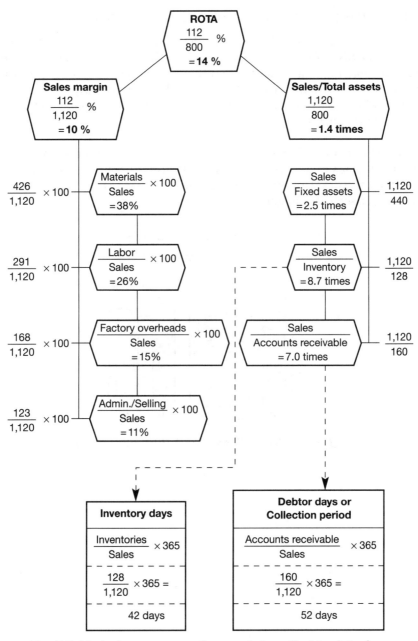

Fig. 7.5 Variations to operating model applied to data from the Example Co. plc

'Sales to fixed assets' ratio – international standards

This ratio, which is one of the strong determinants of company perform-ance, is heavily influenced by the nature of the industry. It is, therefore, less amenable to management action than are many of the other perform-ance drivers. For many years, it has been difficult very capital-intensive sectors of industry to earn high returns except where there has been some element of monopoly.

 The chart in figure 7.6 shows consistent rates around the world. A value of 3.0 to 4.0 times recurs across both international boundaries and many industrial sectors. However, it can be seen from chart 3.5 in appendix 3 that certain sectors can deliver values of up to 5.0 times.

Sales/Fixed Assets by Country

Fig. 7.6 Sales to fixed assets ratio by country

Inventory days – international standards

The 2000 UK data shown in figure 7.7 produced a mean value of 36 days with a 50 percent range of 11 to 60 days. More recent research on a broader geographical spread shows this to be consistent with both the US and the UK. Across all sectors of US business a figure of 40 days emerges.

However in Japan this figure is much lower at approximately 30 days. Chart 3.6 in appendix 3 shows that in Japan, numbers as low as 20 days emerge for both the food and retail sectors.

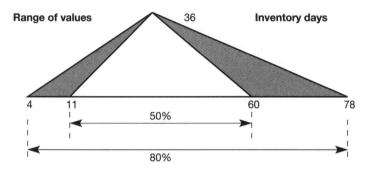

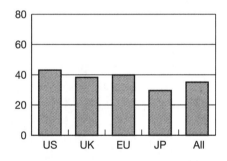

Fig. 7.7 Range of values for inventory days of top UK companies in 2000

Debtor days – international standards

We observe in figure 7.8 that both the US and the UK have low values of approximately 40 days. In these two countries also the sectors show a remarkable similarity. Food and retail have particularly low values, but these are counterbalanced by the machinery and drug sectors.

When we look beyond the US and the UK, we see a remarkable change. Debtor levels are almost 100 percent higher in the EU and 50 percent higher in Japan.

We can trace the impact of these various performance drivers right up through the system to the return that companies make to their shareholders. Both the US and the UK deliver high sales/asset ratios and also much higher sales margin ratios, with the result that shareholders in these regions achieve more than twice the return than shareholders in the rest of the EU or Japan.

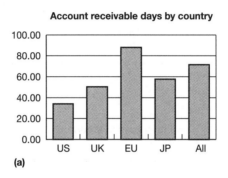

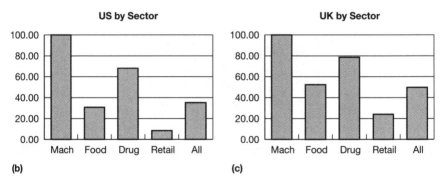

Fig. 7.8 Accounts receivable days

Part III Corporate liquidity

Cash flow cycle

Corporate liquidity · The cash cycle
· Measures of liquidity – long and
short analysis

Every branch of knowledge has its
fundamental discovery. In mechanics it is
the wheel, in science fire, in politics the vote.
Similarly, in economics, in the whole
commercial side of man's social existence,
money is the essential invention on which
all the rest is based.
SIR GEOFFREY CROWTHER (1907–1972)

Corporate liquidity

A company must maintain sufficient cash resources to pay all legitimate bills as they arise. A company that cannot do so has run out of liquidity and is in a very serious financial condition. Ironically, this is so even if it is currently generating good profits.

Cash in this case can be a bank account with a positive balance, or it can be a loan facility that the company has authority to draw down.

When cash runs out, the company's management has lost the power to make independent decisions. An outside agency, such as an unpaid creditor or a bank whose loan is in default, will decide the fate of the company.

That fate could be bankruptcy, a forced reconstruction, an involuntary takeover, or the company could be allowed to continue in some altered form. The reality is that management has lost its authority. It is also likely that the owners have lost their entire investment.

One may well ask, 'How can this happen if profits are good?' The answer is that it does happen and for reasons that will become clearer later.

Loss of profits is often the immediate cause of the disaster, but as we have said, it can happen even when companies are making good profits. Indeed, profitable and rapidly growing small companies very often run out of cash. They then pass out of the hands of the original owner or entrepreneur who is left with nothing, while others reap the benefits of his enterprise.

This chapter will examine corporate liquidity and the factors that drive it. It will look at how we can measure a company's liquid health. It will identify the forces that bring benefit or harm to it.

*Refer to appendix 1 where the technical term EBITDA is explained and discussed.

The cash cycle

The flow of cash through an organization is sometimes compared with the flow of blood through the body. When we look at the cash flow diagram in figure 8.2, the reason for this is obvious. Cash is in continuous circulation through the 'arteries' of the business carrying value to its various 'organs.' If this flow is stopped, or even severely reduced for a time, then serious consequences result.

This diagram shows part of the total cash cycle, the part that we refer to as the working capital cash flow. Central to the system is a cash tank, or reservoir, through which cash flows constantly.

> It is crucial to the independent survival of the business that this tank does not run dry.

Supporting the cash tank is a supplementary supply, representing unused short-term loan facilities. These provide a first line of defense against a cash shortage. Day-to-day liquidity consists of these two separate cash reservoirs

The main flow of cash into the reservoir comes from 'accounts receivable.' These are the customers who pay for the goods or services received from the company.

The main cash out-flows can be identified under two headings:

- payments to 'accounts payable,' that is the suppliers of raw materials and services.

- payments of staff salaries/wages, and payments of all other operating expenses.

We can trace the steps in the cycle. 'Accounts payable' supply 'raw materials.' In time these pass through 'work in process' into the 'finished goods' category. During this conversion, cash is absorbed in the form of labor and expenses and payments to suppliers.

In due course, these 'finished goods' are sold. Value passes down the artery into the 'accounts receivable' box, from which it flows back into the 'cash' reservoir to complete the cycle.

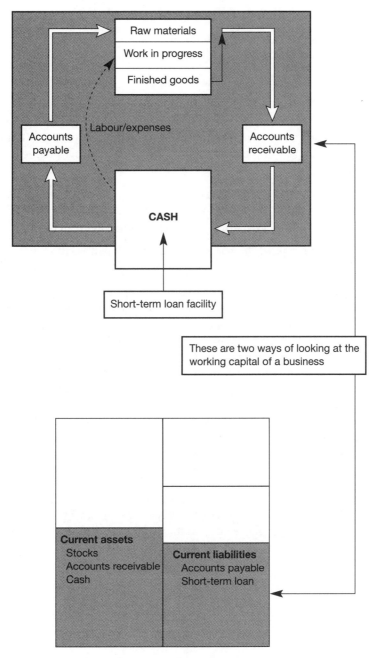

Fig. 8.1 The operating cash cycle

Cash flow – the role of profit and depreciation

In figure 8.2, two further input values are shown that produce an increase in the cash in circulation:

- profit
- depreciation.

The input from profit is easy to understand. Normally goods are sold at a price that exceeds total cost. For instance if goods that cost $100 are sold at a price of $125, the $25 profit will quickly flow into the business in the form of cash.

It is a little more difficult to understand the input from 'depreciation.' But depreciation is often quoted as a source of funds and we may have seen the definition:

operating cash flow = operating profit + depreciation

It is not easy to see why this should be. What is so special about depreciation? The answer is that, for most companies, depreciation is the only cost item in the profit and loss account that does not have a cash out-flow attached to it. While referred to as a source of cash, it is really the avoidance of a cash out-flow. This point is more fully developed in the following section.

It must be emphasized that, even though depreciation does not have a related cash out-flow, it is a true cost nevertheless. The relevant cash out-flow has simply taken place at an earlier time. At the time the associated fixed assets were purchased, the cash cost was not charged against profits. It was, instead, charged to the balance sheet. As the asset is used up, an appropriate amount of cost is released into the profit and loss account. This is what depreciation is all about.

What figure 8.2 shows is that, with every full cycle, the amount of cash in circulation is increased by the profit earned plus the depreciation charged.

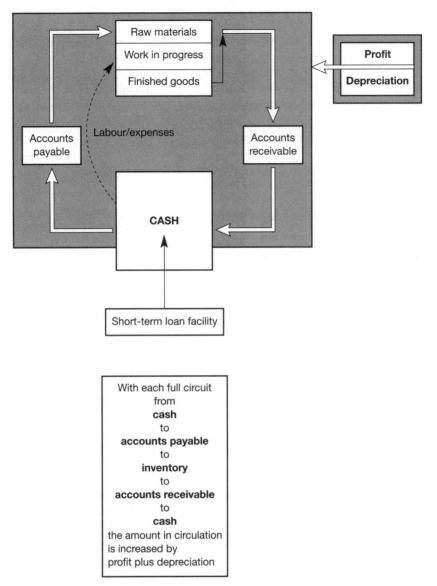

Fig. 8.2 The operating cash cycle and the role of profit and depreciation

Depreciation and cash flow

The example in figure 8.3 illustrates the relationship between depreciation and cash flow. It is one that gives rise to much confusion.

The example uses the illustration of a very small haulage business. It has one single asset, namely a vehicle valued at $20,000 that the owner uses to transport goods on a jobbing basis. The business has no inventories or accounts receivable. It has no bank or other loans and all its transactions are carried out for cash.

The opening balance sheet is simple. It shows a single asset of $20,000 that is represented by capital of the same amount.

The profit and loss account highlights are:

- sales of $30,000
- total costs of $27,000
- profit of $3,000.

The closing balance sheet shows a cash figure of $8,000. The company started with no cash and ended up with $8,000, but the profit was only $3,000. How can this be?

We run down through the items of cost and find that the depreciation charge is $5,000. No cash was paid out under this heading. The trading cash receipts were $30,000 and the trading cash costs were $22,000. Therefore the net cash from trading was $8,000. However from this net cash we must deduct depreciation to give the profit of $3,000.

Therefore it is simply a convenient shortcut to arrive at cash flow by adding back depreciation to profit.

An interesting aspect of the depreciation effect is that certain types of companies can suffer serious trading losses without suffering from cash shortages. These are companies where depreciation is a big percentage of total cost, e.g., transportation, and utility companies. So long as losses are less than the depreciation charged in the accounts, operations are cash positive.

Opening balance sheet

Assets		Funds/liabilities	
Vehicle	$20,000	Capital	$20,000

Operating cash flow
=
Operating profit
+
Depreciation

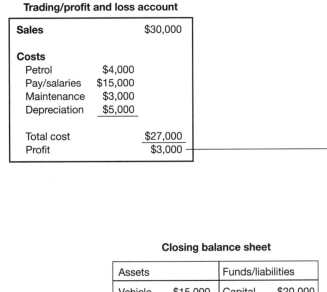

Trading/profit and loss account

Sales		$30,000
Costs		
Petrol	$4,000	
Pay/salaries	$15,000	
Maintenance	$3,000	
Depreciation	$5,000	
Total cost		$27,000
Profit		$3,000

Closing balance sheet

Assets		Funds/liabilities	
Vehicle	$15,000	Capital	$20,000
Cash	$8,000	Profit	$3,000
	$23,000		$23,000

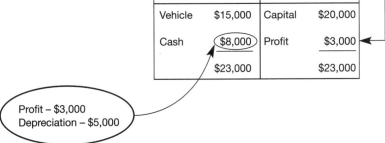

Profit – $3,000
Depreciation – $5,000

Fig. 8.3 The relationship between depreciation and cash flow

Non-operating cash out-flows

In figures 8.1 and 8.2 we saw cash flowing round in a closed circuit. If there were no leaks from this circuit, there would be few problems. However, this is not the case and we must now add further sections to the diagram to allow for cash out-flows that are not related to day-to-day operations.

In figure 8.4 the principal additional out-flows are shown as:

- interest, tax and dividends
- loan repayments
- capital expenditure.

We will discuss each in turn.

Interest, tax and dividends

These three items are deducted from EBIT in the 'profit and loss account.' They represent a distribution of most of the profit earned for the period. Possibly 75 percent of the profit in any year goes out under these headings, to leave approximately 25 percent that is permanently retained in the business.

Therefore we expect cash flow to remain positive even after these charges. Furthermore, as regards timing, the profit is realized in cash well ahead of these out-flows. So this first set of payments should not, of themselves, be a cause of cash embarrassment.

Loan repayments

These can be substantial in amount. They are also deducted from after-tax income and are in no way connected with the profit for the period. Therefore they can give rise to heavily negative cash positions. However, the amounts required are known well in advance and, in most situations, can be planned and provided for.

Capital expenditure

This final item is nearly always a matter of policy. It can probably be deferred in unfavorable circumstances. It is subjected to much thought, analysis and planning. Nevertheless heavy expenditure on projects that do not perform to plan is one of the major causes of cash difficulties.

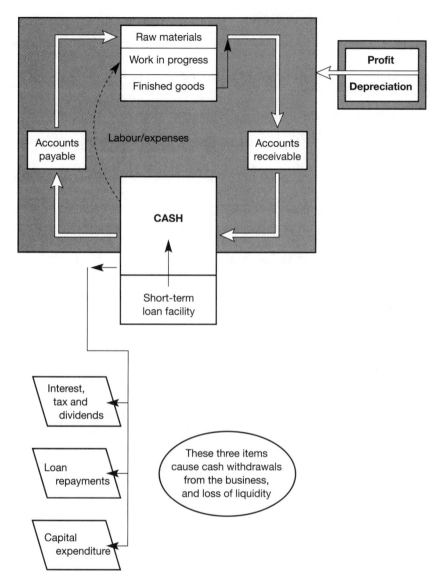

Fig. 8.4 The main non-operating cash out-flows

Non-operating cash in-flows

In figure 8.5, the right-hand final branch of the diagram has been completed.

 Three sources of cash from external sources are shown feeding into the cash reservoir. These are:

- new equity capital
- new long-term loans
- sale of fixed assets.

In many parts of the world a fourth source of cash is available in the form of grants from government to stimulate investment and employment, but this has been ignored here.

The first two headings cover the two principal sources of long-term finance to a company, i.e., equity and loan capital. In comparing these sources three matters must be given attention:

- cost
- risk
- control.

New equity capital

It is a function of the stock exchange to raise funds for commercial enterprises. There is a constant stream of public companies coming to the stock exchange to raise cash from the general public or from financial institutions.

The great advantage of equity capital is that it is permanent and it carries no risk to the company. However, it is high-cost money and expensive in terms of control.

New long-term loans

Companies are continually repaying old debts and raising new ones. They must have long-term loan capital, but banks are structured to provide loans for relatively short fixed periods. Companies draw these down but they rarely eliminate them. They simply replace them with new loans.

However, each time a company goes looking for new funds it must prove itself to be credit worthy; it must show strong evidence that it can service both the interest and principal.

In many ways, debt has features that are the opposite of equity: it is less costly, it does not dilute control, but it brings extra risk.

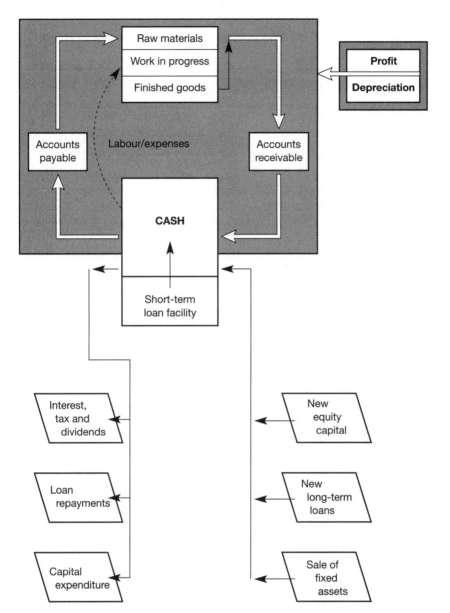

Fig. 8.5 The main non-operating cash in-flows

Sale of fixed assets

This is not one commonly resorted to. However, it may be the only way out of a liquidity crisis. Indeed, sometimes it can be a very beneficial move even in a non-crisis situation.

Measures of liquidity – long and short analysis

When we look at a company's liquidity position we must make a distinction between long-term and short-term sections of the balance sheet. Figure 8.6 shows the five-box balance sheet and highlights this distinction.

'Current assets' and 'current liabilities' both fall into the short-term area. The remaining three boxes – 'owners funds,' 'long-term loans' and 'fixed assets' occupy the long-term area.

A certain balance should exist between the long-term assets and funds on the one hand and the short-term assets and funds on the other. As a general rule, long-term assets in a company should be matched by corresponding long-term liabilities.

Company profiles

A balance sheet with its five boxes drawn to scale can highlight the profile of a company. By profile we mean the shape of the balance sheet in terms of the relative weight of each of the five boxes. These profiles are determined by the operating characteristics of the industrial sector in which a company operates.

Such profiles throw useful light on how a company will respond to certain conditions. Companies that are heavy in current assets will be adversely affected by an increase in the rate of inflation very quickly. Companies that have borrowed heavily are, of course, very responsive to changes in overall levels of interest rates.

Examples of two contrasting companies are shown in figure 8.7. On the left we see the balance sheet outline of a company from the brewing sector. A very high percentage of the total assets are in the long-term investment area and there is a corresponding reliance on equity and long-term loans.

The balance sheet on the right-hand side represents a company from the textile sector. The heavy investment here is in short-term current assets. We see that a mix of funds follows. There are very high current liabilities and relatively little long-term loans.

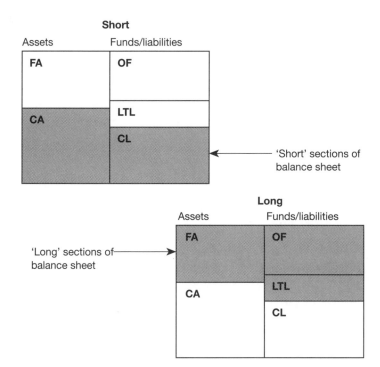

Fig. 8.6 Long and short balance sheet analysis

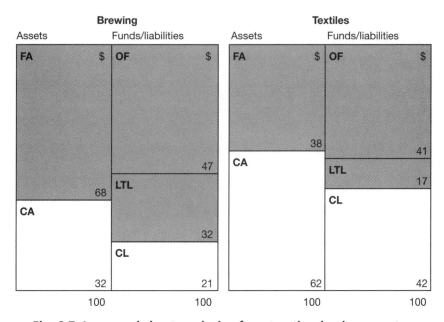

Fig. 8.7 Long and short analysis of contrasting business sectors

9

Liquidity

Short-term liquidity measures
· Current ratio · Quick ratio
· Working capital to sales ratio
· Working capital days

*Money is the most important thing in the
world. It represents health, strength, honour,
generosity and beauty as conspicuously and
undeniably as the want of it represents illness,
weakness, disgrace, meanness and ugliness.*
GEORGE BERNARD SHAW (1856–1950)

Short-term liquidity measures

The first test of a company's financial position is, 'Will it have sufficient cash over the immediate future to meet its short-term liabilities as they fall due?' Unless the answer here is positive, the company is in a financial crisis irrespective of its profit performance.

Normally short-term liabilities amount to a considerable part of the total borrowings of the company. They are always greater than the company's pure cash resources. The question we ask is, 'Where will the cash come from to pay them?'

Cash is in constant movement through the company. It flows in daily from accounts receivable as as customers pay their bills. Each payment reduces the balance outstanding, unless it is in turn topped up by transfers from the finished goods inventory as new sales are made. The finished goods inventory is likewise fed from raw materials and work in process. We can visualize these assets as temporary stores for cash, i.e., inventories in various forms and accounts receivable. These are the assets that collectively make up 'current assets.' They amount to a high percentage of a company's total investment.

At the same time, goods are being purchased on credit from suppliers, thereby creating short-term liabilities. Normally other short-term loans are being availed of also. It is these that we collectively refer to as 'current liabilities.'

We measure a firm's short-term liquidity position by comparing the values of 'current assets' with its 'current liabilities.'

Three ways of expressing this relationship are illustrated:

- current ratio
- quick ratio
- 'working capital to sales' percentage.

We illustrate these measures in this chapter. In chapter 10 measures of long-term liquidity are discussed.

Current ratio

The current ratio is a favorite of the institutions that lend money. The calculation is based on a simple comparison between the totals of 'current assets' and 'current liabilities.'

The former represent the amount of liquid, i.e., cash and near-cash, assets available to the business. The latter give an indication of its upcoming cash requirements. Institutions expect to see a positive cash surplus here. We therefore look for a value comfortably in excess of 1.0 for this ratio. While this is the standard for most types of businesses, certain types of operation are capable of operating at a much lower value.

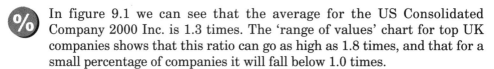

In figure 9.1 we can see that the average for the US Consolidated Company 2000 Inc. is 1.3 times. The 'range of values' chart for top UK companies shows that this ratio can go as high as 1.8 times, and that for a small percentage of companies it will fall below 1.0 times.

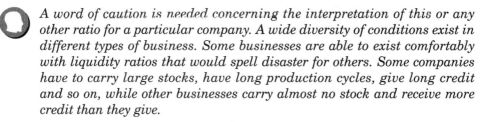

A word of caution is needed concerning the interpretation of this or any other ratio for a particular company. A wide diversity of conditions exist in different types of business. Some businesses are able to exist comfortably with liquidity ratios that would spell disaster for others. Some companies have to carry large stocks, have long production cycles, give long credit and so on, while other businesses carry almost no stock and receive more credit than they give.

One ratio value in isolation tells us little. To get a good picture of a situation we must use a series of tests and we must apply appropriate benchmarks. These benchmarks can be derived from many sources, such as historical data, competitors' accounts and published data of all kinds.

It can be said regarding liquidity ratios, that it is the trend over time rather than the absolute value that gives the most valuable information. A current ratio of 1.2 could give either a good or bad signal depending on past results.

A disadvantage of this ratio is that it does not distinguish between different types of current assets, some of which are far more liquid than others. A company could be getting into cash problems and still have a strong current ratio. This issue is addressed in the next section.

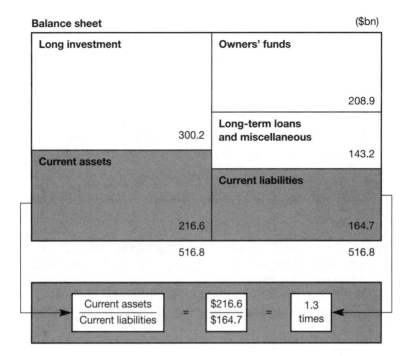

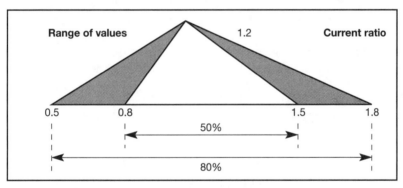

Fig. 9.1 *Current ratio applied to data from the top UK companies in 2000*

Quick ratio

The calculation here is very similiar to that of the 'current ratio.' Simply remove the 'inventories' value from the 'current assets' and divide the result by the 'current liabilities' total.

The reason for excluding the inventory figure is that its liquidity can be a problem. You will recall that the term 'liquidity' is used to express how quickly, and to what percentage of its book value, an asset can be converted into cash if the need were to arise.

For instance, a cargo of crude oil in port at Rotterdam has a high liquidity value, whereas a stock of fashion garments in a warehouse probably has a low one.

We can meet with a situation where a company has a constant current but a falling quick ratio. This would be a most dangerous sign. It tells us that inventory is building up at the expense of receivables and cash.

Lending institutions have difficulty is ascertaining the liquidity of many types of inventory. They feel much more comfortable when dealing with receivables and cash. Accordingly they pay quite a lot of attention to the 'quick ratio.'

Both the current and quick ratios are the most widely used measures of short-term liquidity but a problem with them is that they are static. They reflect values at a point in time only, i.e. at the balance sheet date. It is possible to 'window dress' a company's accounts so that it looks good on this one day only. To deal with this shortcoming it is argued that cash flow over the short-term future would be a better indicator of ability to pay. The 'working capital to sales' ratio illustrated in figure 9.3 meets this objection to a certain extent.

Figure 9.2 shows an average value of 0.9 times with 50 percent of companies falling within the range of 0.6 to 1.1 times. A value of 1.0 is very strong. It means that the company can pay off all its short-term liabilities from its cash balances plus its accounts receivable. Most companies decide that such a level of liquidity is unnecessary. An alternative name for this ratio is the 'acid test.'

Calculation

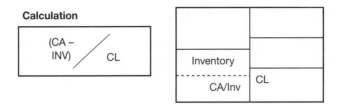

$$\frac{(CA - INV)}{CL}$$

Inventory	
CA/Inv	CL

US Consolidated Company Inc.

Balance sheet ($bn)

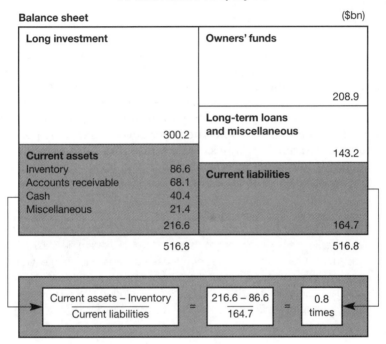

Long investment		Owners' funds	
			208.9
	300.2	Long-term loans and miscellaneous	
			143.2
Current assets			
Inventory	86.6	**Current liabilities**	
Accounts receivable	68.1		
Cash	40.4		
Miscellaneous	21.4		
	216.6		164.7
	516.8		516.8

$$\frac{\text{Current assets} - \text{Inventory}}{\text{Current liabilities}} = \frac{216.6 - 86.6}{164.7} = 0.8 \text{ times}$$

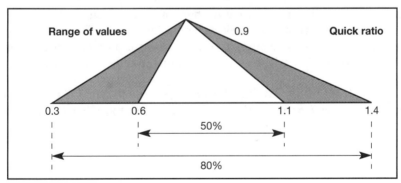

Range of values   0.9   Quick ratio

0.3   0.6   1.1   1.4

50%

80%

Fig. 9.2 Quick ratio applied to data from the top UK companies in 2000

Working capital to sales ratio

The ratio illustrated in figure 9.3 gives us a glimpse of the liquidity position from yet another angle. This measure shows up some features that cannot be ascertained easily from the previous two measures.

In chapter 3, working capital was defined as 'current assets' less 'current liabilities.' We express this value as a percentage of 'sales.'

Whereas the current and quick ratios use balance sheets figures only, here we take into account the ongoing operations by including a value from the profit and loss account. The 'sales' figure reflects, to some extent, the operating cash flow through the whole system. This ratio, therefore, relates the short-term surplus liquidity to the annual operating cash flow.

It will often highlight a trend the other ratios miss. It is possible to have a stable 'current' or 'quick' ratio while this ratio is falling. This would happen if sales were increasing rapidly but levels of working capital were static. A condition known as 'overtrading' could develop.

The term 'overtrading' is used to describe a situation where there are not sufficient resources in the balance sheet to carry the level of existing business. It arises in a company that has grown too fast or has been underfunded in the first place. The symptoms show up as a constant shortage of cash to meet day-to-day needs. There is a danger of bankruptcy. Probably the only solution to the condition is an injection of long-term liquid funds.

There is a difference between being short of 'working capital' and so managing the business that less 'working capital' is needed. The latter is a sign of good management. The modern trend is towards a lower 'working capital to sales' ratio, particularly in the form of much reduced inventories.

We can see from figure 9.3 that the average value for the US Consolidated Company Inc. is 7 percent. Research in 2000 on top UK companies suggested values of between 10 and 21 percent.

Calculation

$$\frac{(CA - CL)}{Sales}$$

Sales ← CA
CL

A: US Consolidated Company Inc.

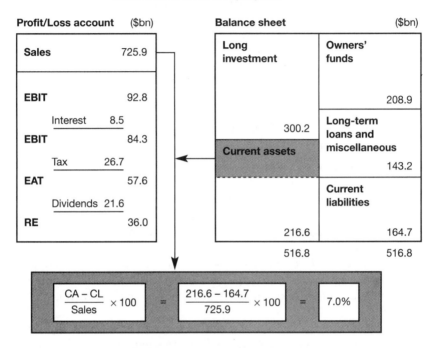

Profit/Loss account	($bn)
Sales	725.9
EBIT	92.8
Interest	8.5
EBIT	84.3
Tax	26.7
EAT	57.6
Dividends	21.6
RE	36.0

Balance sheet ($bn)

Long investment	Owners' funds
	208.9
300.2	**Long-term loans and miscellaneous**
Current assets	143.2
	Current liabilities
216.6	164.7
516.8	516.8

$$\frac{CA - CL}{Sales} \times 100 = \frac{216.6 - 164.7}{725.9} \times 100 = 7.0\%$$

B: UK top companies, 1992

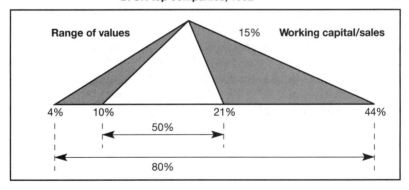

Range of values   15%   Working capital/sales

4%   10%   21%   44%

←——— 50% ———→

←——————— 80% ———————→

Fig. 9.3 Working capital to sales ratio applied to data from (A) the US Consolidated Company Inc., (B) UK top companies, 2000

Working capital days

Possibly the clearest way of looking at the role of working capital in a company's operations is illustrated in figure 9.4.

Data has been extracted from accounts of the US Consolidated Company Inc. for 'inventory,' 'accounts receivable' and 'accounts payable.' The significance of these accounts is that they are 'spontaneous.' They react very quickly to changes in levels of company turnover. The company will have policies regarding levels of inventory, etc., but these policies will not fix absolute values, they will be expressed in terms of sales. A sustained growth in sales will inevitably result in growth in these three accounts.

We express each account in terms of 'days' sales' (see figure 7.4), i.e:

	Amount	**Days**
Inventory	$86.6 (bn)	44
Accounts receivable	$68.2	34
Accounts payable	$56.1	28

This data is plotted in figure 9.4. The objective is to show the number of days that lapse from the time money is paid out to the suppliers of materials until the corresponding cash is received back from the customer that buys the goods.

We nominate Day 0 to indicate when goods are received from suppliers. Given the average stockholding period, day 44 indicates when the goods are sold. The customer takes on average 34 days to pay, so cash is received on day 78.

In the meantime the company, given its average number of days credit, will have paid the supplier on day 28. The time gap between the cash out on day 28 and its return to the company on day 78 is 50 days. (In addition the company will have have paid out in respect of wages, salaries and overheads all through the period.)

It is this time gap the creates in a company the need for working capital. The amount is easily quantified. Given a gap of 50 days, each $1m of sales requires $136,000 ($1m × 50/365) of working capital. Every increase of $1m will create a need for an additional $136,000 in cash resources. This point is often missed by small rapidly growing companies who find themselves in cash difficulties in the midst of high sales and profits.

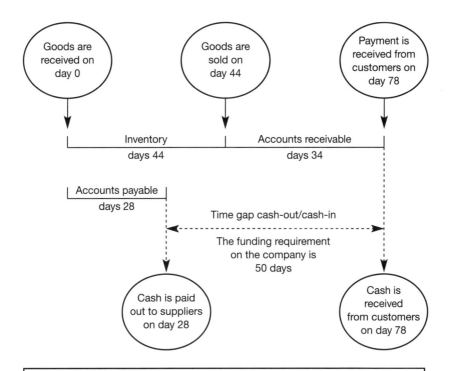

(We have used the term "working capital" here to include three items only, i.e., "inventory," "accounts receivable" and "accounts payable," but the classic definition covers all items in "current assets" and "current liabilities."

The reason is that they are (1) the dominant accounts, and (2) their behavior is spontaneous. The main items excluded are "cash" and "short loans" which depend on policy decisions. For operating management purposes, this narrow definition is more useful.)

Fig. 9.4 Working capital days for US Consolidated Company Inc.

Financial strength

Interest cover · 'Debt to equity'
ratio (D/E) · Leverage · Summary

*Over-trading is among tradesmen as over-
lifting is among strong men; such people, vain
of their strength…at last lift at something
too heavy for them, over-strain their sinews,
break some of nature's bands and are
cripples ever after.*
DANIEL DEFOE (1660–1731)

By 'financial strength' we mean a company's ability to to withstand operating setbacks. In the previous chapter we looked at the short-term position. The long-term situation is even more important. To arrive at an assessment for this we look at a company's total borrowings, and we relate them to its trading cash flow. The first measure we use is referred to as 'interest cover.'

Interest cover

This ratio is of fairly recent vintage. It is unique in that it is a measure derived solely from the profit and loss account.

The 'interest' charge is divided into the 'EBIT' figure to give the 'cover' expressed as 'so many times.'

Previous ratios looked only at the amount of borrowing. This ratio measures a company's ability to service those borrowings.

Three factors determine its value:

- The operating profit
- The total amount borrowed
- The effective rate of interest.

A highly profitable company can have very adequate interest cover even though the balance sheet may appear to be over-borrowed.

The level of interest rates in an economy will impinge significantly on this ratio, which may partly explain why low-interest economies seem to accept more highly leveraged balance sheets.

The term 'financial leverage' is used to reflect the relationship between profit and the fixed interest charge. If financial leverage is high, that is, if interest is a high part of pre-interest profits, a small change in operating profit will be greatly magnified in its effect on return to the shareholders. A highly leveraged company does well in boom times, but quickly falls into difficulty in recession.

We can see in figure 10.1 that the average for the US Consolidated Company Inc. is 10.9 times. UK research has shown that most successful companies operate at a value of approximately 5.5 times. A prudent value for a company is 5 times.

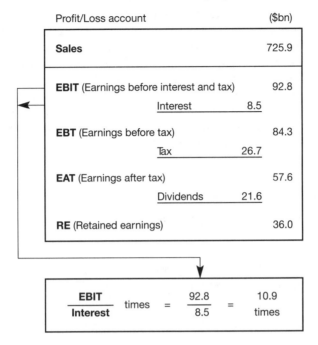

A: Interest cover applied to data from the US Consolidated Company Inc.

Profit/Loss account   ($bn)

Sales	725.9
EBIT (Earnings before interest and tax)	92.8
Interest 8.5	
EBT (Earnings before tax)	84.3
Tax 26.7	
EAT (Earnings after tax)	57.6
Dividends 21.6	
RE (Retained earnings)	36.0

$$\frac{\text{EBIT}}{\text{Interest}} \text{ times} = \frac{92.8}{8.5} = 10.9 \text{ times}$$

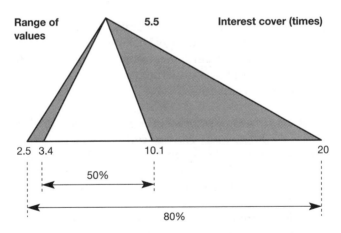

Fig. 10.1 Interest cover applied to data from top UK companies in 2000

'Debt to equity' ratio (D/E)

The 'debt to equity' ratio is one of the most fundamental measures in corporate finance. It is the great test of the financial strength of a company. Although used universally, it unfortunately turns up under many different names and with different methods of calculation. This causes some confusion which we will try to remove in this chapter.

The purpose of the ratio is to measure the mix of funds in the balance sheet and to make a comparison between those funds that have been supplied by the owners (equity) and those which have been borrowed (debt). This distinction is illustrated in figure 10.2.

The idea seems a very simple one. Nevertheless difficulties arise in two areas:

- 'What do we mean by debt?'
- 'How exactly will we express the calculation?'

We will first consider different meanings given to the term 'debt.' In figure 10.3 you will see the three interpretations in common use:

- long-term loans only
- long- and short-term loans (i.e., all interest-bearing debt)
- long-term loans plus all current liabilities (i.e., total debt)

Note that the first two definitions concentrate on formal interest-bearing debt, i.e., that sourced from banks or other financial institutions. In bank calculations, these are the definitions most commonly used. The final definition includes trade creditors plus all accruals, such as dividends, tax and other miscellaneous amounts.

The reason bank analysts use the more restricted view of debt is understandable. Their claims usually rank ahead of trade and other creditors. (Note that, at this point, we leave out the important question of creditors with statutory preference.) From the banks' point of view, the only debt that matters is that which ranks equal to or ahead of their own position.

However, from the companies' viewpoint, debt due to a supplier is just as real and as important as that due to a bank. There are therefore good arguments for including all debt in the calculation of the debt to equity ratio.

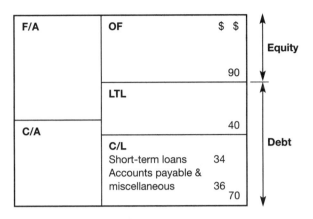

Fig. 10.2 The debt to equity ratio

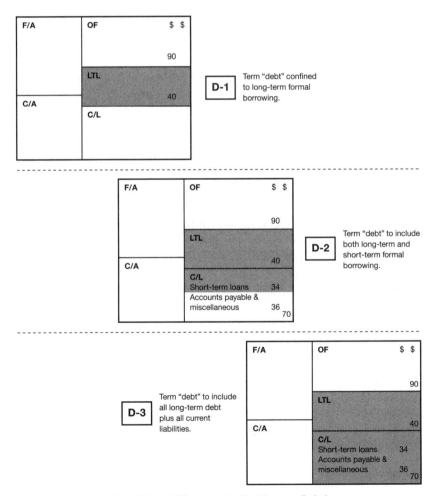

Term "debt" confined to long-term formal borrowing. **D-1**

Term "debt" to include both long-term and short-term formal borrowing. **D-2**

Term "debt" to include all long-term debt plus all current liabilities. **D-3**

Fig. 10.3 Different definitions of debt

Debt/equity – methods of calculation

As stated previously, one kind of debt is as important as another from a management point of view. For that reason, we will use the broadest definition – long-term loans plus current liabilities – for the remainder of this book. This done, we will examine the various ways in which the ratio can be calculated.

First we should emphasize that it matters little which method of calculation we use. Different methods simply give different numbers that mean the same thing. We can measure length in either inches or centimetres and the different numbers express the same length. So also we express the relationship between equity and debt in different ways. The true ratio is the same irrespective of how it is expressed.

This point is worth noting. There are a relatively small number of independent financial ratios that are absolutely fundamental; this is such a one. Sometimes it seems that there are dozens of business ratios of all kinds.

Figure 10.4. shows three methods for expressing the 'debt to equity' ratio:

Method 1 – debt over equity
This is the classic approach and it is used widely, i.e. all formal interest bearing debt is expressed as a ratio to equity. When a debt to equity value is quoted for a company, then, in the absence of evidence to the contrary, it should be assumed that this method has been adopted.

Method 2 – equity over total funds
An approach that is not so common. The answer is almost the reciprocal of the third method shown below and one which is more often encountered.

Method 3 – total debt over total funds
This approach is favored by the author, i.e. all debt in the balance sheet, whether interest bearing or not, is expressed as a percentage of total funds. It gives an instant picture of the funding side of the total balance sheet. The numbers are easily extracted from the most complex set of accounts.

(The thorny question of how to treat deferred tax and other miscellaneous funds is being ignored for the present. While these items can give rise to nice academic debates, in practice they do not cause serious difficulties. They are usually insignificant in terms of the total balance sheet – see appendix 1.)

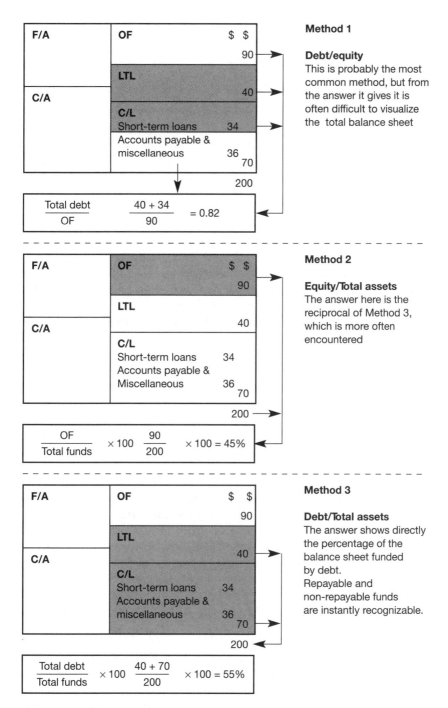

Fig. 10.4 Different methods of expressing the debt into equity ratio

Debt/equity – why it is important

> We place a lot of emphasis on this ratio because, if it goes wrong, the company has a real long-term problem; one which may become terminal.

The greater the debt, the greater the risk. All debt in the balance sheet gives third parties legal claims on the company. These claims are for interest payments at regular intervals, plus repayment of the principal by the agreed time. The principal is repaid either by periodic instalments or a single lump sum at the end of the loan period.

Therefore when a company raises debt, it takes on a commitment to substantial fixed cash out-flows for some time into the future. The company does not have a guaranteed cash in-flow over the same period. Indeed the in-flow may be most uncertain. A fixed cash out-flow combined with an uncertain cash in-flow gives rise to financial risk. It follows that the greater the loan, the greater is the risk.

Why, then, do companies take on debt and incur this extra risk? The answer lies in the relative costs. Debt costs less than equity funds. By adding debt to its balance sheet, a company can generally improve its profitability, add to its share price, increase the wealth of its shareholders and develop greater potential for growth.

> Debt increases both profit and risk. It is the job of management to maintain a proper balance between the two.

Where should the line be drawn? The increased return to the equity shareholder that results from debt leverage can rarely be forsaken altogether even though some companies do just that. Most companies must take a view on the degree of uncertainty of future cash receipts and arrange their level of debt in line with this uncertainty.

We find that companies in business sectors with very predictable income streams, e.g. property leasing, incur high levels of debt. Companies in highly volatile sectors, e.g. mine exploration, fund mainly from equity.

We find geographical as well as sectoral differences in companies' approach to debt (see figure 10.5). In the US as well as in the UK the approach is more conservative than we find in the EU. In the former locations it is unusual for debt/total assets to exceed 60 percent. In the latter we often encounter ratios of 70 percent and over.

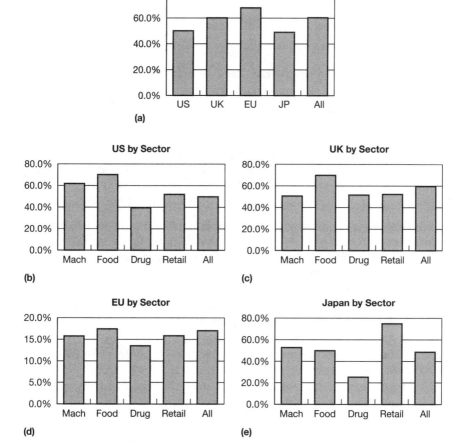

Fig. 10.5 Analysis of debt/total assets ratio by country and by sector

Much has been written exploring the reasons for these variations. The general conclusion seems to be that they arise because of attitudinal, cultural and historical, rather than financial, factors.

Leverage

This subject is covered in greater depth in chapter 13, but it is appropriate here to consider the impact of different debt to equity ratios on shareholders' returns.

In figure 10.6, section A, we see a company for which the mix of funds has not yet been decided. It has assets of $100,000, sales of $120,000 and an operating profit of $15,000. The effects of different levels of gearing or leverage on the shareholders are illustrated in Sections B and C. (Note: For simplicity, tax is ignored and the interest rate is set at 10 percent.)

In section B, just one level of leverage is analyzed to show you how the figures work. Option 1 in the first row illustrates a situation with $100,000 equity and no debt. Accordingly there is no interest charge. The total profit of $15,000 is applied to the shareholders' investment of $100,000. The ROE is 15 percent.

In the second row, the funding mix has changed to $80,000 equity and $20,000 debt. The interest charge at 10 percent is $2,000. This is deducted from the profit of $15,000 to leave $13,000 for the shareholders. Because the equity investment is now $80,000 the ROE is 16.25 percent ($13,000/$80,000 × 100).

As a result of introducing 20 percent debt into the company, the ROE has increased from 15 percent to 16.25 percent. This is financial leverage in action.

In section C, the leverage has been extended in steps all the way up to 90 percent. With each additional slice of debt, the ROE increases until it reaches 60 percent at the 90 percent level of debt. Extraordinarily high levels of return can thus be achieved from very highly leveraged companies. The price that is paid for these high returns is the additional exposure to risk.

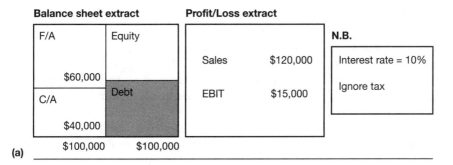

Balance sheet extract

F/A	Equity
$60,000	
C/A	Debt
$40,000	
$100,000	$100,000

Profit/Loss extract

Sales	$120,000
EBIT	$15,000

N.B.

Interest rate = 10%

Ignore tax

(a)

Funding mix options and calculations

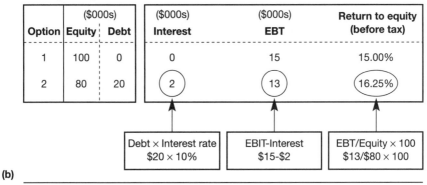

	($000s)		($000s)	($000s)	Return to equity
Option	Equity	Debt	Interest	EBT	(before tax)
1	100	0	0	15	15.00%
2	80	20	2	13	16.25%

Debt × Interest rate	EBIT-Interest	EBT/Equity × 100
$20 × 10%	$15-$2	$13/$80 × 100

(b)

Degrees of leverage and impact on ROE

	($000s)				Return to equity
Option	Equity	Debt	Interest	EBT	(before tax)
1	100	0	0	15	15.00%
2	80	20	2	13	16.25%
3	60	40	4	11	18.33%
4	50	50	5	10	20.00%
5	40	60	6	9	22.50%
6	20	80	8	7	35.00%
7	10	90	9	6	**60.00%**

(c)

Fig. 10.6 Effects of different levels of leverage

Summary

The debt/equity or leverage decision is one of great importance to management. There is a risk return trade-off. The impulse to achieve high returns for the shareholders must be restrained by the company's risk profile. Even a very well managed company can suffer an unexpected deterioration in its financial position either from a default on the part of a major debtor or a general worsening of business conditions. Such a deterioration can be very difficult to recover from. It is prudent to keep some liquidity in reserve to guard against such an eventuality.

Cash flow

The cash flow statement · Sources
and uses of funds – method ·
Opening and closing cash
reconciliation · Long and short
analysis · Financial reporting
standards

*But when times are bad and the breath of
fear has already chilled the markets, the
banker must be cautious, conservative, and
severe. His business has been aptly compared
to that of a man who stands ready to lend
umbrellas when it is fine and demand them
back when it starts to rain.*
SIR GEOFFREY CROWTHER (1907–1972)

The cash flow statement

The cash flow statement completes a company's set of published accounts. Its purpose is to track the flow of funds through the company. It identifies where cash has gone to and where it has come from and it is a very powerful tool for explaining movements in the various liquidity ratios.

There are those who would contend that the cash flow statement is more reliable and less subject to manipulation than the profit and loss account.

Many operating cash movements do not appear in the profit and loss account. One reason is that the profit and loss account uses the accruals concept to adjust a company's cash flows to bring them into line with revenue earned and costs incurred for a specific period. While it is most important that true revenue and costs are identified, these adjustments sometimes hide important aspects of a company's affairs.

The cash flow statement has in the past been presented in many formats, but it has now been standardized into the layout shown (in slightly simplified form) in figure 11.6.

The rules relating to cash flow are very simple. Every time a company writes a cheque, a cash out-flow occurs. When a cheque is received, there is a cash in-flow. This is the only rule, and its very simplicity means that it is difficult to find mechanisms to hide unpleasant truths about a company's affairs.

However, despite its clarity, it cannot, as is occasionally suggested, replace the profit and loss account. The latter correctly distinguishes between cash paid for electricity consumed last month and cash paid for a building that will be occupied by the company for the next 20 years.

This chapter looks at the logic of the cash flow statement and how it can be of use to management.

Sources and uses of funds – method

To get at the data needed in order to build a cash flow statement, we go through a sources and uses exercise. The mechanics of this exercise are easy to grasp and are shown in figure 11.1 opposite.

In figure 11.1 a simplified balance sheet is shown for the two years 2000 and 2001. It has been laid out in vertical columns to facilitate comparison between the two years. The assets are in the upper section of the statement and the liabilities in the lower. To the right of the balance sheet, two extra columns have been added – respectively 'Source' and 'Use.'

 An entry will be made in one of these columns for every change that has taken place in a balance sheet item.

- If the change has caused a cash out-flow, the entry will be entered in the 'Use'column.
- For a cash in-flow, the entry will be made in the 'Source' column.

Two entries have been illustrated:

1 Fixed assets $10,000   Use of funds

2 Tax $500   Source of funds

The logic of the first entry is fairly obvious. The fixed assets have increased from $22,500 to $32,500. The company has had to write a cheque for $10,000. (For the purposes of this exercise we ignore revaluation and depreciation.)

The second entry is less obvious. The amount shown under 'Tax' has increased from $2,500 to $3,000. How can an increase in tax be a source of funds? The answer is that the tax amount of $3,000 shown as a liability in the closing balance sheet is unpaid. The company now has the use of $500 more government money than it had one year ago, so for the present it is a source of funds. This liability will have to be paid off in due course. It will then disappear from the balance sheet and be picked up as a use of funds.

Balance sheets ($000s)	2000 $	2001 $	Source	Use
Assets				
Fixed assets	22,500	32,500		10,000
Current assets				
Inventory (stocks)	12,500	14,350		
Accounts receivable (debtors)	15,000	16,000		
Cash	1,750	0		
Total assets	$51,750	$62,850		
Liabilities				
Issued capital	18,000	18,000		
Reserves	9,500	10,750		
Long-term loans	8,000	9,000		
Current liabilities				
Accounts payable (creditors)	13,750	17,000		
Bank short-term loans	0	5,100		
Current tax due	2,500	3,000	500	
Total liabilities	$51,750	$62,850		

Increase in liability
=
source of funds

Increase in assets
=
use of funds

Fig. 11.1 Sources and uses of funds – example

Rules of construction

The completed statement is shown in figure 11.2. All changes in balance sheet values have been identified and classified as sources or uses. The total sources agree with the total uses. This will always be the case.

It can be difficult at first to distinguish sources from uses and to put items into the wrong columns. Fortunately there is a rule that makes the classification very simple:

	Increase	**Decrease**
Asset	Use	Source
Liability	Source	Use

Therefore to complete the statement one simply needs to identify a change in any balance sheet value and answer the the following questions:

- 'Is the item an asset or liability?'
- 'Has its value increased or decreased?'

then the item automatically slots into its correct column.

The exercise illustrates a technique for translating all balance sheet changes into corresponding movements of funds. The reader will appreciate the this method does not in fact identify all cash payments and all cash receipts. What it does is track net movements in assets and liabilities that will impinge on a company's cash position. The method demonstrated is called the 'indirect method'.*

Hidden movements

A word of caution is needed here. The indirect method picks up only the net movements in balance sheet values. Of course a net change can be the result of two oposing movements that partly cancel out. A full cash flow statement should pick such items. Even more importantly some movements in balance sheet values do not give rise to cash flow – revaluation of fixed assets is an example (see appendix 1). It may be necessary to get behind some of the numbers to find out if there are any hidden or non-cash movements. Notwithstanding these qualifications, the method illustrated here is a powerful tool of analysis.

---

*One sometimes sees a 'payments and receipts' form of cash statement that gives summaries of all cheques paid and received. Such a statement has little analytical value but is crucial for control purposes.

Balance sheets ($000s)	2000 $	2001 $	Source	Use
Assets				
Fixed assets	22,500	32,500		10,000
Current assets				
Inventory (stocks)	12,500	14,350		1,850
Accounts receivable (debtors)	15,000	16,000		1,000
Cash	1,750	0	1,750	
Total assets	$51,750	$62,850		
Liabilities				
Issued capital	18,000	18,000		
Reserves	9,500	10,750	1,250	
Long-term loans	8,000	9,000	1,000	
Current liabilities				
Accounts payable (creditors)	13,750	17,000	3,250	
Bank short-term loans	0	5,100	5,100	
Current tax due	2,500	3,000	500	
Total liabilities	$51,750	$62,850	$12,850	$12,850

Hidden movements
This figure gives the net change in fixed assets.
It probably masks a depreciation charge counterbalanced
by an even greater figure for new investment, e.g.
if depreciation of $2,500 had been charged in the period,
then the total new investment is $12,500.

Fig. 11.2 Completed allocation of sources and uses funds

Opening and closing cash reconciliation

Once the sources and uses have been identified and reconciled, we can use various layouts of the cash flow statement to draw management's attention to specific issues.

For instance, the company's cash position could deteriorate even though high profits have been achieved. To explain why, we could use a layout that would reconcile opening and closing cash with the net cash flow for the period. It would show:

- the opening cash balance,
- the itemized cash out-flows,
- the itemized cash in-flows,
- the closing cash balance.

The layout shown in figure 11.3 illustrates such a reconciliation.

(Note: A cash balance can be positive or negative. A positive position is where there is cash asset whereas a negative position shows up as short-term bank loan.)

The various entries are taken straight from the 'sources/uses' statement (see Figure 11.2). 'Cash-out' items are taken from the 'use' column and 'cash-in' from the 'source' column. There is one exception to this rule: movements in 'cash' and 'short loan' are not listed because they are absorbed in the 'opening/closing' cash positions.

- The total for cash-out comes to: $12,850 (negative)
- The total for cash-in comes to: $ 6,000 (positive)
- The net cash flow is the difference: – $ 6,850 (negative)

This net cash flow, added to the opening cash figure of $1,750 (positive) gives the closing cash position of $5,100 (negative).

The statement clearly identifies major movements in the cash position. Even a cursory examination of the figures shows the reason for the negative cash flow. The company has expended $10,000 on fixed assets. This relatively large sum has not been matched by any corresponding large cash in-flows. The assets have been purchased from day-to-day operating cash.

The heavily negative net cash flow also explains why the 'current ratio' has dropped from 1.8 to 1.2 times, and the 'debt to total assets' ratio of the company has increased from 47 percent to 54 percent.

This issue is pursued further in the next section.

Balance sheets ($000s)	2000 $	2001 $	Source $	Use $
Assets				
Fixed assets	22,500	32,500		10,000
Current assets				
Inventory (stocks)	12,500	14,350		1,850
Accounts receivable (debtors)	15,000	16,000		1,000
Cash	1,750	0	1,750	
Total assets	$51,750	$62,850		
Liabilities				
Issued capital	18,000	18,000		
Reserves	9,500	10,750	1,250	
Long-term loans	8,000	9,000	1,000	
Current liabilities				
Accounts payable (creditors)	13,750	17,000	3,250	
Bank short-term loans	0	5,100	5,100	
Current tax due	2,500	3,000	500	
Total liabilities	$51,750	$62,850	$12,850	$12,850

Cash reconciliation statement

(A) Opening cash position		$1,750
Cash out		
Fixed assets	(10,000)	
Inventory	(1,850)	
Accounts receivable	(1,000)	
(B) Total cash out		($12,850)
Cash in (sources)		
Reserves	1,250	
Long-term loans	1,000	
Accounts payable	3,250	
Current tax due	500	
(C) Total cash in		$6,000
(D) Net cash flow (C-B)		($6,850)
Closing cash position (A-D)		($5,100)

Fig. 11.3 Opening and closing cash reconciliation

Long and short analysis

The information provided in figure 11.3 adds considerably to knowledge of the company's affairs that we could have derived from the balance sheet and profit and loss account. Alternative layouts of the cash flow data provide more insights.

In figure 11.4, the same original data has been plotted into a grid that distinguishes between 'long' and 'short' sources on the one hand, and 'long' and 'short' uses on the other (refer back to page 111 where the 'long' and 'short' sections of the balance sheet were identified).

Each item in the 'Source' column has been slotted into its appropriate 'long' or 'short' box. Ditto for all items in the 'Use' column. The boxes are totaled to give four major values for comparison.

The main expenditure has taken place in the 'Long-Use' box. We identify here the large fixed asset purchase of $10,000.

The corresponding 'Long-Source' box shows $2,250. The total amount of long-term cash received into the business by way of 'Reserves' and the 'Long-term loan' falls considerably short of the fixed asset expenditure.

Because 'sources' and 'uses' must balance, the above deficit must be made good from the 'Short-Source' box. We see that this is indeed the case. The bulk of the cash in-flow falls into the short-term box.

Most of the money that has come into the business has come from 'accounts payable' and 'bank overdraft.' These are be due to be repaid within 12 months. The company has used short-term sources to fund long-term assets.

This layout of the cash flow highlights the fact that 'current liabilities' have increased by much more than 'current assets' and has brought about the deterioration we have already seen in the 'current ratio.'

The 'debt to total assets ratio' has also deteriorated over the 2000–01 period. This is analyzed in further detail in the next section.

Balance sheets ($000s)	2000 $	2001 $	Source	Use
Assets				
Fixed assets	22,500	32,500		10,000
Current assets				
Inventory (stocks)	12,500	14,350		1,850
Accounts receivable (debtors)	15,000	16,000		1,000
Cash	1,750	0	1,750	
Total assets	$51,750	$62,850		
Liabilities				
Issued capital	18,000	18,000		
Reserves	9,500	10,750	1,250	
Long-term loans	8,000	9,000	1,000	
Current liabilities				
Accounts payable (creditors)	13,750	17,000	3,250	
Bank short-term loans	0	5,100	5,100	
Current tax due	2,500	3,000	500	
Total liabilities	$51,750	$62,850	$12,850	$12,850

	Source	$	Use	$
Long	Reserves	1,250	Fixed assets	10,000
	Long-term loans	1,000		
		2,250		10,000
Short	Bank loan	5,100	Inventory	1,850
	Accounts payable	3,250	Accounts receivable	1,000
	Current tax	500		
	Cash	1,750		
		10,600		2,850
		12,850		12,850

Fig. 11.4 Long and short analysis of sources and uses of funds

Long and short strategy

In figure 11.5, the long and short grid of figure 11.4 is repeated, but the detail has been removed to show only the total values in each section. Arrows show the movements of funds. The largest single movement of funds in the company for the 2000–01 period has been the $7,750 raised short and invested long.

The problem with this strategy is that short-term funds have to be repaid quickly, but they cannot be withdrawn from the investment to meet this repayment. Therefore a new source of funds must be found to meet the repayments. Conditions could deteriorate to the extent that the company would be unable to raise new money and it would then be in a financial crisis. The grid has identified a movement of funds that is loaded with risk.

A well-known principle of finance is that funds for long-term uses should come from long-term sources – the matching principle. Short-term uses can be largely funded from short-term sources, but not entirely as we shall see.

A second principle of finance is that the new funds into the company should be sourced in the proportions of a good 'debt to equity ratio.'

For example, if the company had an existing ratio of 60 percent debt to 40 percent equity, then we would expect the new funds to reflect this mix approximately. In the example used, however, the funds have been raised as approximately 90 percent debt ($11,600 including LTL) and 10 percent equity ($1,250). It is this high level of debt in the new funds has damaged the 'debt to equity ratio' of the company by moving it from 47 percent to 54 percent

A third principle it is advisable to follow is that the totals in the two short-term boxes should show the same relationship as 'current assets' to 'current liabilities' in the opening balance sheet.

This must be so if we wish to maintain the existing 'current ratio.' In the example used the short-source box should have a total that is just little in excess of 50 percent of the short-use box. In fact the figure that emerges is almost 400 percent.

The analysis has shown that the company has breached all three principles of cash flow management.

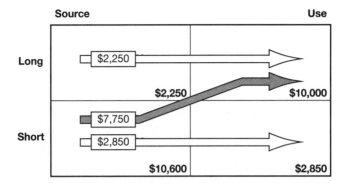

Source   Use

Note:
The most significant movement of funds illustrated above
is the $7,750 raised in the short source box and invested
in the long use box.
When a company raises funds short and invests them
long, it increases the risk of bankruptcy.

An ideal pattern of cash flows

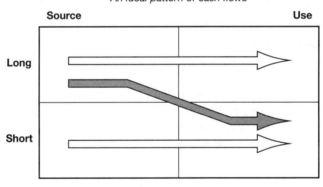

Source   Use

Note:
Over a long period we would expect to see a cash pattern
as illustrated above, with these elements:
(1) long investments being funded from long sources
(2) short investments being funded from short sources
(3) some long-term funds being invested in short-term assets.

The reason for item (3) is that working capital needs to
expand in line with company growth. The funds to meet this
requirement must be drawn from a long source.

Fig. 11.5 Strategy for long and short movements of funds

Financial reporting standards

In recent years there have been a number of highly publicized situations where it emerged after the event that fully audited published financial statements had not provided satisfactory information to the investors or bankers involved. Criticism has been voiced of existing standards of reporting.

As a result the Financial Accounting Standards Boards (FASB) of the various developed countries have stepped up their efforts to impose more rigorous reporting standards. The cash flow statement has been one to receive particular attention.

Phrases such as: 'to give users information on the liquidity, viability and financial adaptability of the entity concerned,'; 'improved understanding of a reporting entity's cash generating or cash absorption mechanisms,'; 'basis for the assessment of future cash flow,' give a flavor of the desired objectives.

The standards arrived at lay great stress on identifying the following separate components of the flow of cash and its equivalents:

- operating activities
- servicing of finance and taxation
- investing activities
- financing activities.

They further require a reconciliation of the figure shown for operating profit and operating cash flow, as well as a total showing the net cash inflow or out-flow before financing.

Figure 11.6 identifies the main headings but omits much of the detail in the interest of clarity.

The terminology in the Reporting Standards will be widely used in boardrooms and management meetings over the coming years. It is important that managers be familiar with this terminology and appreciate the significance of the various components of cash flow. The sources and uses statement has been dropped as a reporting requirement, but it still remains a powerful tool of analysis for managers to use for their own benefit.

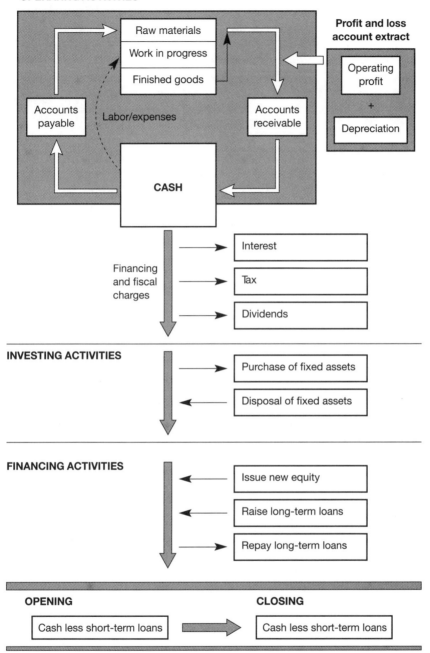

OPERATING ACTIVITIES

Raw materials
Work in progress
Finished goods

Profit and loss account extract

Operating profit

+

Depreciation

Accounts payable

Labor/expenses

Accounts receivable

CASH

Financing and fiscal charges

Interest

Tax

Dividends

INVESTING ACTIVITIES

Purchase of fixed assets

Disposal of fixed assets

FINANCING ACTIVITIES

Issue new equity

Raise long-term loans

Repay long-term loans

OPENING

Cash less short-term loans

CLOSING

Cash less short-term loans

Fig. 11.6 Main headings of a corporate cash flow report

Part IV Determinants of corporate value

Corporate valuation

Introduction · Share values

He used to watch the market most precisely,
and got in first, and so he did quite nicely.
GEOFFREY CHAUCER (1380)

Introduction

The value of public companies is determined by the stock market. The value of companies not publicly quoted will be greatly influenced by the same market. In this chapter, therefore, we will look at the main stock-market-related ratios.

These are:

- market capitalization
- share values, nominal, book, market
- earnings per share (EPS)
- dividends per share (DPS)
- dividend cover and the pay-out ratio
- earnings yield
- dividend yield
- price to earnings ratio (PE)
- market to book ratio.

When we talk about the value of a company we mean its market capitalization or the combined value of the common stock. We have already looked at the position that common shares occupy in the balance sheet and have seen where they stand in the queue for participation in profits. Both these issues are important for an understanding of this chapter.

In figure 12.1 we again see the balance sheet for the Example Co. plc. The top right-hand box shows common or owners funds totaling $360. Various accounting rules have been applied over many years in arriving at this value, e.g., how much depreciation has been charged to the profit/loss account?

A more pragmatic approach to determine the value of owners funds is to take the total assets figure of $800 and deduct from it the total loans figure of $440 (200 + 240). This approach gives us the same answer in our example but it emphasizes the importance of the asset values in determining shareholders' funds. The authentic value for owners funds is derived simply by taking the total value of all assets in to-days terms and deducting all third party liabilities.

Some adjustments to assets values (and, possibly, liabilities) will probably be necessary.

The more likely areas for adjustment are shown in figure 12.1, i.e.:

- fixed assets
- inventories
- certain liabilities.

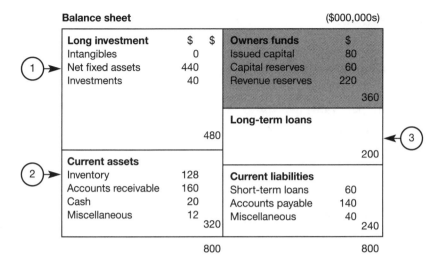

Balance sheet ($000,000s)

Long investment	$	$	Owners funds	$
Intangibles	0		Issued capital	80
Net fixed assets	440		Capital reserves	60
Investments	40		Revenue reserves	220
				360
			Long-term loans	
		480		
				200
Current assets				
Inventory	128		Current liabilities	
Accounts receivable	160		Short-term loans	60
Cash	20		Accounts payable	140
Miscellaneous	12		Miscellaneous	40
		320		240
		800		800

While all asset values can be queried, and one or two liabilities, the main areas where difficulties can be expected are listed.

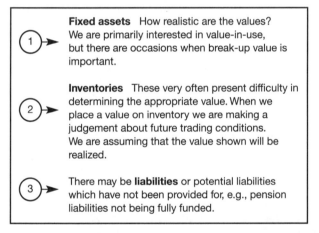

Fixed assets How realistic are the values? We are primarily interested in value-in-use, but there are occasions when break-up value is important.

Inventories These very often present difficulty in determining the appropriate value. When we place a value on inventory we are making a judgement about future trading conditions. We are assuming that the value shown will be realized.

There may be **liabilities** or potential liabilities which have not been provided for, e.g., pension liabilities not being fully funded.

Fig. 12.1 Company valuation applied to data from the Example Co. plc

Share values

In Chapter 2, three types of share value were mentioned. We now look at these in detail using figures from the Example Co. plc (figure 12.2). There are 32 million issued common shares, for each of which there is a:

Nominal (par) value of $2.50

Book (asset) value of $11.25

Market value of $22.50.

Let us now look at each of these in turn.

Nominal (Par) value $2.50

The nominal value is largely a notional low figure arbitrarily placed on a company's stock. It serves to determine the value of 'issued common stock,' i.e., in the Example Co. the number of issued shares is 32m. The par value is $2.5 to give a value of $80m. If new shares are issued, they will hold this same nominal value even though the issue price will be much above it, probably close to the current market price. Say new shares go out at a price of $17.50, there is a surplus of $15.00 over the nominal value. This surplus is called the 'share premium' and it forms part of the capital reserves. Many companies have shares of 'no par value.' They simply put it in the books at the price they were sold at.

Book value (asset value, or asset backing) $11.25

This value is arrived at by dividing the number of issued shares – 32m – into the owners' funds of $360m. The book value of all the shares is $360m. Therefore each share has a book value of $11.50. You will recall that we discussed the need to validate that sum of $360m. For instance, if an examination of the inventories produced a more prudent valuation of $20m less than the balance sheet value ($108m), this write-down would reduce the common funds from 360m to 340m. The book value would fall from $11.26 to $10.62 per share.

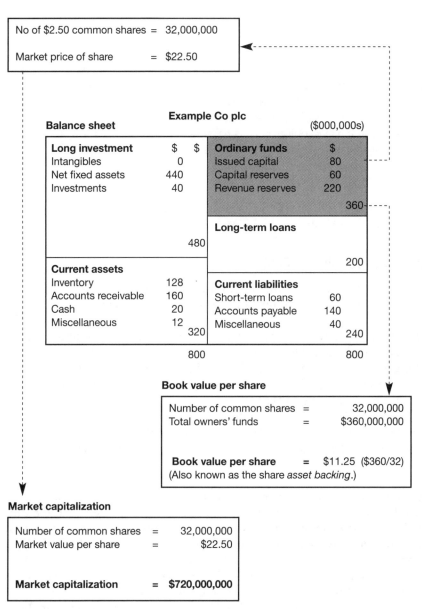

Fig. 12.2 Share value and market capitalization applied to data from the Example Co. plc

Market value $22.50

This is the price quoted in the Stock Exchange for a public company or an esti-mated price for a non-quoted company. On the Stock Exchange the figure changes daily in response to actual or anticipated results and overall or sectoral sentiment of the market as reflected in the Stock Exchange indices. It is sug-gested that the main objective of management is to secure the best price possible under any set of conditions.

These different values will be used to derive the various ratios explored in the rest of the chapter.

Earnings per share (EPS)

'Earnings per share' is one of the most widely quoted statistics when there is a discussion of a company's performance or share value.

Figure 12.3 shows how this ratio is calculated. Remember that the common shareholder comes last in the queue for participating in profit. The profit used in the calculation is the figure after all other claimants have been satisfied. The most common prior charges in the profit and loss account are interest and tax.

Therefore it is the earnings after tax (EAT) figure that is divided by the number of common shares to calculate the value of earnings per share. This figure tells us what profit has been earned by the common share-holder for every share held.

It serves no purpose to compare the earnings per share in one company with that in another because a company can elect to have a large number of shares of low denomination or a smaller number of a higher denomina-tion. A company can also decide to increase or reduce the number of shares on issue. This decision will automatically alter the earnings per share. We cannot say, therefore, that a company with an earnings per share value of 50p is any better than one with a value of 40p.

While the absolute amount of earnings per share tells nothing about a company's performance, the growth in EPS over time is a very important statistic. Indeed, many chairpersons stress it as a prime target in annual reports. Furthermore, growth in earnings per share has a significant influence on the market price of the share.

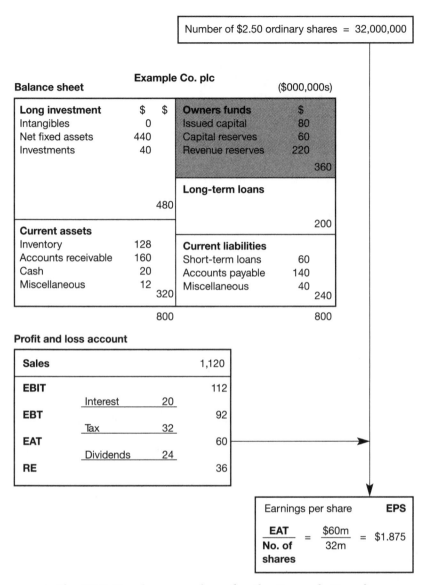

Fig. 12.3 Earnings per share for the Example Co. plc

Growth in EPS tells us more about a company's progress than growth in absolute profits. Growth in profits can result from a great many things. For instance, a company could acquire another for shares and thereby increase its profit. However, if the percentage increase in profit is less than the percentage increase in the number of shares, earnings per share will fall even with higher profits.

Not only is growth in EPS most important, so also is its stability. Investors look closely at the quality of earnings. They dislike the erratic performance of companies with widely fluctuating profits. A high-quality rating is given to earnings that are showing steady, non-volatile growth.

Dividends per share (DPS)

Figure 12.4 shows how to calculate this value. Only a fraction of the earnings accruing to the shareholders is paid out to them in cash. The remainder is retained to consolidate and expand the business.

It is a well-established rule that dividends are paid only out of profits, not from any other source. However, the earnings need not necessarily fall into the same year as the dividends. Therefore situations can arise when dividends exceed earnings. In such cases, dividends are being paid from earnings that have been retained in the business from previous years.

The total return to the shareholder over any given time consists of the dividend received plus the growth in the share price. While for some investors growth is most important, many shareholders and potential investors – both private individuals and institutions such as pension funds who need income for their day-to-day affairs – pay very close attention to dividends. They look at the absolute dividend per share and for a history of stable but growing payments.

Therefore companies dislike intensely to have to reduce the dividend because this will drive away investors with possibly serious effects on share price. A company in a difficult year will often decide that it must pay a dividend in excess of earnings rather than cut the pay-out. Of course, this policy can be followed only for a short time and when there is reason to believe that earnings will recover to a figure greater than the dividends.

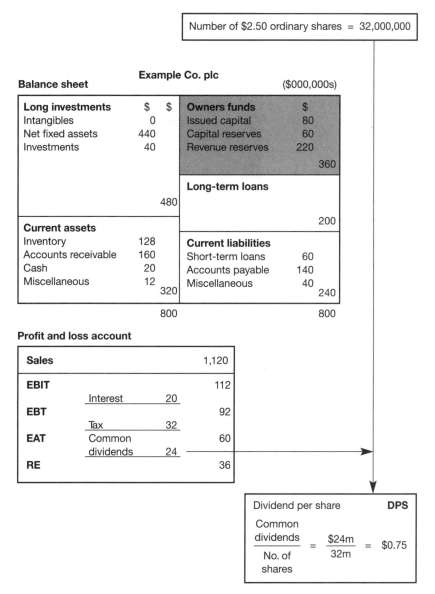

Number of $2.50 ordinary shares = 32,000,000

Example Co. plc

Balance sheet ($000,000s)

Long investments	$	$	Owners funds	$
Intangibles	0		Issued capital	80
Net fixed assets	440		Capital reserves	60
Investments	40		Revenue reserves	220
				360
		480	**Long-term loans**	
				200
Current assets				
Inventory	128		**Current liabilities**	
Accounts receivable	160		Short-term loans	60
Cash	20		Accounts payable	140
Miscellaneous	12		Miscellaneous	40
		320		240
		800		800

Profit and loss account

Sales		1,120
EBIT		112
Interest	20	
EBT		92
Tax	32	
EAT	Common	60
	dividends 24	
RE		36

Dividend per share **DPS**

$$\frac{\text{Common dividends}}{\text{No. of shares}} = \frac{\$24m}{32m} = \$0.75$$

Fig. 12.4 Dividends per share for the Example Co. plc

Dividends cover and the pay-out ratio

These two ratios are mirror images of one another and give the same information. Both express the relationship between a company's earnings and the cash paid out in dividends. Figure 12.5 shows the calculations. For the first ratio divide EPS by DPS. For the second reverse the numbers.*

Companies adopt dividend policies to suit their business needs. These will reflect the sectors in which they operate and the specific strategies they adopt. Fast-growing companies have a great need for cash and they pay out little. On the other hand stable low-growth companies pay out a high percentage of earnings.

We therefore see that public utility companies are noted for high stable pay-out policies. They are therefore, very popular with investors for whom income is the most important consideration. On the other hand, some computer companies have never paid a dividend, even though they have made large profits over many years. These companies attract investors who look for capital growth.

The importance of the dividend's cover is the indication it gives of the future stability and growth of the dividend:

- a high cover (low pay-out ratio) suggests that the dividend is fairly safe, because it can be maintained in the face of any expected downturn in profit.

- a high cover also indicates a high retention policy, which suggests that the company is aiming for high growth.

---

*These calculations use the earnings and dividend for a single share to arrive at the results. We can also use the earnings and dividend for the total company to derive the same results, as has been done for the US Consolidated Company Inc. in figure 12.6.

From previous calculation

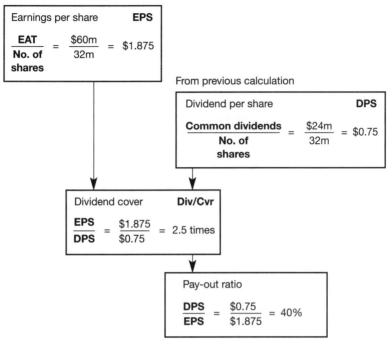

Fig. 12.5 Dividends cover and pay-out ratio for the Example Co. plc

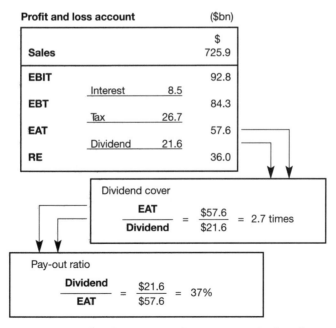

Fig. 12.6 Dividends cover and pay-out ratio for the US
Consolidated Company Inc.

Figures 12.6 and 12.7 show what level of cover is normal. In US Consolidated Inc., it is 2.7 times (equal to a 37 percent pay-out ratio). This tells us that in most companies more that 50 percent of available profit is ploughed back into the operation.

The country and sectoral analysis charts in figure 12.7 show how closely international companies cluster around the average (Japan is the exception with an interest cover greater than 6 times). It is not surprising, given their high historic growth rates.

It is worthwhile considering the implication of these numbers. Companies in the main retain more profits than they distribute. More than 50 percent of equity returns, therefore, should come from capital growth, not dividends. However, capital growth depends on the share price.

Most share prices show significant fluctuations around a central trend line. Therefore, the actual capital gain delivered to a particular investor is heavily dependent on the timing of the investment and its later conversion back into cash.

For instance, an investor in a high growth stock would suffer a capital loss if he bought at the high and sold at the low point in the cycle.

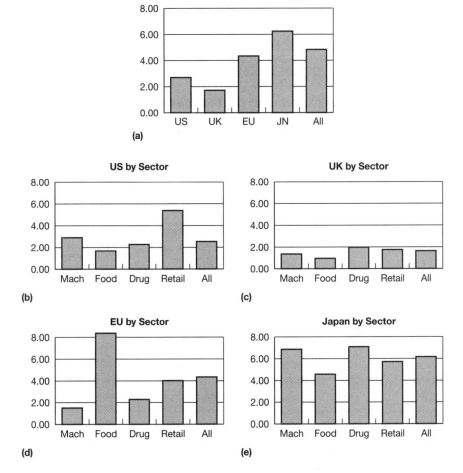

Fig. 12.7 Dividend cover by country and by sector

Earnings and dividend yield ratios

> The yield on a share expresses the return it provides in terms of earnings or dividends as a percentage of the current share price. Both measures are important for both the investor and the company.

Figure 12.8 shows calculations for the Example Co. plc.

The earnings yield shows the relationship that EPS bears to the share price. For instance, if the EPS is $1.50 and the share price is $10.00 the earnings yield is 15 percent. If the share price moved up to $15.00 the corresponding yield would be 10 percent. As the share price increases the yield falls. Paradoxically, a low yield indicates a share that is in much demand by investors. We will see in the next section its link to the price earnings ratio.

From the company point of view, the ratio indicates the return the company must provide to attract investors. If a company falls out of favor in the market-place the share price falls and the company is faced with a higher yield. It follows that a company with a poor image has to pay a high return to attract capital.

For the investor, yield calculations allow comparisons to be made between the return on shares and other types of investment, such as government stocks (gilts) or commercial property.

Managers of large investment funds constantly balance their portfolios between these different investment outlets. In doing so, they take account of the relative yields which change daily, together with the stability and capital growth expected in each area.

Whereas the earning yield specifies the total return, the dividend yield is more important for investors dependent on income from the shares. It allows them to compare the cash flow that they will receive from investing a fixed sum in different stocks or other investment outlets. As we have seen in the previous section, public utility companies with high pay-out ratios tend to produce high dividend yields and would be popular with pension fund managers.

The degree of variation in yield values is shown in the country variations illustrated in figure 12.8. The most striking result is the dividend yield for Japan at less than 1 percent. This is brought about by the low pay-out ratio already mentioned and high share prices.

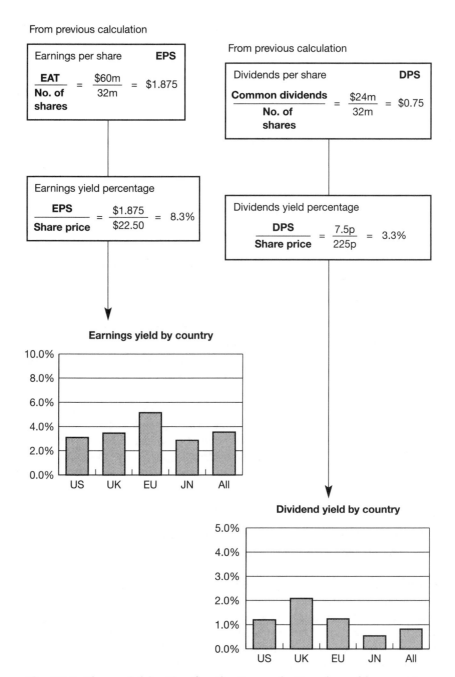

From previous calculation

Earnings per share	**EPS**
$\dfrac{\textbf{EAT}}{\textbf{No. of}}$ shares $= \dfrac{\$60m}{32m} = \$1.875$	

From previous calculation

Dividends per share	**DPS**
$\dfrac{\textbf{Common dividends}}{\textbf{No. of}}$ shares $= \dfrac{\$24m}{32m} = \$0.75$	

Earnings yield percentage
$\dfrac{\textbf{EPS}}{\textbf{Share price}} = \dfrac{\$1.875}{\$22.50} = 8.3\%$

Dividends yield percentage
$\dfrac{\textbf{DPS}}{\textbf{Share price}} = \dfrac{7.5p}{225p} = 3.3\%$

Earnings yield by country

Dividend yield by country

Fig. 12.8 Share yield ratios for the Example Co. plc and by country

These yield values are low in comparison to gilt yields. The expression 'reverse yield gap' is used to highlight the shortfall in dividend yields as opposed to those for gilts.

Price to earnings ratio (PE)

The price to earnings ratio or 'multiple' is a widely quoted parameter of share value. Figure 12.9 shows the method of calculation. The share price is divided by the EPS figure. The answer gives the number of years' purchase that the price bears to earnings.

While the calculation of the ratio is based on figures from the past, its value is determined by investors whose focus is on the future. They are primarily interested in the prospects for **earnings growth**. To estimate this they will look to the industrial sector, the company's products, its management and its financial stability and growth history.

The company has no direct control over the PE ratio. It may influence it over the short-term by a good public relations exercise. In the long-term, however, it must deliver a good return to the equity shareholder to secure a continued high rating.

The advantages of a high price to earnings ratio value are considerable. The wealth of the company's owners is increased in proportion. New funds can be raised at a favorable price. The possibility of a successful hostile takeover bid is much reduced. Most importantly, the company has the means to make acquisitions on favorable terms by using its 'paper' (shares), as opposed to cash.

When we look at the PE ratio across international boundaries (see figure 12.9), we see that the US and the UK show similiar values just about 30 times. The returns for the EU are considerably lower, but we notice a considerable jump when we come to Japan. Here the current value is approximately 35, even though the market has fallen by 50 percent.

Japanese PE values have puzzled western investors for years. A short while ago, many companies were in the 50 to 60 range. Attempts to explain this mentioned very low inflation rates, strong currency, low cost of capital etc. However stockmarket prices fell sharply and rates, while still high, are now more in line with western world norms.

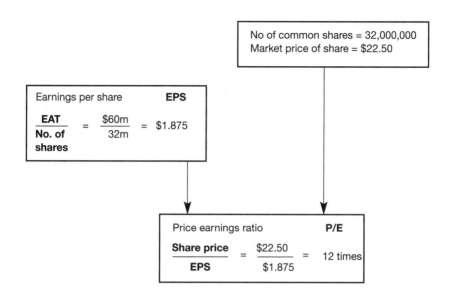

No of common shares = 32,000,000
Market price of share = $22.50

Earnings per share   **EPS**

$$\frac{\textbf{EAT}}{\textbf{No. of shares}} = \frac{\$60m}{32m} = \$1.875$$

Price earnings ratio   **P/E**

$$\frac{\textbf{Share price}}{\textbf{EPS}} = \frac{\$22.50}{\$1.875} = 12 \text{ times}$$

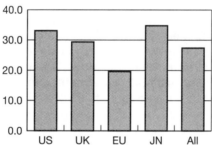

Price to earnings ratio by country

Fig. 12.9 Price earnings ratios for the Example Co. plc and by country

Market to book ratio

The market to book ratio gives the final and, perhaps the most thorough assessment by the stockmarket of a company's overall status. It summarizes the investors' view of the company overall, its management, its profits, its liquidity, and future prospects.

Figure 12.10 shows the calculation. The ratio relates the total market capitalization of the company to the shareholders' funds. To express it in another way, it compares the value in the stockmarket with the shareholders' investment in the company.

The answer will be less than, greater than or equal to unity. It is the investors' perception of the performance of the company in terms of profits, balance sheet strength or liquidity and growth that determines this ratio.

A value of less than unity means that the shareholders' investment has diminished in value; it has wasted away. The investing community have given a 'thumbs down' signal to the company. They do not anticipate that future profits will be sufficient to justify the current owners' investment in the company.

On the other hand, when this value is well in excess of unity, it means that the investment has been multiplied by the market/book factor. A high ratio does not simply mean that the worth of the company has increased over time by means of its retained earnings. The multiplier acts in addition to this. Each \$1 of original investment, plus each \$1 of retained earnings is multiplied by a factor equal to the market to book ratio.

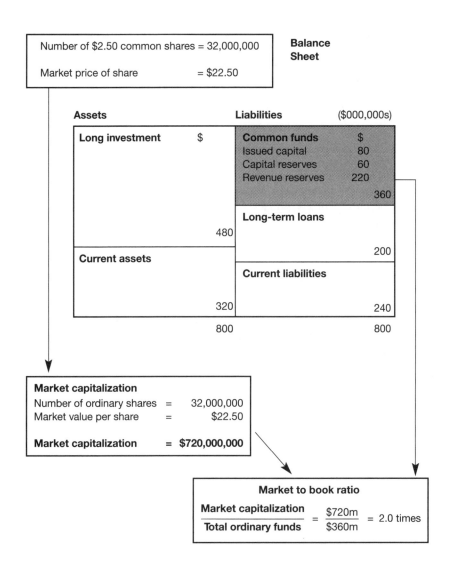

Number of $2.50 common shares = 32,000,000   **Balance Sheet**

Market price of share   = $22.50

Assets		Liabilities		($000,000s)
Long investment	$	**Common funds**	$	
		Issued capital	80	
		Capital reserves	60	
		Revenue reserves	220	
			360	
	480	**Long-term loans**		
			200	
Current assets		**Current liabilities**		
	320		240	
	800		800	

Market capitalization
Number of ordinary shares   =   32,000,000
Market value per share   = $22.50

Market capitalization   = **$720,000,000**

Market to book ratio

$$\frac{\text{Market capitalization}}{\text{Total ordinary funds}} = \frac{\$720m}{\$360m} = 2.0 \text{ times}$$

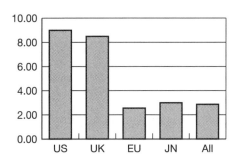

Fig. 12.10 Market to book ratio for the Example Co. plc

Two important questions must be kept in mind when considering this ratio:

- Do the shareholders' funds reflect a realistic value for the assets?
- Is the market rating going through an exceptionally high or low phase?

Refer to appendix 1 for various items that can affect this ratio.

The country analysis in figure 12.10 shows widely differing values between the US and UK on the one hand and the rest of the EU and Japan on the other. In normal circumstances we would expect a value of between 2 and 3 times for this ratio, and these are the values we see for the EU and Japan. The extraordinary high values we encounter in the US and UK can only be accounted for by:

- the extraordinary exuberance in the market at the time;
- the understatement of owners' equity as a result of goodwill write-downs.

The fall in the overall market will have reduced the numbers considerably.

The absolute minimum that management must achieve for this ratio is 1.0. Good companies produce a factor of 2.0.

13

Financial leverage and corporate valuation

Introduction · Financial leverage
· V chart · Market to book ratio

*Auditors are the troops who watch battle
from the safety of a hillside and when the
battle is over come down to count the dead
and bayonet the wounded.*
ANONYMOUS

Introduction

This chapter will integrate material from previous chapters into one single web supporting corporate value and it will show the relationships that exist between many of the ratios covered so far. Specifically it will:

1. establish the financial leverage links between ROTA and ROE

2. examine further the great importance of ROE

3. tie together – operating efficiency measures

   – leverage ratios

   – valuation factors

so as to identify and quantify the drivers of corporate value.
    To accomplish this we will make much use of the V chart (valuation chart).

Financial leverage

The term 'financial engineering' has become quite popular. It is used in relation to schemes that increase the return to the shareholders from a given return earned by the company.

The material that follows will give some appreciation of this.
    The concept of leverage, or gearing, was looked at briefly in chapter 10. It was seen that high leverage could substantially increase the return to the shareholder. This chapter will explore further the impact of leverage and the specific elements that link ROTA and ROE.

We have seen in chapter 6, figure 6.3, that the US Consolidated Company Inc. showed the following values:

- ROTA   13.3%
- ROE   19.6%

Financial mechanisms have been used to transform a pretax return of 13.3 percent from the total company into an after-tax return of 19.6 percent to the shareholders. This is leverage in action. The financial variables that link these two values are laid out diagrammatically in figure 13.1, viz:

debt to equity ratio	1.8 times
average interest cost	3.3%
tax rate	38%

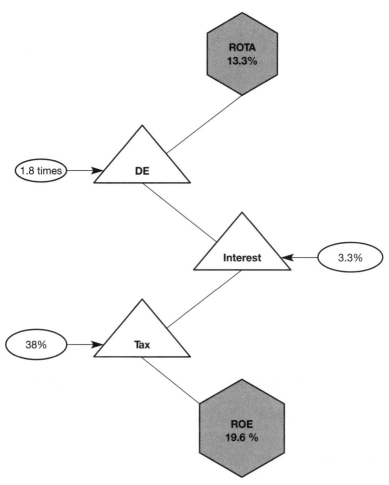

Fig. 13.1 The links between return on total assets and return on equity

In figure 13.2, the US Consolidated Company Inc. accounts are displayed together with a chart that that shows in geometric form the relationships between all these elements. The chart is referred to as the V Chart (valuation chart). It integrates in one diagram the financial variables that determine a company's valuation in the stockmarket.

V chart

Figure 13.2 shows the chart and the accounts of the US Consolidated Company Inc. from which it has been constructed. It looks formidable at first sight because there seem to be so many parts to it.

However, we will work carefully through it. There are approximately six separate steps. Each step is simple in itself. The result of the exercise will be total comprehension of quite a difficult subject. Once this is achieved the remaining material will be very easy to follow.

Step 1 The chart is constructed on a base that represents the total funds in the business divided between total equity ($77.4) and total non-equity ($142.6).

Step 2 Where equity and non-equity meet we draw to scale a vertical line representing ROTA (13.3 percent).

Step 3 At the extreme left of the base we place a vertical line representing the average cost of all non-equity funds (3.3 percent). (The amount of 'free' funds in the balance sheet, e.g. accounts payable, accounts for this apparently low value.)

Step 4 At the extreme right of the base we erect a vertical line to represent ROE (before tax).

Step 5 We join the upper limit of the 'Interest' line (step 3) to the upper limit of the 'ROTA' line (Step 2) and extend this diagonal to meet the ROE line (Step 4)

Step 6 The point where these two lines meet represents ROE value (before tax).

For the US Consolidated Company Inc. the ROE (before tax) figure is 31.6 percent. Corporation tax charged in the accounts averages 38 percent. We deduct this amount to arrive at ROE (after tax) 19.6 percent.

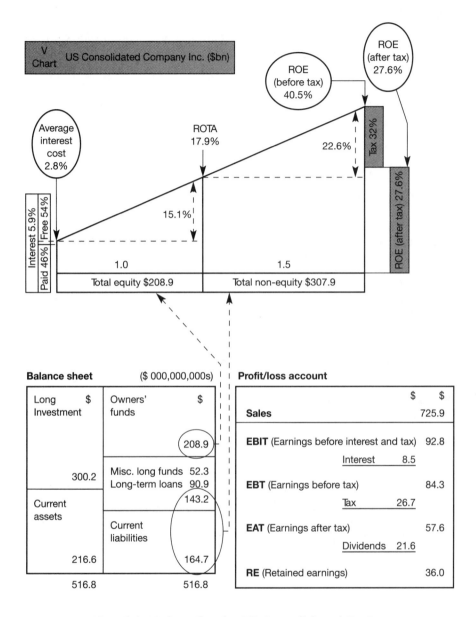

Balance sheet | ($ 000,000,000s)

Long Investment	$	Owners' funds	$
			208.9
	300.2	Misc. long funds	52.3
		Long-term loans	90.9
Current assets			143.2
		Current liabilities	
	216.6		164.7
	516.8		516.8

Profit/loss account

	$	$
Sales		725.9
EBIT (Earnings before interest and tax)		92.8
Interest	8.5	
EBT (Earnings before tax)		84.3
Tax	26.7	
EAT (Earnings after tax)		57.6
Dividends	21.6	
RE (Retained earnings)		36.0

Fig. 13.2 V chart for the US Consolidated Co. Inc.

V chart dynamics

To understand the dynamics of financial leverage, we can look on the upper diagonal of the chart as a cantilevered beam that is anchored at its left extremity to the 'Interest' vertical. It is pushed upwards by the ROTA piston.

The point of intersection with the ROE (before tax) line is determined by three factors:

1. its 'anchor,' i.e., average interest cost

2. ROTA value

3. the relative values for 'equity' and 'non-equity.'

We can write this in an equation:

$$\text{ROE (pre-tax)} = \text{ROTA} + [(\text{ROTA} - \text{Interest}) \times \text{D/E}]$$
$$40.5\% = 17.9\% + [(17.9\% - 2.8\%) \times 1.5]$$

We can use either the chart or the formula to track a change in any of the input values to its effect on ROE (before tax). By allowing for tax, we can get to ROE (after tax).

Three examples are shown in figure 13.3.

Example A. Increase ROTA by 1% to 18.9%.
                    Answer: ROE (before tax) = 43%

Example B. Increase non-equity/equity to 2.0 times
                    Answer: ROE (before tax) = 48%

Example C. Increase interest cost by 0.5%
                    Answer: ROE (before tax) = 39.8%

We have identified and quantified the variables that link the ROTA to ROE. It only remains to link ROE to company value. When this is complete we will be able to trace a path from the shop-floor variables right through to stock-market value. This will be addressed in the next section.

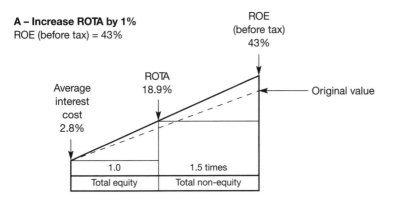

A – Increase ROTA by 1%
ROE (before tax) = 43%

ROE
(before tax)
43%

ROTA
18.9%

Average
interest
cost
2.8%

Original value

1.0 | 1.5 times
Total equity | Total non-equity

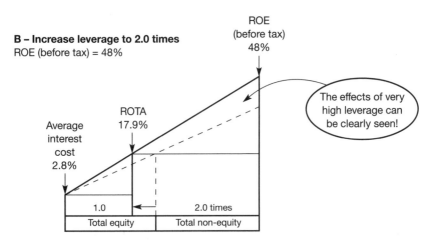

ROE
(before tax)
48%

B – Increase leverage to 2.0 times
ROE (before tax) = 48%

The effects of very
high leverage can
be clearly seen!

ROTA
17.9%

Average
interest
cost
2.8%

1.0 | 2.0 times
Total equity | Total non-equity

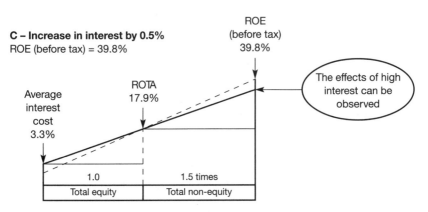

ROE
(before tax)
39.8%

C – Increase in interest by 0.5%
ROE (before tax) = 39.8%

The effects of high
interest can be
observed

ROTA
17.9%

Average
interest
cost
3.3%

1.0 | 1.5 times
Total equity | Total non-equity

Fig. 13.3 Effects of changes in values on V chart

Market to book ratio

In figure 13.4, the accounts for the Example Co. plc are repeated together with data relating to the number of shares and their market price.

The following ratios have already been calculated in chapter 12:

Book/asset value per share	$11.25
Market capitalization – company	$720
Return on equity (ROE)	16.6%
Earnings yield	8.3%

> With the market/book ratio we express the relationship that exists between a company's value on the stock exchange and the underlying asset/book value as shown in the balance sheet. This ratio can be calculated for the company in total or for one share in the company.

The company:

Markey capitalization	$720
OF – balance sheet	$360
Market/book ratio ($720/$360)	2 times

One share

Share market price	$22.5
Book/asset value	$11.25
Market/book ratio ($2.25/$1.125)	2 times

However neither of these calculations identify the factors that drive the market/book ratio. For this we must look to a third set of relationships.

The ROE figure tells us the rate of return that the company is delivering to the shareholders. The earnings yield figure is the rate of return investors require to hold the share. The market/book ratio falls out of the relationship between these two:

ROE	16.6%
Earnings yield	8.3%
Market/book ratio (16.6%/8.3%)	2 times

> This concept is of crucial importance. It illustrates the fact that investors decide on the rate necessary for a particular business. Then they mark that business at a premium or a discount, depending on whether the return delivered by the business is greater or less than the required rate.

Example Co plc

Number of 25c ordinary shares	=	32,000,000
Market price of share	=	$2.25

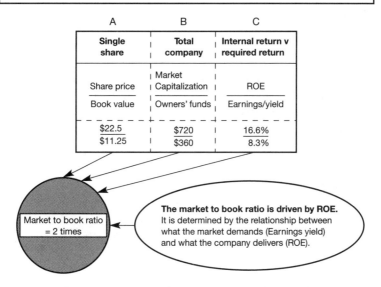

Profit and loss account ($000,000s)

	$
Sales	1,120
Operating costs	1,008
EBIT	112
Interest	20
EBT	92
Tax	32
EAT	60
Dividend	24
RE	36

Balance sheet ($000,000s)

FA	$	$	OF	$	$
			Issued	80	
			Capital reserves	60	
			Revenue reserves	220	
					360
		480	LTL		
					200
CA			CL		
		320			240
		800			800

Important ratios

Book value per share	Owners' funds/No. of shares	$360/32	$11.25
Market capitalization	No. of shares × Market price	32 × $22.5	$720
Return on equity (ROE)	EAT/Owners funds	$60/$360	16.6%
Earnings yield	EPS/Share price	$1.875/$22.5	8.3%

A	B	C
Single share	**Total company**	**Internal return v required return**
Share price / Book value	Market Capitalization / Owners' funds	ROE / Earnings/yield
$22.5 / $11.25	$720 / $360	16.6% / 8.3%

Market to book ratio = 2 times

The market to book ratio is driven by ROE. It is determined by the relationship between what the market demands (Earnings yield) and what the company delivers (ROE).

Fig. 13.4 The importance of ROE in the market to book ratio

Importance of ROE

> **ROE drives company value.** There are those who will dispute this statement. With good logic they will argue this is too simple an explanation because ROE is a short-term accounting measure. It does not take into account future growth prospects, etc. Nevertheless we can say that, other things being equal, the most important driver of value is ROE.

We have identified the drivers of ROE in the previous section. The most important are ROTA and the debt/equity ratio. The factors that drive ROTA are 'margin' and 'turn' (sales/total assets ratio) as we saw in chapter 7. Standing behind the 'margin' and 'turn' are all the operating ratios. So it is ROE that brings together all the operating and financing characteristics of the business.

We therfore can trace a path from the shop floor to stockmarket value.

However we need to examine a little more the factors that help the stockmarket decide on the earnings yield it will demand from a particular company.

Figure 13.5 list the main influencing factors. Under the headings:

- Company
- Industry
- Economy.

Investors are buying the expected future returns of the company. If growth prospects are good this will promise high returns. However they trade off risk against return. For a high perceived risk they will look for a high return.

So they weigh up the prospects for:

- The economy overall
- The industrial sector
- The particular company.

The main items for consideration under each heading are shown in figure 13.5.

The market/book ratio is a reflection of the internal rate of return being delivered by the company to the shareholder i.e., ROE versus earnings yield which is the rate of return demanded externally by the market. Below we show the main factors that influence both these variables.

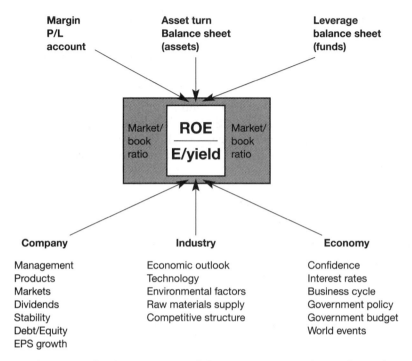

Fig. 13.5 The importance of the return on equity ratio and earnings yield relationship

Corporate valuation model

In figure 13.6 we are now able to pull together the various sections of the overall corporate valuation model.

Section A repeats the operating performance model given in chapters 6 and 7.

Section B shows the financial gearing model given earlier in this chapter.

Section C brings in the stockmarket ratios covered in chapter 12.

This completes the chain that links shop floor value drivers to the stockmarket value. Figures from the US Consolidated Company Inc. accounts are used for the various nodes in the model. There is an arithmetical link between each node in the chain that produces the final corporate value of $1,876.5bn.

The total number of independent variables in the model that can be influenced by management can now be identified:

- the cost percentages in the profit and loss account:
  - material
  - labour
  - overheads
- the main asset groups in the balance sheet:
  - fixed assets
  - inventories
  - accounts receivable
- debt to equity ratio
- interest rate/free v paid borrowings
- tax rate.

Note: An increase in the debt/equity value has a double effect, it increases return on equity but it also increases risk and therefore normally results in a higher 'earnings yield' value. The increase in return on equity should increase corporate value but if debt/equity is pushed beyond a prudent level the resulting increase in the yield will actually reduce total value.

One can work back from a desired end result to determine what the value of any single input variable must be, if other inputs remain constant. For instance, if the management set a target of 21.5 percent for ROE, they could work back to determine that the value of ROTA needed to deliver that is 14.4 percent.

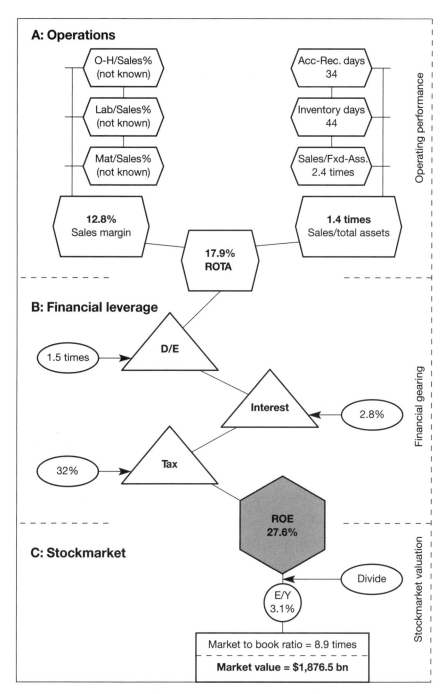

A: Operations

O-H/Sales%
(not known)

Lab/Sales%
(not known)

Mat/Sales%
(not known)

Acc-Rec. days
34

Inventory days
44

Sales/Fxd-Ass.
2.4 times

12.8%
Sales margin

17.9%
ROTA

1.4 times
Sales/total assets

Operating performance

B: Financial leverage

1.5 times

D/E

Interest

2.8%

32%

Tax

Financial gearing

C: Stockmarket

ROE
27.6%

Divide

E/Y
3.1%

Market to book ratio = 8.9 times

Market value = $1,876.5 bn

Stockmarket valuation

Fig. 13.6 Overall corporate valuation model for the US
Consolidated Co. Inc.

Growth

Growth · Analysis · Growth
equilibrium · Application to
acquisitions

Commerce defies every wind, outrides every
tempest and invades every zone.
GEORGE BANCROFT (1800–1891)

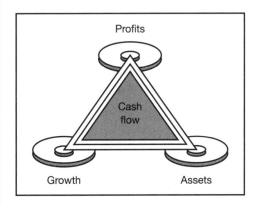

Fig. 14.1 Growth and the need for balance

Growth

Growth to a company is like medicine is to a patient – beneficial up to a certain level, but dangerous and possibly fatal when that level is exceeded. There is a need for balance between profits, assets and growth (see figure 14.1). Any imbalance between these factors will impact strongly on cash flow. Given the opportunities and corresponding dangers of growth, particularly in times of high inflation, it is wise to consider whether there is some way in which we can specify for a company what level of growth it can safely absorb. This chapter illustrates one particular method that many companies have found useful.

To assist in our analysis, we will take the case of the CABCO Construction Company shown in figure 14.2. This is a company that is suffering from severe problems of growth.

We see that it has been growing, in terms of sales, at approximately 15 percent per annum. However, it has a rapidly deteriorating financial position. The current ratio has dropped from 2.3 to 1.4 times over the four years and the debt to total assets ratio has risen from 37 percent to 61 percent over the same period. The liquidity ratios were very strong in 1997 but have sunk to their lowest acceptable level by 2001. The most worrying aspect of the case is the speed at which the liquidity position has deteriorated.

Performance, as measured by return on equity, was low but improved significantly in 2001. It made a passable return of almost 20 percent before tax to its shareholders, but it is now close to a liquidity crisis. Accordingly, management must take urgent action to stop the downward trend and change the direction in which the company is going.

This chapter is concerned with the problem of identifying and quantifying the options open to management, but, more importantly, it will extract general rules relating to company growth and how it can be handled.

Balance sheets	1997 $	1999 $	2001 $
Capital and reserves	661	654	696
Current liabilities	388	584	1,096
Total	1,049	1,238	1,792
Fixed assets	159	272	271
Current assets	890	966	1,521
Total	1,049	1,238	1,792

Income statistics

Sales*	1,325	1,766	2,280
EBIT	85	56	184
Tax	41	14	67
Dividends	23	19	23
Retained earnings	19	3	44

Ratios

Current ratio (times)**	2.3	1.6	1.4
Debt/assets (%)**	37%	47%	61%
ROE (before tax)	13%	6%	20%
Share price	90¢	70¢	110¢
No of shares	320	320	320

Fig. 14.2 CABCO Construction Ltd – summary accounts for years 1997, 1999, 2001

* Note – growth 15% per annum
** Note – rapid deterioration

In figure 14.3 the CABCO balance sheets for 1997 and 2001 are shown roughly to scale. The total assets of the 2001 balance sheet are 70 percent greater than that for 1997. From the size of the individual balance sheet boxes we see that the major expansion in both current assets and current liabilities. An explosion in the value of current assets has been financed almost entirely by an increase in current liabilities. Because of this the company has drifted from a strong liquidity base into an unstable, high-risk financial position. If the drift continues, bankruptcy is the likely result – or at least a change of ownership and control.

The immediate problem is an excess of short-term borrowings. They cannot be increased and, if possible, they should be reduced. Possible courses of action to which management has already given consideration are:

- reducing investment in current assets in absolute terms or at least as a proportion of sales

- introducing long-term funds in the form of loans or equity.

Because of industry custom and the situation of the business, management were of the opinion that current assets could not be reduced relative to sales, so attention was, therefore, concentrated on the possibility of finding additional long-term funds. The questions they had to answer were:

- 'How much?'
- 'What form – equity or loan?'
- 'If loan, what term of years?'

When cash flow forecasts were produced, it quickly became evident that a long-term loan would not solve the problem as such borrowed money could not be repaid. Instead, more and more borrowings would be required because of the negative cash flow that this company generated each year. By negative cash flow is meant that sufficient funds are not being generated internally to fund the assets required by the operations.

Companies in such a heavily negative cash flow position have a form of financial diabetes. They have a perpetual cash haemorrhage because the values of certain operating parameters are out of balance. It is necessary to identify and quantify the factors behind this condition.

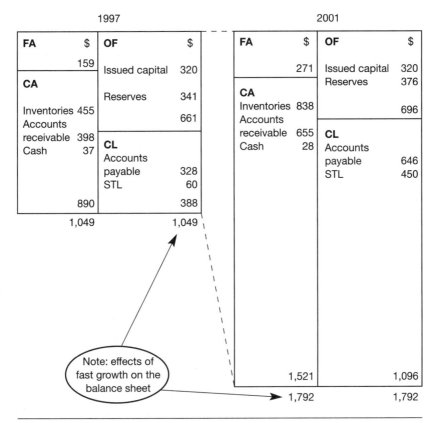

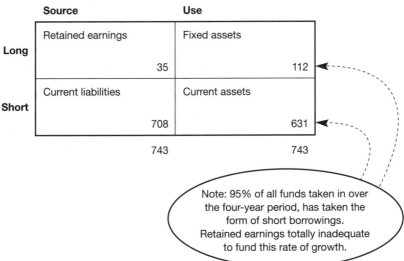

**Fig. 14.3 CABCO Construction Ltd – balance sheet movements
over four years**

Analysis

Figure 14.4 extracts some of the basic figures for 1995. The following are the critical values:

Sales	$2,280
Current assets	$1,521
Retained earnings	$44

It will be shown that it is the interrelationships between these three values, combined with the company's rate of growth that has given rise to its present financing problem. These three values, with a growth rate of 15 percent collectively, give rise to a strong negative cash flow.

- **The relationship of current assets to sales is 0.67** ($1,521/$2,280): each $1 of sales requires 67¢ to carry it. For every increase of $1,000 sales next year, $670 of extra current assets will be needed. This will require $670 of extra funds in the balance sheet.*

- **The relationship of retained earnings to sales is 0.02** ($44/$2,280): each $1 of sales generates 2¢ of retained earnings which goes into balance sheet funds. But each extra $1 sales requires 67¢. Therefore $33 of sales in any year are needed to fund $1 of extra sales following year.*

This ratio of $1 extra sales for every $33 existing sales is the self-financing ratio and it gives a growth rate of 3 percent. This rate of 3 percent is the rate of growth in current assets the company can fund from its retained earnings. The company has been growing at 15 percent over the last 4 years. The excess growth of 12 percent has been funded by borrowing. In this company, all the borrowing has been short term, hence the financing problem.

Current sales are $2,280. If 12 percent of this has to be funded externally next year at the rate of 67¢ for each $1 sale, the company will have to borrow an extra $180. The following year it will need to borrow $180 plus 15 percent and so on, indefinitely.

There is a fundamental problem here that arises from the fact that the relationships identified above are out of balance. This problem is analyzed in the next section.

---

* In Figure 14.4, we use the symbol 'T' to denote the first ratio, 'R' the second and 'G' the growth percentage.

2001 $000s

FA	$	OF	£
	271		
		Issued	320
CA		reserves	376
Inventories	838		696
Accounts			
receivable	655	**CL**	
Cash	28	Accounts	
		payable	646
		STL	450
	1,521		1,096
	1,792		1,792

Extract from income statement

	$000s
Sales	2,280
Retained earnings	44

Critical relationships   Symbol

(1) Working capital per $1 sales $\dfrac{\$1{,}521}{\$2{,}280}$ **$0.67**   T

(2) Retained earnings per $1 sales $\dfrac{\$44}{\$2{,}280}$ **$0.02**   R

(3) Growth in sales/historic rate 1997–2001   **15%**   G

Note: It takes a few moments to realize that the relationship between these two values is 3% and that this is the growth rate in current assets that can be funded directly from retained earnings.

Actual growth is 15%, therefore only a fifth of growth has been funded from the internal resources. The remaining 12% has been funded by borrowed money.

Fig. 14.4 CABCO Construction Ltd – critical asset, profit and growth relationships

Growth equilibrium

We use the term 'growth equilibrium' to identify the rate of growth that a company can sustain from its operating cash flow. It means that cash is in equilibrium in the sense that it is driven neither into surplus nor deficit as a result of growth.

A growth equilibrium equation applicable to CAMCO is given in figure 14.5. The values for 'R,' 'T' and 'G' have been identified in figure 14.4 and these are combined together to produce the equilibrium factor 'E' (Section A).

When E = 1, cash flow is neutral; values greater than 1 indicate a positive cash flow and vice versa.*

The values for CABCO give a result of one over five, 20 percent (Section B). This is the fraction of the growth that is self-funded. It tells us that 80 percent is funded from outside sources. The heavy borrowing that the company has experienced derives from this fact.

The model has identified the three powerful cash flow drivers in this company:

- current assets to sales
- retained earnings to sales
- growth in sales.

The company requires very high levels of inventory and accounts receivable to support sales. As sales expand rapidly these do likewise, thereby creating a great demand for cash. Retained profits are not adequate to meet this need.

The model enables management to focus on the fundamental issues facing this company. These relate to profit, current assets and growth. Management must take steps to balance the relationship between these three so that the equilibrium value ('E') is increased from .02 up to 1.0.

Some scenarios are illustrated in figure 14.6.

---

*Many readers will have valid questions at this stage about the underlying assumptions in the model. However, this is an early and primitive, but useful, version of a more generalized growth model that will be developed later in the chapter.

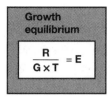

Growth equilibrium

$$\frac{R}{G \times T} = E$$

A

Symbols	Critical relationships	Values as decimal
T	(1) Current assets/sales	0.67
R	(2) Retained earnings/sales	0.02
G	(3) Growth in sales	0.15

B

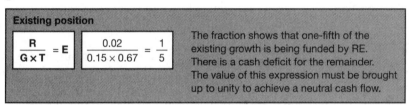

Existing position

$$\frac{R}{G \times T} = E \qquad \frac{0.02}{0.15 \times 0.67} = \frac{1}{5}$$

The fraction shows that one-fifth of the existing growth is being funded by RE. There is a cash deficit for the remainder. The value of this expression must be brought up to unity to achieve a neutral cash flow.

Fig. 14.5 CABCO Construction Ltd – growth equilibrium equation

Growth equilibrium – scenarios

As stated above, management can focus on the essential elements of the problem. The three variables must be brought into balance so that the resulting equilibrium value 'E' is increased to at least 1.0. This is the position where the company does not have to seek any further outside funds.

In figure 14.6 three single-value scenarios are worked out, one each for:

1. Growth
2. Retained profit
3. The current assets/sales ratio.

Each one shows the change in that variable alone that would be required to achieve equilibrium. It is not likely that any one of these in isolation would be the most practical solution. A strategy involving elements of all three would be more likely to bring results. The final combination strategy is shown as an illustration.

This version of the growth model is built up from the relationship that exist between between current assets, retained earnings and growth in a particular company.

It gives valid results for a company in the situation of CABCO Construction Company. This company is heavily current-assets-based and very heavily borrowed. The version is also useful, with slight amendments, for trading companies and rapidly growing small businesses.

However for companies with a more regular asset structure and with normal debt potential, a model with a more general application is needed. Such a model is introduced in the next section.

$$\boxed{\dfrac{\mathbf{R}}{\mathbf{G} \times \mathbf{T}} = \mathbf{E}} \quad \boxed{\dfrac{0.02}{0.03 \times 0.67} = \dfrac{1}{1}}$$

Option 1
Reduce growth to 3%

- -

$$\boxed{\dfrac{\mathbf{R}}{\mathbf{G} \times \mathbf{T}} = \mathbf{E}} \quad \boxed{\dfrac{0.10}{0.15 \times 0.67} = \dfrac{1}{1}}$$

Option 2
Increase retentions to 10%

- -

$$\boxed{\dfrac{\mathbf{R}}{\mathbf{G} \times \mathbf{T}} = \mathbf{E}} \quad \boxed{\dfrac{0.02}{0.15 \times 0.135} = \dfrac{1}{1}}$$

Option 3
Reduce assets/sales ratio to 13.5%

$$\boxed{\dfrac{\mathbf{R}}{\mathbf{G} \times \mathbf{T}} = \mathbf{E}} \quad \boxed{\dfrac{0.05}{0.10 \times 0.50} = \dfrac{1}{1}}$$

Example: Combination strategy
- increase retention to 5%
- reduce growth to 10%
- reduce assets/sales ratio to 50%
These three will wipe out the cash deficit.

Fig. 14.6 CABCO Construction Ltd – growth equilibrium calculation

General model of growth equilibrium

The model used in figures 14.5 and 14.6 suited the limited situation where the company was a low user of fixed assets and it was also very highly borrowed. The limitations of that first model were that:

- it looked at current assets only rather than total assets
- it ignored the fact that most companies can supplement retained earnings with funds from other sources.

Figure 14.7 illustrates the changes that are required in order to make the model more generally applicable.

First: include all the assets in the balance sheet that will be affected by growth.

Second: allow for funding by a mix of both loans and and equity. Each $1 of retained earnings will support borrowings in proportion to target D/E.

These steps arc illustrated in figure 14.7.

Section A: Current assets only are included in the model.

Section B: Fixed assets are taken into account.

Section C: LTL and CL are removed on the other side to leave that section of the balance sheet called OF (owners' funds).

The final growth equilibrium equation (RE/OF) in figure 14.7 tells us that the self-funding rate of growth for a company is calculated by expressing the retained earnings as a percentage of owners' funds (using the opening balance sheet for the period). Growth in excess of this rate will require extra equity or will cause a weakening in ratios.

The assumptions that lie behind this formula are important. They are that growth in sales will be matched exactly by growth in both current and fixed assets. It is further assumed that profits, interest, tax and dividends will grow likewise. Finally, it is assumed that a constant debt to equity ratio will apply.

It is not necessary to emphasize that a company cannot be managed by formulae. What formulae can do, however, is provide a shorthand approach that will quickly identify potential problems.

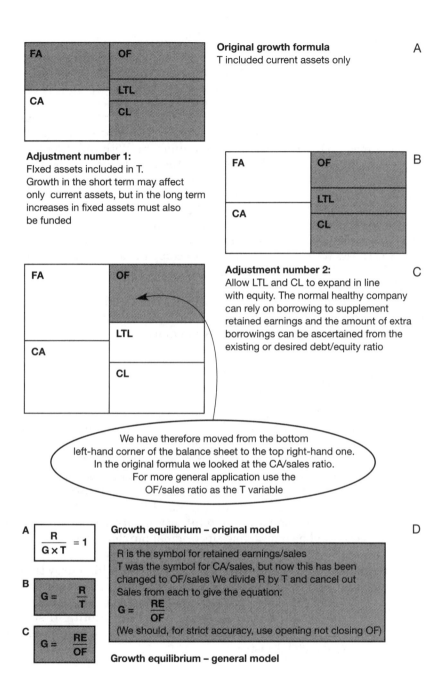

Fig. 14.7 Adjustments to growth equilibrium model

Self-funding growth – international standards

Figure 14.8 shows two charts relating to the international scene.

Chart A is derived from research done with top UK companies in 2000, and chart B relates to research on international companies.

Both indicate that large international companies have sustainable growth rates of between 10 and 20 percent, except Japan with approximately 7 percent. These are all very high numbers. With inflation as low as 3 to 4 percent it suggests that they have the capacity to expand in real terms at well over 8 percent. If their actual growth is less then they will simply accumulate cash in the balance sheet.

Given that the developed economies, in stable times over the long term, grow at 4 percent maximum, these companies are significantly outgrowing the economy. One can see why so many of them are involved in takeover activity. We have seen that these companies are also very profitable and many of them find it difficult to acquire companies that will not dilute their profit performance.

Some have found another outlet for surplus cash which is to buy back their own shares in the marketplace. This is a phenomenon that can now be observed with many large profitable companies.

Application to acquisitions

Many groups acquire fast-growing businesses in order to sustain or enhance the growth rate of the parent. The cash flow characteristics of such acquisitions are of crucial importance.

A company that has heavy asset requirements and that grows rapidly, will need substantial funds to keep its balance sheet in good condition. If the company is very profitable, these funds may be generated internally. However, if it has only medium or low profits, then funds will have to be provided by the parent company. The total cost of such a company over a number of years could be many times its original purchase price.

The most valuable business to own or buy is one with high growth and high profits. The least valuable one is not a low growth, low profit company. Such a company is not worth very much, but it is not dangerous. The worst company is one with high growth and low profits. If such a company also has a high asset to sales ratio, then it has, within itself, all the makings of a financial disaster.

Chart A

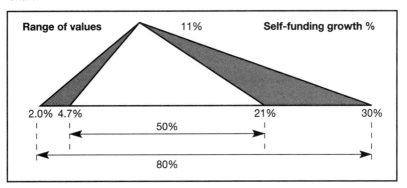

Chart B

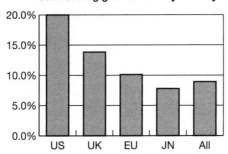

Fig. 14.8 Self-funding growth rate %

Part V Management decision-making

Cost, volume and price relationships

Introduction · Costing illustration · Contribution · Break-even (B/E) · Contribution to sales percentage (CPS) · Summary

Annual income twenty pounds, annual expenditure nineteen pounds, nineteen six, result happiness. Annual income twenty pounds, annual expenditure twenty pounds, ought and six, result misery.
CHARLES DICKENS (1812–1870) (*Mr Micawber*)

Introduction

The material covered to date has concerned itself with the company as a single overall unit. In this chapter we probe down into the detailed operations. Of course we find at this level that there are a multitude of separate products within the overall company. Each of these is a small business in itself, and each has its own associated revenue and cost.

The internal operating dynamics of these sub-units can be quite complicated. We use a cost/management accounting system to give information and help to make decisions at this level. We would like to be in a position where we can establish a total cost for a product, add on a profit margin and then sell at the target selling price. Rarely are we able to do this. The price we would like to charge is generally 10 percent above that of our competitors. The manager is constantly being asked to get costs down or to sell at or below the total cost figure.

How is it possible to make profits in this scenario? There is no magic answer, but what we can do is to recognize that the main function of cost accounting is not to arrive at a selling price but to identify the areas where profit is possible. This means understanding how costs behave – in particular, how they respond to changes in the variables: price, volume and, above all, product mix.

It was mentioned earlier that the performance model which copes well with the big business scene is not good at this level of detail. However, it is at this level that profits are made and lost. Also, it is at this level that day-to-day decisions are made as to what price to quote for a job, whether to accept or reject a price on offer, whether and how to pay commission to salespeople and so on.

The monthly management accounts supplied to managers are used by them for decision-making. However, the way in which the information is presented is often not helpful for this purpose. For instance, costs may be classified in a way that does not allow their recalculation on the basis of an alternative course of action.

This chapter will illustrate a series of calculations around this subject that enable managers to tread their way safely through these difficulties. These are essential, interesting and powerful tools. In the following pages we will work through a number of examples that show their application.

Costing illustration

Figure 15.1 shows a budget for the company Lawnmowers Ltd. We will use the numbers to illustrate some fundamental facts about the behavior of costs. These numbers are kept very simple so that they will embed themselves in the mind very quickly. We will then do many calculations around them.

The crucial facts are:

- this company has only one product, which it sells for a unit price of $200
- it plans to manufacture and sell 1000 units in the coming year at a profit of $20 each
- the total cost of $180 consists of the elements shown in figure 15.1.

The company has received an offer from a very large retailer to purchase 200 extra units at the special price of $160. The sales manager is faced with the dilemma of whether the company can sell at a price that is below the calculated total cost and still bring benefit to the company. (Of course the marketing implications of selling at a special low price are very significant, but, for this exercise, they will be ignored in order to tease out the financial aspects.)

We instinctively know that the total cost as shown in the budget will change if the forecast number of units is changed. The manager could, therefore, recalculate the total cost per unit after allowing for the extra volume of 200 units. This would give a revised overall profit.

A decision could be made on the basis of this type of calculation, but it would not help much in determining the lowest price that could be charged in a really competitive situation. Neither would it be of very much use for producing a whole set of scenarios for sales of different volumes at different prices.

An alternative approach is illustrated in the following pages.

Lawnmowers Ltd
Budget 2001

	No. of Units	Per Unit	Totals
Sales	1,000	$200	$200,000
Direct costs			
Materials	1,000	$75	$75,000
Labor	1,000	$45	$45,000
		$120	$120,000
Overhead costs			
Administration		$40	$40,000
Selling		$20	$20,000
Total cost		$180	$180,000
Profit		$20	$20,000
		$200	$200,000

Total cost = $180
Question: Can the firm sell
at $160 and make a profit?

Fig. 15.1 Summary budget of Lawnmowers Ltd

Cost classification

Of the many ways in which costs can be classified, possibly the most useful for decision-making purposes is on the basis of their response to volume changes. This well-known classification uses the following terms:

- **Fixed costs:** These are costs where the total expenditure does not change with the level of activity. For instance rent of a factory will not increase or decrease if volume of throughput goes up or down by 10 percent.
- **Variable costs:** These vary directly with changes in output. The cost of materials consumed in the product will vary almost in direct proportion to changes in volume.

An interesting paradox is that a fully variable cost is always a fixed charge per unit irrespective of volume. On the other hand, fixed costs charged to each unit fall with volume increases.

In practice, there are very few, if any, costs that are either totally fixed or totally variable across the whole range of possible outputs. However, it is useful for our example to make some simplifying assumptions. The fixed and variable costs for Lawnmowers Ltd are shown in figure 15.2.

The variable costs are:

- material
- labour

(In practice, while direct materials are almost always fully variable, direct labor is more than likely to be largely fixed.)

The fixed costs are assumed to be:

- administration
- selling costs.

(This assumption implies that these amounts will not change at all with any changes in volume.)

The variable and fixed costs per unit are $120 and $60 respectively. They sum to a total cost of $180. Note that management is faced with the question of whether or not to accept a large order at a price of $160 per unit.

Lawnmowers Ltd
Budget 2001

	No. of Units	Per Unit	Totals
Sales	1,000	$200	$200,000
Direct costs			
Materials	1,000	$75	$75,000
Labor	1,000	$45	$45,000
	1,000	$120	$120,000
Overhead costs			
Administration		$40	$40,000
Selling		$20	$20,000
Total cost		$180	$180,000
Profit		$20	$20,000
		$200	$200,000

Costs classification

Fixed costs – – – – – – – – – – – – – – – –
Totals not effected
by volume

Variable costs – – – – – – – – – – – – – –
Totals vary directly with volume

Fig. 15.2 Fixed and variable costs for Lawnmowers Ltd

Contribution

The division of costs into fixed and variable allows us to re-examine unit costs. Figure 15.3 shows two different approaches to cost reporting:

- total cost (traditional) approach
- contribution approach.

In the traditional breakdown the unit selling price of $200 is split into:

- variable cost $120
- fixed cost $60
- profit $20.

With the contribution approach, however, the selling price is split into just two components:

- variable cost of $120
- contribution of $80.

Contribution, therefore, replaces the figures of fixed cost of $60 and profit of $20. We remove the fixed cost charge from the product. The concept of contribution is important and useful. It is worthwhile spending some time examining it.

Cash flow and contribution

We have arrived at the contribution figure of $80 by adding back the fixed cost of $60 to the profit of $20. However, we can see that the same figure is arrived at when we deduct variable cost from the selling price, i.e. $200 – $120. This latter definition is the most useful one.

We will extract cash flow meaning from it. Each extra unit sold at the budget price results in a cash in-flow of $200. However, this extra unit also increases variable costs by $120. These are direct cash costs which will give rise to a corresponding cash out-flow. One extra unit sold gives rise to extra revenue of $200 and extra cash costs of $120. The difference of $80, which we call contribution, is the net cash in-flow resulting from an extra unit sold.

The $80 cash sacrificed from the loss of one unit is even more obvious. If the company suffers the loss of one unit it loses $200 revenue but it saves only $120. So the cash loss is $80.

Contribution can therefore be defined as the net cash flow from a single transaction. In other words, it is the cash gained from the sale of an extra unit or the cash lost from the sale of one unit less.

The relationship of contribution to profit will be pursued in the following pages.

Traditional total cost breakdown

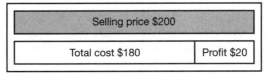

| Selling price $200 | |
| Total cost $180 | Profit $20 |

Contribution approach

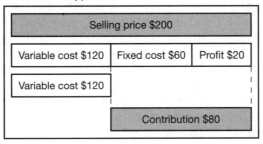

Selling price $200		
Variable cost $120	Fixed cost $60	Profit $20
Variable cost $120		
	Contribution $80	

The difference between the two approaches is that the upper one has got the fixed costs allocated to individual units of product.

The contribution approach is to charge units with the variable costs only.

Fig. 15.3 Alternative costing approaches applied to Lawnmowers Ltd's figures

Contribution and profit

Contribution flows into the business as cash from the sale of each unit. However, it is not free cash because it must first be assigned to the payment of fixed costs. But once these fixed costs have been paid in full, the contribution stream goes straight into profit.

Figure 15.4 illustrates the process. It shows two water tanks that represent volumes of fixed costs and profit respectively. The fixed cost tank has a capacity of $60,000 representing the total fixed costs of the company. Each unit sold pumps $80 into this tank. When a sufficient number of $80s have filled this tank with cash, then all the extra contribution overflows into the profit tank.

It is easy to see that the cash from the first 750 units (750 × $80 = $60,000) remains in the fixed cost tank, it is only the cash from units in excess of 750 that goes to profit. If the company sells its budgeted volume of 1,000 units, then the final 250 units will provide profits of $20,000 (250 × $80). So the budgeted profit figure is not built up at the stated rate of $20 per unit. Rather it accrues at the rate ot $80 per unit after fixed costs have been covered.

This important figure of $80 is referred to as contribution per unit (CPU). It is used a great deal in profit/volume calculations and you will find it to be a very useful tool of analysis.

Figure 15.4 also highlights a second important concept, which is **total contribution**. The total contribution in this plant is $80,000. In the upper part of the diagram it is shown as 'units multiplied by CPU.' In the lower part, the same figure is produced from 'fixed costs plus profit.' We will find ourselves making use of this formula in many situations.

A fundamental principle underlying the material of this chapter is that our objective in decision making should be to 'maximize contribution.' In following this principle the greatest profit will be achieved.

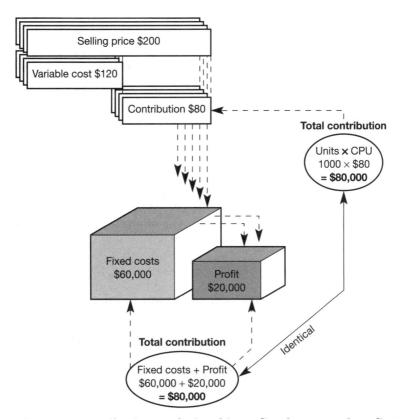

Fig. 15.4 Contribution's relationship to fixed costs and profit

Total contribution

This view of the cost dynamics of the company facilitates calculations to do with volume, cost and profits. For instance, we can start at units, and ascertain without difficulty what the profit would be at any level of unit sales. Alternatively we can work from the profit side and ask what unit sales are needed to deliver any desired level of profit. Finally we can combine price and volume changes and instantly translate them into profit.

For instance:

1. What profit would result from an increase in sales of 10 percent?
   Answer $28,000

2. How many units must be sold to provide a profit of $32,000?
   Answer 1,150 units

3. Finally, a very important question, how many units must be sold to break even, i.e., make neither a profit nor a loss?
   Answer 750 units.

This latter calculation gives the break-even point, a concept that is used widely in business. The formula for its calculation in terms of units is derived directly from the above equation. We simply set profit equal to zero and solve for the number of units. We will look at this concept some more in the following pages.

It is important to remember that we are still thinking in terms of physical units. The formulae and methods illustrated above work only in the case of a business that sells one type of unit. However, these limited formulae provide a useful stepping off point for the next stage. As soon as the fundamentals have been grasped, it is possible to move easily to the more general case where we can do calculations for a company that produces many different units.

Basic equation

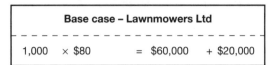
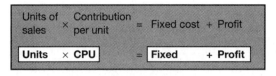

Units of sales	×	Contribution per unit	=	Fixed cost	+	Profit
Units	×	**CPU**	=	**Fixed**	+	**Profit**

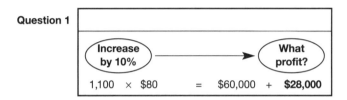

Base case – Lawnmowers Ltd

| 1,000 | × | $80 | = | $60,000 | + | $20,000 |

Question 1

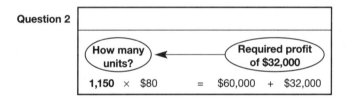

Increase by 10% ⟶ What profit?

| 1,100 | × | $80 | = | $60,000 | + | **$28,000** |

Question 2

How many units? ⟵ Required profit of $32,000

| **1,150** | × | $80 | = | $60,000 | + | $32,000 |

Break-even calculation

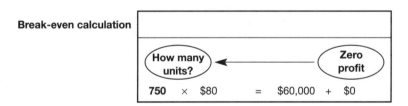

How many units? ⟵ Zero profit

| **750** | × | $80 | = | $60,000 | + | $0 |

Fig. 15.5 Calculations using contributions per unit

Break-even (B/E)

> The importance of the break-even level of output has been mentioned. It is the level at which the company makes neither a loss nor a profit, but just covers its fixed costs. It is, therefore, a most important cross-over point in a plant's level of activity and managers pay much attention to it.

The break-even chart is a well-known illustration of the concept. It shows the relationship between three important components over the total possible range of outputs:

- fixed costs
- variable costs
- revenue.

The horizontal axis in figure 15.6 is used to represent activity, which can be expressed in different ways, e.g., percentage of capacity, machine hours, etc. For our purposes here, both the number of units produced and capacity percentages are used. The chart covers the full output range – from zero to the full plant capacity of 1,500 units.

The vertical axis is used to plot costs and revenue. Figures from Lawnmowers Ltd are used for each of the three components (fixed costs, variable costs and revenue). These are plotted in three separate charts in figure 15.6.

Chart A illustrates the fixed costs, represented by a horizontal line at the $60,000 point on the vertical axis. This line is absolutely horizontal because fixed costs do not go up or down with changes in the level of output.

Chart B illustrates the variable costs. At zero output there are no variable costs, but, with each unit sold, the total grows by $120. At 600 units variable costs amount to $72,000. The relationship with output is strictly linear, hence the straight line sloping upwards.

Chart C illustrates the revenue. Again, at zero output, total revenue is zero. For every unit sold, revenue increases by $200. At 600 units, total revenue amounts to $120 000 (600 × $200). The relationship between revenue and output is also linear, and this is reflected in the more rapidly rising total revenue line.

Chart A

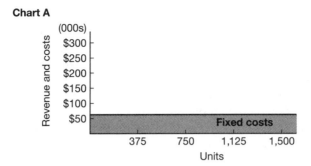

Chart B

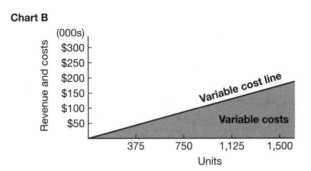

Chart C

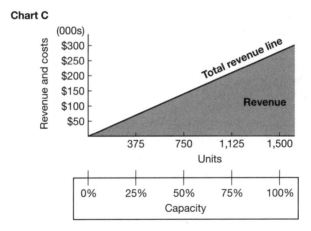

Fig. 15.6 The elements of break-even chart

Break-even (B/E) Chart

In figure 15.7, the three separate charts of figure 15.6 have been combined to show how the three sections come together. First we see the band of fixed costs at the base of the chart. Positioned above this is the variable costs wedge. Along the upper boundary of this wedge is the total cost line. Finally, the total revenue line is shown rising from the zero revenue at zero output up through the two areas of cost until it breaks through the total cost line about 50 percent of capacity. This is the break-even point. To the left of it lies loss, to the right profit.

The break-even point here occurs at a level of 750 units which equates to revenue of $150,000. Remember from figure 15.5 that 750 units will result in a contribution of $60,000 (750 ¥ $80), which just equals the fixed cost.

A line is plotted representing the budgeted sales of 1,000 units at a unit price of $200. This puts the company a little way to the right of the break-even point. The surplus output over break even is sometimes referred to as the 'margin of safety.' This margin of safety here is 25 percent, which means that sales can fall by this percentage before the break-even point is reached.

A number of simplifying assumptions are incorporated into this chart. It has been assumed that (1) fixed costs are totally fixed for all levels of output, (2) that unit variable costs do not change irrespective of numbers produced and (3) that unit revenue is the same for all levels of sales. These assumptions may be valid over a fairly narrow range on each side of existing levels of activity. At very low or very high levels, however, the assumptions break down and the chart ceases to be accurate.

Notwithstanding these limitations, the break-even chart is a useful tool for presenting information, for explaining the dynamics of a production unit, for pointing out the essential features of the volume, cost and revenue system and for setting minimum sales targets.

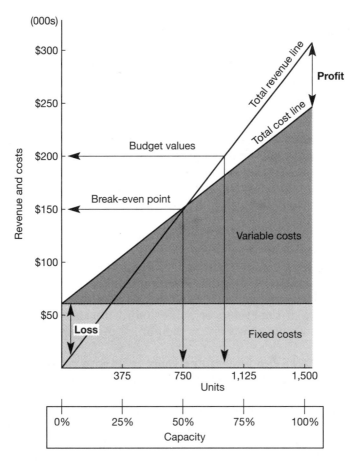

Fig. 15.7 Break-even chart for Lawnmowers Ltd

This chart can also be used to identify companies with different cost structures and therefore different levels of what is called 'operating leverage.' Operating leverage identifies the change in profit that results from a small change in sales, e.g., if a 10 percent change in sales produces a 40 percent change in profit, then we say that the company has a high operating leverage of 4 times.

Figure 15.8 shows charts for two types of company. The first (A) has a high operating leverage. With high fixed costs and low unit variable costs it has a total cost line that starts high on the chart but has a relatively flat trajectory. The total revenue line cuts the total cost line at quite a wide angle, which means that profit increases rapidly to the right of the break-even point. Unfortunately, to the left of this point, the negative gap also widens rapidly, meaning that the company gets into heavy losses very quickly as output falls away.

The second (B) has a low operating leverage. This company has low fixed costs but high unit variable costs. The total cost line starts low but climbs steeply with increased volume. The total revenue line produces a much narrower angle at the crossover point, indicating that both profits and losses both grow more slowly either right or left of the break-even point.

In Company A, we can understand there is intense pressure to achieve volume sales in order to move out of the heavy loss situation to the left of the break-even point. And when the break-even point has been reached, there is the prize of a rapidly increasing profit figure to provide the incentive to achieve even greater volume. When total production capacity exceeds total demand, fierce price competition can erupt between firms of this type as they compete for volume. The companies with this cost profile are those with heavy fixed assets, such as steel and transport companies.

The second situation, with low operating leverage, is frequently found to exist in companies with smaller, flexible production systems and low fixed assets. These companies tend to have less risk, but also less reward, attached to them.

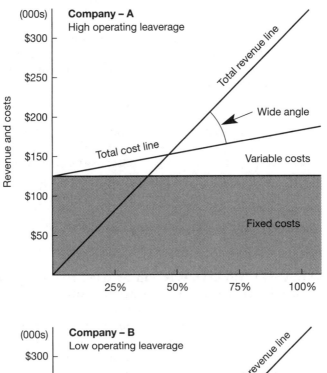

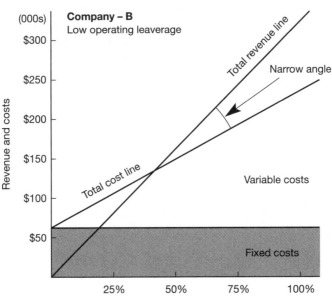

Fig. 15.8 Operating leverage

Contribution to sales percentage (CPS)

As noted earlier, 'contribution per unit' (CPU) is limited in its usefulness because it can be applied only to a one-product company. A more general ratio is therefore needed for the normal multi-product company. The following approach deals with this problem.

Figure 15.9 shows the familiar diagram of unit selling price, variable costs and contribution. However one extra calculation has been added. The contribution figure of $80 is expressed as a percentage of the selling price of $200 to give the answer 40 percent.

This is a very important percentage and a very important ratio. It has several different names in financial literature, such as, profit to volume (PV) ratio. As we have used the term 'contribution per unit' (CPU) when dealing with units, we will for consistency adopt the term 'contribution percentage of sales' (CPS) for this value.

This power of this ratio is that it can be used to convert any revenue figure into its corresponding contribution. Therefore it can be applied to the output of a total company or any sub-section of a company such as a particular product or market. It can be used to analyze separate individual products, groups of similar products or the total mix of products for a multi-unit business. When it is used to convert sales into contribution, the profit figure can be derived simply by deducting the fixed costs.

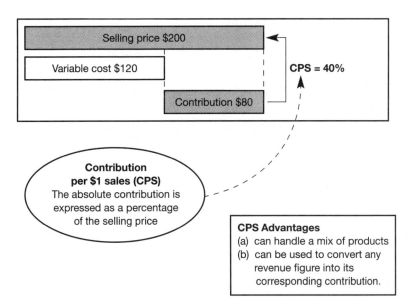

Fig. 15.9 Contribution to sales percentage

Total contribution – Alternate views

It is important at this point to distinguish between **unit contribution** and the **total contribution** of the whole plant.

Unit contribution is simply the selling price less the variable costs figure for one unit.

Similarly **total contribution** is total revenue less total variable costs.

However it can also be derived from three separate sources (see figure 15.10):

- units × CPU
- revenue × CPS
- fixed costs + profit.

We can take the latter two and derive the identity:

Revenue × CPS = Fixed costs + Profit

Given the four variables in this equation, if we know any three of them we can find the remaining one.

Revenue	?	×	$35,000	×
CPS	×	?	22%	×
Fixed costs	×	×	?	×
Profit	×	×	$3,800	?

Answer: ($35,000 × 22% – $3,800) = $3,900

Further examples are given in the next section.

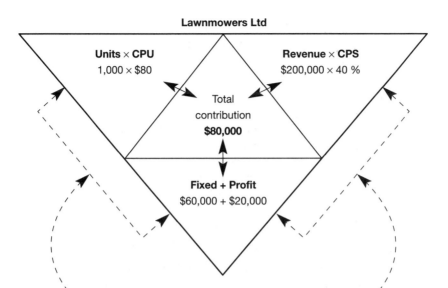

Lawnmowers Ltd

Units × CPU
1,000 × $80

Revenue × CPS
$200,000 × 40 %

Total
contribution
$80,000

Fixed + Profit
$60,000 + $20,000

Units x CPU = Fixed costs + Profit
We used this equation in figure 15.5
to solve problems relating to number
of units.

Revenue x CPU = Fixed costs + Profit
This is a more general equation.
We will use it in figure 15.11 to
solve problems relating to revenue.

Fig. 15.10 Alternative views of total contribution

Problem solving using CPS

We use the identity between the expressions:

1. Revenue x CPS and
2. fixed costs plus profit

to solve problems in figure 15.11.

The problems illustrated here are the same as in figure 15.5, except that 'contribution to sales percentage' (CPS) has been used in place of 'contribution per unit' (CPU). Results are expressed in money terms rather than in units which is generally more useful. By converting units @ $200 sales price we see that the answers achieved by both approaches are identical.

 As an extra example, consider the following:

- Budgeted sales for Lawnmowers Ltd are $200,000.
- At a CPS of 40 percent the budgeted contribution is $80,000.
- If the revenue figure were to fall to $180,000, the resulting contribution would be $72,000 ($180,000 × 40 percent).
- The profit from this reduced level of sales would be $12,000.
- ($72,000 contribution – $60,000 fixed cost = $12,000 profit).

Basic equation

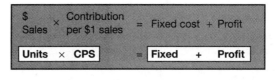

$$\frac{\$}{\text{Sales}} \times \frac{\text{Contribution}}{\text{per \$1 sales}} = \text{Fixed cost} + \text{Profit}$$

$$\text{Units} \times \text{CPS} = \text{Fixed} + \text{Profit}$$

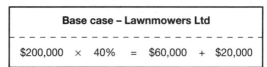

Base case – Lawnmowers Ltd

$$\$200,000 \times 40\% = \$60,000 + \$20,000$$

Question 1 | What profit would result from an increase in revenue of 10%?

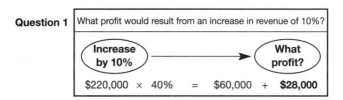

Increase by 10% ⟶ What profit?

$$\$220,000 \times 40\% = \$60,000 + \mathbf{\$28,000}$$

Question 2 | What revenue in needed to produce $32,000 profit?

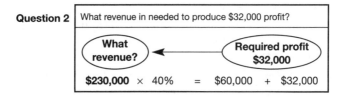

What revenue? ⟵ Required profit $32,000

$$\mathbf{\$230,000} \times 40\% = \$60,000 + \$32,000$$

Break-even calculation | What revenue is required to break even?

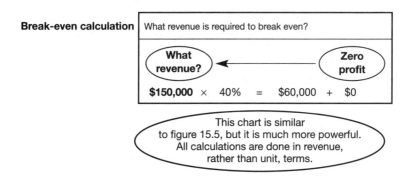

What revenue? ⟵ Zero profit

$$\mathbf{\$150,000} \times 40\% = \$60,000 + \$0$$

This chart is similar to figure 15.5, but it is much more powerful. All calculations are done in revenue, rather than unit, terms.

Fig. 15.11 Working out the effects of change using the contribution to sales percentage for Lawnmowers Ltd

Weighted CPS

We now know how to convert sales revenue into contribution by applying the 'contribution to sales percentage.' However if a company's sales increase by 10 percent will contribution increase by the same amount? The answer is 'yes' if the CPS remains constant. However we can ask how constant is this factor likely to be? What drives it?

The selling prices of products are determined not by cost but by the market-place. Most companies do not have the luxury of fixing prices to give secure margins, they must accept or reject, within a range, the generally accepted price. For some products, the prices will be more satisfactory than for others.

A single product can have more than one price as discounts are given to bulk purchasers and so on. Therefore, the 'contribution to sales percentage' will vary widely for different products and in different markets. The overall contribution to sales percentage is a weighted average of the individual CPSs of the separate products and markets.

Figure 15.12 shows an example of a product that is sold though two different distribution channels. First it is sold direct to the public at a price of $500. It is also sold through agents at a discount of 20 percent. The variable costs figure in both situations is $350.

The contribution for sales through the direct channel is $150 per unit, to yield a CPS of 30 percent. Sales through agents give a contribution of only $50, to yield a CPS of 12.5 percent.

As shown in Box 3, with revenues budgeted at $300,000 for direct sales and at $100,000 for agent sales the average CPS for all sales amounts to 25.6 percent.

In Box 4 it is shown what happens when sales to agents increase substantially. the average CPS falls to 19 percent. A change in the mix of sales has brought on a dramatic fall in the weighted CPS. The result in this exaggerated example is that a significant increase in sales volume has not produced a corresponding increase in profit.

Many companies work on the basis of average values. This can be dangerous. The average is determined by the mix of high and low contribution products and this mix must be managed. This point is illustrated more fully in the next section.

(1) Sales direct to public

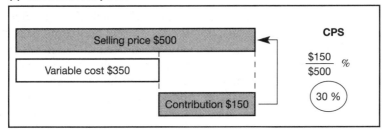

	CPS
Selling price $500	
Variable cost $350	$\dfrac{$150}{$500}$ %
Contribution $150	30 %

(2) Sales through agent – less (20% discount)

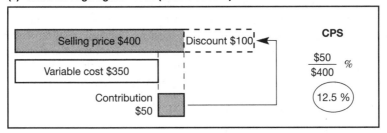

	CPS
Selling price $400	Discount $100
Variable cost $350	$\dfrac{$50}{$400}$ %
Contribution $50	12.5 %

(3) Original sales mix

Channel	Sales	CPS	Contribution
Direct	$300,000	30%	$90,000
Agent	$100,000	12.5%	$12,500
	£400,000		$102,500

CPS – Average = 25.6%

(4) New sales mix following substantial growth

Channel	Sales	CPS	Contribution
Direct	$300,000	30%	$90,000
Agent	$500,000	12.5%	$62,500
	$800,000		$152,500

CPS – Average = 19.0%

Fig. 15.12 Overall contribution to sales percentage as a weighted average for a mix of sales

Product mix

In figure 15.13, data is given about a company that sells three products (A, B and C) through two distribution networks (direct and through agents). There are, therefore, six product-market segments as shown in the matrix in the top right-hand corner. The contribution to sales percentage for each segment is shown in the matrix in the upper right-hand corner.

Budgeted and actual sales of the product market segments are shown. Beneath these, the contributions from the two sets of data have been calculated.

As shown by the arrows, the sales value in each segment is multiplied by its corresponding CPS to arrive at its contribution. The contributions from the individual segments are accumulated to give the total contribution.

Fixed costs are $75,000 for both budgeted and actual results, and these are deducted to give the final budgeted and actual profit. A budgeted profit of $16,000 has turned into an actual loss of $1,000.

In comparing budgeted with actual figures, note the following:

- total revenue of $300,000 is unchanged
- selling prices are unchanged
- cost per unit figures are unchanged
- fixed costs are unchanged
- budgeted profit is converted into an actual loss.

The sole reason for this adverse turnaround is to be found in the mix of products.

The bulk of sales has moved from high to low contribution segments. For example, in the bottom right-hand last segment, which has the lowest CPS value (Product C sold through agents), sales have increased from a budgeted $20,000 to an actual $60,000. This increase has been offset by reductions in the better segments. Similiar other adverse movements can be identified. the overall product mix has been diluted and the company has suffered grievously.

Product mix is a potent driver of profit. It must be identified, understood by all and positively managed to achieve maximum potential.

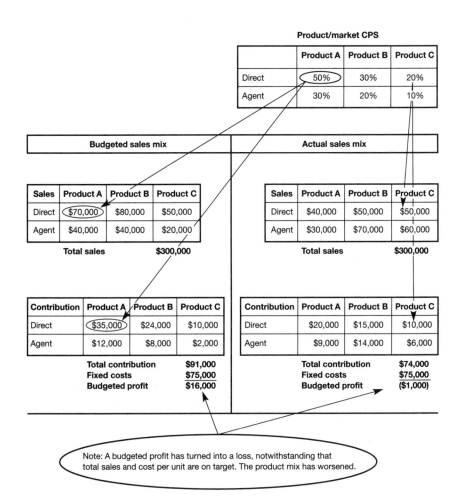

Product/market CPS

	Product A	Product B	Product C
Direct	50%	30%	20%
Agent	30%	20%	10%

Budgeted sales mix	Actual sales mix

Sales	Product A	Product B	Product C
Direct	$70,000	$80,000	$50,000
Agent	$40,000	$40,000	$20,000

Total sales $300,000

Sales	Product A	Product B	Product C
Direct	$40,000	$50,000	$50,000
Agent	$30,000	$70,000	$60,000

Total sales $300,000

Contribution	Product A	Product B	Product C
Direct	$35,000	$24,000	$10,000
Agent	$12,000	$8,000	$2,000

Total contribution $91,000
Fixed costs $75,000
Budgeted profit $16,000

Contribution	Product A	Product B	Product C
Direct	$20,000	$15,000	$10,000
Agent	$9,000	$14,000	$6,000

Total contribution $74,000
Fixed costs $75,000
Budgeted profit   ($1,000)

Note: A budgeted profit has turned into a loss, notwithstanding that total sales and cost per unit are on target. The product mix has worsened.

Fig. 15.13 Product mix

A step beyond contribution to sales percentage

Product mix expressed in terms of CPS by product/market segment is, as noted previously, a powerful tool to enable management to achieve the best from the market-place. It is difficult to exaggerate the importance to a company's financial health of directing sales away from low to high contribution areas.

However this is not the end of the story. This technique alone will not always succeed in maximizing contribution. There are situations in which the promotion of sales of products with high CPS is not to the advantage of the company.

This is often true when a company is working close to maximum capacity and when different products are competing for this capacity. In such situations, additional output of one product means a reduction in the output of another. So a gain from one product may be more than offset by loss from the other.

 Consider a manufacturing situation where a high-value machine is used to manufacture two products, each of which sells for $5,000 (see figure 15.14). Product A has a CPS of 30 percent while that of product B is 20 percent. The absolute contribution from product A is $1,500 and from product B is $1,000.

From all that has been said so far, it would seem that management should always favour product A over product B. However, it is possible for product B to be more profitable than product A. How can this be?

When a company is operating at, or close to, maximum capacity, a further calculation beyond CPS is necessary. We extract a value that we call 'contribution per unit of capacity' or 'contribution per unit of the limiting factor.' It can be a great identifier of sources of profit to a company, and so it will be explored in the next section.

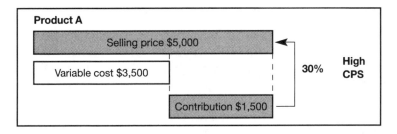

Product A

Selling price $5,000

Variable cost $3,500

Contribution $1,500

30% **High CPS**

It apears as first sight that product A, with a CPS value of 30%, is a more profitable product for the company than product B with a CPS value of only 20%.

Normally this is true, but there are circumstances where product B is more profitable.

We must check its usage of capacity.

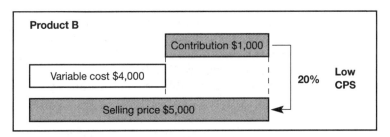

Product B

Contribution $1,000

Variable cost $4,000

Selling price $5,000

20% **Low CPS**

Fig. 15.14 Selling price to cost relationships of products A and B

Contribution per unit of capacity

Central to figure 15.15 is an illustration of machine capacity. We will assume that the machine can (after allowing for downtime, maintenance, cleaning and so on) deliver 2,000 productive hours per annum. We further assume that these productive hours can be more than fully utilized by existing products. Is it possible to increase the profitability of this machine?

We start our analysis by looking at what proportion of this capacity is used by each product, and we then relate this usage of capacity to the total contribution of each product.

Product A

One unit of product A takes 10 hours of machine capacity. The total contribution of this unit is $1,500. Therefore, the contribution per hour (CPH) of this product is $150. The capacity of the machine, remember, is 2,000 hours per annum, so, at $150 per hour, the maximum contribution attainable from the machine for this product in one year is $300,000.

Product B

One unit of product B takes four hours of machine capacity. The total contribution of this unit is $1,000. Therefore, the CPH of this product is $250. At $250 per hour, the maximum contribution attainable from the machine for this product in one year is $500,000

Product B is by far the more profitable product in this situation, even though it has a lower CPS.

The determining conditions for these circumstances to exist is that capacity is limited, and there is competition between products for this capacity. In this situation contribution will be maximized – and, therefore, so will profit – when activity is directed into those products that have, not the highest contribution to sales percentage, but the highest contribution per hour value.

We have discussed here a specific instance of the more general case referred to as 'contribution per unit of the limiting factor.' The limiting factor is the constraint that puts a ceiling on output. Machine hours are the most common limitation, but there can be others, such as raw materials, or working capital.

Errors are frequently made in pricing products without reference to this concept.

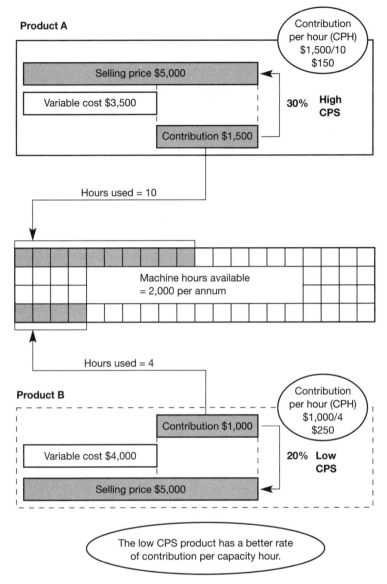

Fig. 15.15 Contribution per machine hour of products A and B

Summary

It is important to:

- Classify costs to distinguish fixed from variable
- Identify contribution by product group
- Actively direct sales from low to high contribution areas
- Where capacity hours are a constraint, identify and direct sales into products with high CPH values.

Investment ratios

Introduction · Product appraisal –
the problem · Product appraisal –
Steps to solution (1) · Product
appraisal – Steps to solution (2)
· Product appraisal – present value
(PV) · Product appraisal – internal
rate of return (IRR) · Product
appraisal – Summary

*The social object of skilled investment should
be to defeat the dark forces of time and
ignorance which envelope our future.*
JOHN MAYNARD KEYNES (1883–1946)

Introduction

The need for a company to earn a return on its investment has been covered in detail. It is clear that this return must meet market expectations if the standing and value of the company is not to suffer.

One of management's critical functions is planning the future of the business to ensure that an adequate rate of return is maintained. Essential to this is adequate new productive investment, as it is the return on this new investment that will provide the ongoing profits on which the company depends. Therefore a careful selection process needs to be applied to competing investment proposals so that only the best qualify.

In the past, many approaches have been adopted to assist managers in this selection. One very well tried and tested one that is still in use, is 'pay-back.' Simply calculate the number of years that the project will take to pay back the money invested in it. As a rule of thumb it can provide a useful 'fix' on a project. However, it is not a mathematically sound approach. Some accounting-type measures have also been used in the past that are mathematically suspect.

This chapter is about the sound and tested techniques used now by all major companies to assist them with investment decisions. It illustrates the various measures and ratios that have proved to be effective in selecting and ranking investment projects.

Project appraisal – the problem

The standard investment profile is that of a large initial cash out-flow followed by a stream of cash in-flows for a certain number of years (section A of figure 16.1). The investor hopes that the in-flows will both repay the initial investment and yield an adequate surplus. The problem has been how to relate the immediate cash outlay with the stream of future repayments so as to determine the true rate of return.

In section B of figure 16.1, the financial numbers are given for Investment 'X.' The investment is $1,000 and the stream of repayments over five years add up to $2,000. What, then, is the rate of return on the investment (ROI)? The increase in value over the five years is 100 percent, which could be interpreted as 20 percent per annum. Is this a correct interpretation? Is the return adequate and how is it affected by inflation? These are the questions investors commonly ask. Before answering them, let us look at one more example.

Section C of figure 16.1 shows the cash flows of Investment 'Y.' The investment here of $1,000 and total repayments of $2,000 is the same as before. However, the pattern of repayments is quite different. For each of the first four years the cash in-flows are $200 but in Year 5 the initial investment of $1,000 is repaid in addition to the annual amount of $200. In other words an investment of $1,000 gives an annual return of $200 and, at the end of its life, the original investment of $1,000 is also repaid in full. This is the pattern of cash flows we would realize if we were to invest in a fixed interest security yielding 20 percent. The true return on this project is 20 percent.

When we look back at Investment X, we see that we do not get our investment back in one lump at the end of the period – it is spread over each year. The yearly cash repayments, then, are both paying interest on the investments and repaying the principal. This is the pattern of returns given by a commercial investment such as a piece of equipment that wears out to nothing over a five year period. The return to the investor here cannot be assessed so easily.

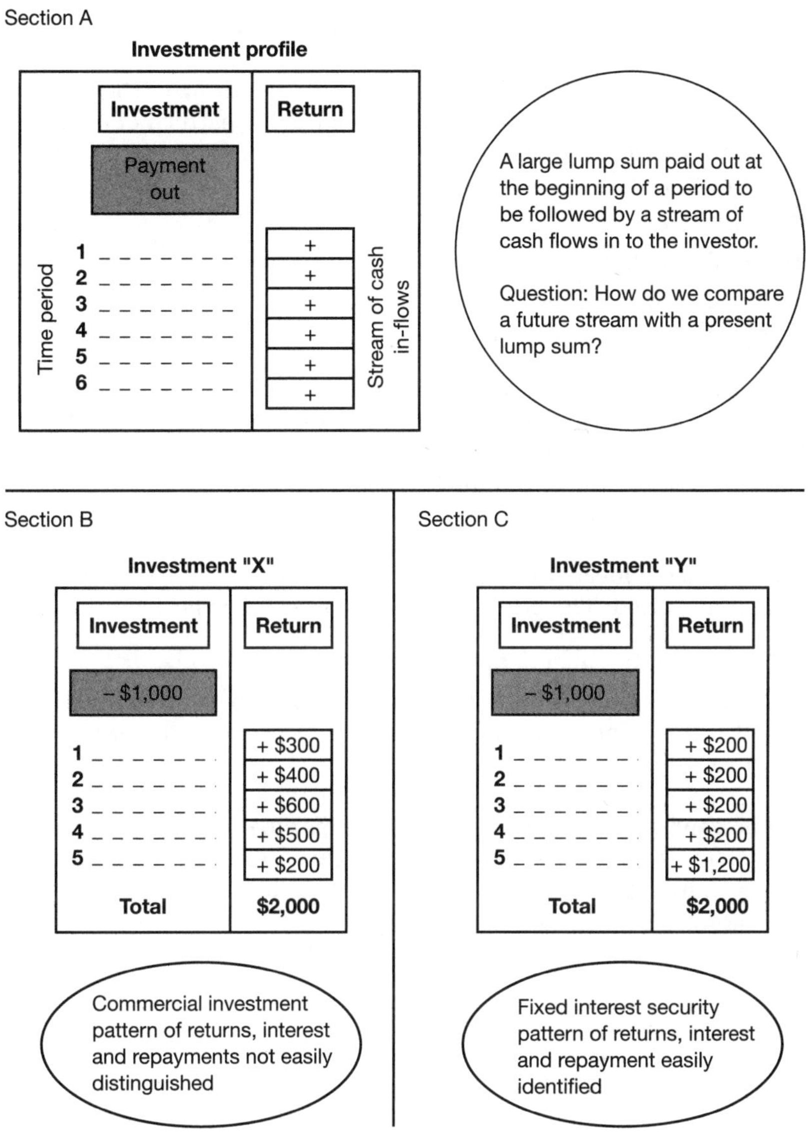
Section A
Investment profile
Investment
Return
Payment out
Time period
1
2
3
4
5
6
Stream of cash in-flows
A large lump sum paid out at the beginning of a period to be followed by a stream of cash flows in to the investor.
Question: How do we compare a future stream with a present lump sum?
Section B
Investment "X"
Investment
Return
– $1,000
1 + $300
2 + $400
3 + $600
4 + $500
5 + $200
Total $2,000
Commercial investment pattern of returns, interest and repayments not easily distinguished
Section C
Investment "Y"
Investment
Return
– $1,000
1 + $200
2 + $200
3 + $200
4 + $200
5 + $1,200
Total $2,000
Fixed interest security pattern of returns, interest and repayment easily identified

Fig. 16.1 Investment profiles

Project appraisal – steps to a solution (1)

The difficulty in assessment arises because of the timing of the cash flows. As already stated the cash flows tend to follow the pattern of a large cash out-flow followed by a stream of smaller cash in-flows over a series of future time periods.

We designate these periods as:

- Period 0: today
- Period 1: one year hence
- Period 2: two years hence, etc.

We know instinctively that money to be received at some distant time in the future has not the same worth as money in our hands now. This is the well-known principle referred to as 'The time value of money.' Because of it we cannot make direct comparisons between sums of money that fall into different time periods.

 We have to use a mechanism to express the value of all cash flows at one specific time period. The period most often selected is Period 0.

This approach is illustrated in figure 16.2. Each of the future cash flows is converted into what is called its 'present value' by the application of a 'discount factor.' The means of calculating this discount factor is shown in the next section.

These present values are now directly comparable. They have been standardized. They are summed together to give a total present value of all future cash in-flows. This amount in turn can be directly compared with the investment's initial cash out-flow. From this comparison we come to a conclusion about the worth of the investment project.

Setting out the problem

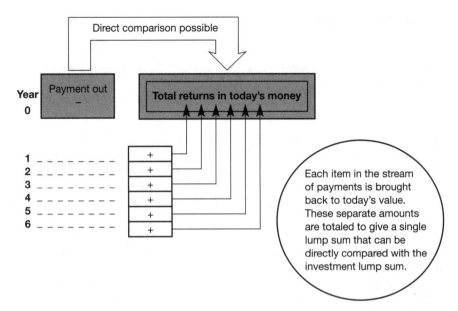

Fig. 16.2 Project appraisal – setting out the problem

Project appraisal – steps to a solution (2)

The discount factor

As stated above, we know that money due in a future time period has less value than money in our hands today. But how much less?

We can approach this question by asking the question 'If I had $100 available for deposit in the bank at an interest rate of 10 percent, what would it be worth one year from now?' The answer is of course $110.

Therefore $100 is the **present value** of $110 due in year 1 at a rate of 10 percent (expressed as a decimal = 0.1). We can bring any value back from the future to the present by applying a factor related to the interest rate. In this case we divide the future value by (1 + decimal interest rate), i.e. $110/ 1.1 = $100. **(It is mathematically identical to multiply by the discount factor .909, i.e., 1/1.1.)**

If the future cash flow was positioned in Period 2, then we would have to do the calculation twice, i.e. $\frac{1}{1.1} \times \frac{1}{1.1}$ = .826. In reality we do not make two calculations, we apply a factor that has the equivalent effect.

Figure 16.3 illustrates the effect of taking the value of a present sum of money either forward in time or back in time.

Centrally placed is the box showing $100 which is aligned with the Period 0. Periods going forward into the future and back into the past are shown on the right- and left-hand sides of zero respectively. An interest rate of 10 percent is used here to keep things simple. As we move to the right of the central zero point, the interest factors are 1.100, 1.210 and 1.331, which is 10 percent compounded for years +1, +2 and +3.

When applied to the sum of $100 they tell us that the equivalent is $133.1 at the end of Year 3.

To the left of the model, the factors are 0.909, 0.826 and 0.751. This last one tells us that $100 carried back three years has a present value of $75.1.

The investment appraisal technique relies mainly on the factors to the left of center, i.e. the discount factors.

To carry out our analysis we first select an appropriate interest rate. A higher rate would give a lower discount factor and vice versa. (See appendix 4 for relevant interest rate tables.) We can calculate the present or future value of any sum of money due in any period past or future by using such tables.

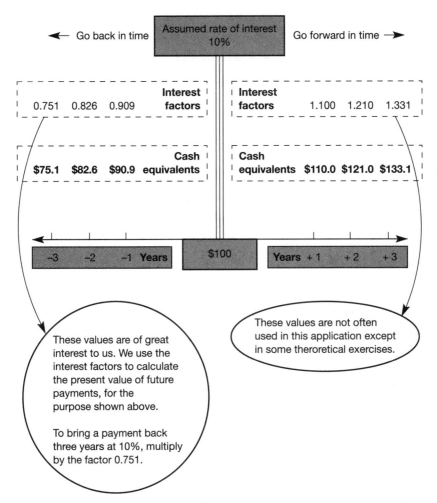

Fig. 16.3 Project appraisal – effects of time on value of a cash flow

Project appraisal – present value (PV)

Figure 16.4 shows an example of a three-year project:

Investment		$5,000
Return in:	Year 1	$1,500
	Year 2	$3,500
	Year 3	$1,400

We wish to ascertain if the rate of return on this investment is greater or less than 10 percent.

In figure 16.2, we saw the method for setting out the problem; figure 16.4 shows how the 10 percent discount factors are applied to the stream of returns. Each future payment is connected by an arrow back to the present time, showing the conversion of future cash flows into present-day values. The discount factor for one year at 10 percent is 0.909, for two years it is 0.826, etc.

The present value of each conversion is shown, i.c., $1,364 for year 1, etc. All individual present values are summed to give a total $5,309. The technical name for this amount of $5,309 is the **present value (PV)** of the project's future cash flows.

This sum can now be directly compared with the initial investment of $5,000. Cash in-flows are shown positive and out-flows negative. The positive sum of $5,309 is offset against the negative sum of $5,000 to give a **net present value (NPV)** of $309 (positive).

What information can be drawn from the NPV? Figure 16.5 will help us to interpret the result.

Example project tested at 10%

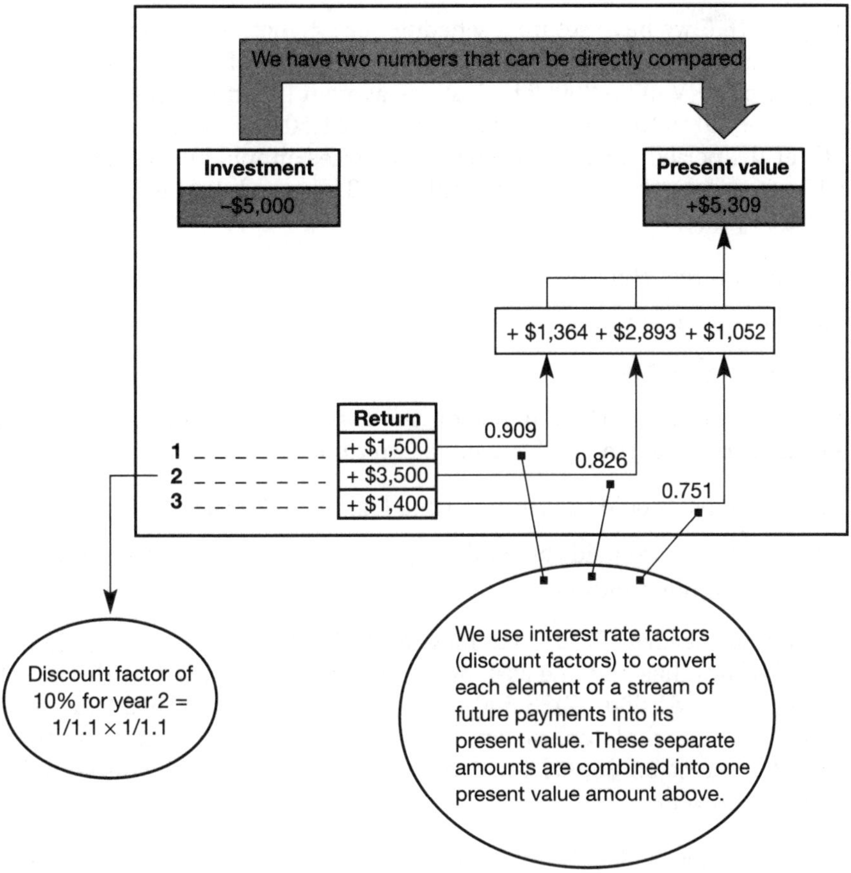

We have two numbers that can be directly compared

Investment
–$5,000

Present value
+$5,309

+ $1,364 + $2,893 + $1,052

Return
+ $1,500
+ $3,500
+ $1,400

1 _ _ _ _ _ _ _   0.909

2 _ _ _ _ _ _ _   0.826

3 _ _ _ _ _ _ _   0.751

Discount factor of 10% for year 2 = $1/1.1 \times 1/1.1$

We use interest rate factors (discount factors) to convert each element of a stream of future payments into its present value. These separate amounts are combined into one present value amount above.

Fig. 16.4 Project appraisal – calculating present value 1

The meaning of Net Present Value (NPV)

In figure 16.5 we have set up a schedule for a hypothetical bank loan that carries an interest rate of 10 percent. The amount of the loan is equal to the project NPV of $5,309. The loan repayment schedule shows payments that are equal to the project's cash flows of $1,500, $3,500, and $1,400.

Over the period of the loan the bank charges annual interest at the rate of 10 percent on the outstanding balance. The schedule shows for each of the three years:

a the interest charge

b the repayment and

c the closing balance.

At the end of Year 3 the balance on the loan is exactly zero. This shows that the three repayments have done two things:

1. they have repaid in full the initial loan of $5,309 and

2. they have also paid the bank 10 percent interest each year on the amount outstanding.

The column headed 'Bank cash movements' will clarify the example further. The bank has had one cash out-flow of $5,309 followed by three cash in-flows of (1) $1,500, (2)$3,500 (3) $1,400 and it has earned exactly 10 percent on the whole operation. Note that the bank has not earned 10 percent interest on $5,309 for three years, but only on the outstanding balance each year.

This example establishes the meaning of 'Present Value.' It is the sum of money today that exactly matches a future stream of income at a given rate of interest. It is obvious that the rate of interest used directly affects the present value. A higher rate of interest produces a lower present value and vice versa.

We will now apply these principles to our example investment project. If the initial investment were $5,309 (as in the case of the bank) the return to the investor would have been exactly 10 percent. It follows that if we can get the same returns from a smaller initial sum, i.e. $5,000, then the return is greater than 10 percent.

The fact that the value derived for NPV (i.e. present value of cash flows less initial investment) has come out positive means that the project is delivering a rate of return greater than the interest rate used in the calculations. If the NPV were negative, it would mean the rate delivered was less than the interest rate used.

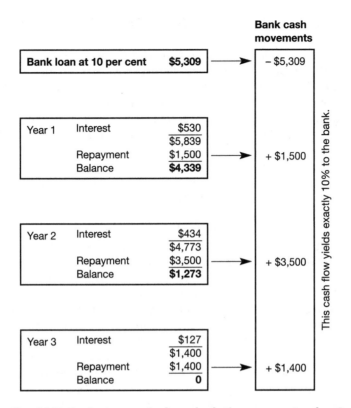

Bank cash movements

				Bank cash movements
Bank loan at 10 per cent		**$5,309**	→	– $5,309
Year 1	Interest	$530		
		$5,839		
	Repayment	$1,500	→	+ $1,500
	Balance	**$4,339**		
Year 2	Interest	$434		
		$4,773		
	Repayment	$3,500	→	+ $3,500
	Balance	**$1,273**		
Year 3	Interest	$127		
		$1,400		
	Repayment	$1,400	→	+ $1,400
	Balance	0		

This cash flow yields exactly 10% to the bank.

Fig. 16.5 Project appraisal – calculating present value 2

Project appraisal – internal rate of return (IRR)

The previous example has shown that the investment of $5,000 earns more than 10 percent. We have established that when the present value of the future cash flows exceeds the investment amount, we know that the rate of return is greater than the interest rate used in the calculation.

However, we do not know what actual rate of return is being delivered by the project. Of course this is very important information and further calculations are needed to establish it.

Unfortunately, there is no mathematical way of going directly to the answer. Instead we carry out a series of tests at various rates and by degrees work our way towards the answer.

We see this approach in figure 16.6. On our first test we got a positive NPV of $309 which told us that the project was delivering a return greater than 10 percent. A second test is carried out using 11 percent discount factors. The present value here is $5,216, yielding an NPV of $216 positive. We conclude that the return is greater than 11 percent.

In section B, a schedule shows calculations for interest rate values between 10 percent and 15 percent, as listed in column 1. In the second column the present values that correspond to these different rates are $5,309, $5,216, $5,126 and so on. Note how these amounts fall in value as higher interest rates are applied. The third column has the unchanged investment figure of $5,000 in all rows. The fourth column shows the result of deducting the investment from the present value.

The NPV at 10 percent is $309 (positive) and at 11 percent it is $216 (positive). Going down the column, the value remains positive as far as 13 percent. At 14 percent cent it becomes negative. It becomes even more negative at 15 percent. It can be concluded from these values, then, that the investment is earning more than 13 percent and less than 14 percent. At approximately 13.5 percent, the figure in the NPV column would equal zero.

This value of 13.5 percent is the rate of return being earned by the project. It is referred to as the **Internal Rate of Return (IRR)**.

The IRR is the rate that makes the present value of the stream of future cash flows exactly equal the investment.

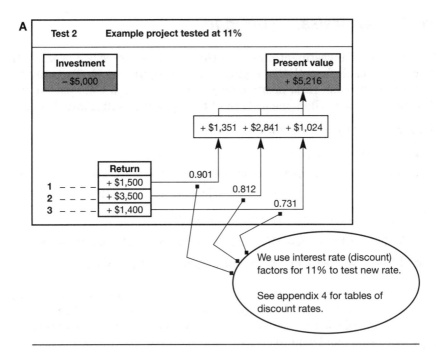

A

Test 2　　Example project tested at 11%

Investment	Present value
– $5,000	+ $5,216

+ $1,351　+ $2,841　+ $1,024

Return
+ $1,500
+ $3,500
+ $1,400

1 – – – –
2 – – – –
3 – – – –

0.901
0.812
0.731

We use interest rate (discount) factors for 11% to test new rate.

See appendix 4 for tables of discount rates.

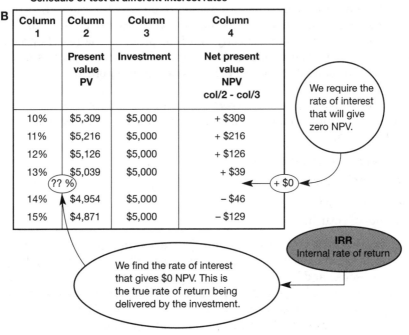

Schedule of test at different interest rates

B

Column 1	Column 2	Column 3	Column 4
	Present value PV	Investment	Net present value NPV col/2 - col/3
10%	$5,309	$5,000	+ $309
11%	$5,216	$5,000	+ $216
12%	$5,126	$5,000	+ $126
13%	$5,039	$5,000	+ $39
?? %			
14%	$4,954	$5,000	– $46
15%	$4,871	$5,000	– $129

We require the rate of interest that will give zero NPV.

+ $0

We find the rate of interest that gives $0 NPV. This is the true rate of return being delivered by the investment.

IRR
Internal rate of return

Fig. 16.6 Calculating the internal rate of return

Project appraisal – summary

The method of investment appraisal that has been described is called the discounted cash flow (DCF) technique. (see figure 16.7). To apply this technique the cash flow, positive or negative, for each time period must first be identified. Then one or both of the approaches illustrated is used:

The NPV (net present value) method

- select the required rate of interest (see below)
- apply it to the stream of cash flows to derive net present value
- if net present value is positive, select the project, otherwise do not.

The IRR (internal rate of return) method

- find the interest rate that makes net present value equal to zero
- if this rate is satisfactory, select project, otherwise do not.

In this chapter we have merely considered how to apply a mathematical technique once the cash flows from a project have been established.

In real life this is the easy part of project appraisal. It requires considerably more effort and skill to arrive at the expected cash flows. Furthermore managers will never have to physically do the calculations themselves because computer programs are available do this for them. However, a manager must understand the reasoning behind the calculations so that he can formulate a problem correctly and interpret the the results produced by the computer. The various ratios produced by these programs can help him to make sound decisions in field of investment appraisal.

Figure 16.7 gives an outline structure for of the inputs that are required to analyze an investment decision. These inputs can be grouped under four headings:

- cost of the investments
- annual returns
- life of project
- rate of return.

A brief description of each is given. The area for which it is hardest to input reliable data is that of 'annual returns.' There are no rules for this. Common sense and business acumen must apply here. It is normal to test a series of scenarios to examine the sensitivity of the project to small changes in input variables. Over time the accuracy of predictions can be monitored and suitable filtering mechanisms adopted.

The name of the technique that has been demonstrated. The short-hand expression is DCF	**D**iscounted **C**ash **F**low	Cash flow is used rather than profit to measure the return on investment, because: (a) it is easier to identitfy in respect of a single project, and (b) it is mathmatically more correct.

The four seperate input elements that have to be quantified are:

(1) Cost of investment
This is probably the easiest amount to establish. Consider incremental cash outlay only, i.e., the total extra cash outflow that results from doing this project as opposed to not doing it. Allow for any savings such as tax. Remember to include working capital outlays such as extra inventory associated with the project. Do not add in any allocated cost, i.e. costs transferred from another part of the organization not giving rise to any extra cash out-flow

(2) Annual returns from project
Again we make a comparison between two situations: (1) the project goes ahead, (2) the project does not go ahead. The appropriate figure here is the incrmental cash inflow after tax. This value is derived from the extra revenue to be received less the extra cash costs to be incurred. Do not include any allocated costs in the calculations.

(3) Life of project
The number of years can be determined by the project's physical, technological or economic life span. A heavy duty vehicle has a physical life of 5 years. A computer could have a physical life of 25 years but a technological life of 3 years. For very long-life project, e.g. a hotel, we look forward a maximum of 6 to 8 years and assume a terminal value at the end of that time. This is treated as a cash in-flow in the DCF model.

(4) Rate of interest
This can be a contentious issue relating to the cost of capital. In practice a rate is laid down by the policy makers in the business. It is a rate that all new projects are expected to exceed. It is often called the "hurdle rate." To allow for different levels of risk in projects, different discount rates may be applied.

Fig. 16.7 Discounted cash flow – the component parts

Shareholder value added (SVA)

*Capital, in the sense of capital value, is
simply future income discounted or, in
other words, capitalised.*
IRVING FISHER (1867–1947)

Introduction

In chapter 12 we looked at various stockmarket ratios and traditional approaches to the measurement of corporate performance and value. These have been in use for many years, they are still widely used and they have served the business community well. However many practitioners have now come to the conclusion that something more is needed.

Global competition, worldwide recession, and complex financial instruments have shown up weaknesses in these traditional aproaches. This has given rise to a search for more precise instruments of assessment. The search has not been in vain, and there are now exciting new developments in this area.

The most robust of these new techniques is that most commonly known as 'shareholder value added' (SVA)*, but the terms 'economic value added' (EVA), and 'market value added' (MVA) are also used.

These systems all have the same underlying approach. They adopt an economic rather than an accounting stance, and they look to the future rather than the past.

One of the problems with the purely accounting approach is that it relies largely on values that are historic. Furthermore these values are derived from accounting statements that are produced according to various accounting conventions. Often these conventions are more useful for auditing purposes rather than for performance assessment or valuation.

There are other issues that traditional approaches do not address explicity such as risk measurement and future capital investment. There is no doubt that SVA methods provide a more comprehensive and philosophically sound basis for managerial decisions than those used in the past.

* Dr Alfred Rappaport (author of *Creating Shareholder Value*) is one of the founders of the movement and the ideas in this chapter owe much to his initiatives.

Description

The economic viewpoint is that value is determined by future cash flows rather than historic profit or balance sheet calculations. Cash is invested today in order to get a surplus back in the future. This future cash flow must fully repay the initial investment and also cover the cost of the funds over the period of investment. This cash flow technique has been used for many years in the assessment of capital projects (see chapter 16).

Let us say that we are faced with a capital project decision on whether we should spend $1m on a particular piece of equipment. We estimate future revenues and costs over the life of the equipment. We convert these into the extra cash in-flow that the equipment will produce. We combine that in-flow with other cash movements arising from working capital etc. Then we discount the total cash flow back to a net present value (NPV) We use that figure to assess the financial value of the investment.

The shareholder value approach is to use the same technique to assess the value of a company's operations either in whole or in part.

However in regard to a company special considerations apply:

1. The returns from a company cannot be so neatly packaged as those from a single piece of equipment. In a company there will be many different operations each giving rise to a separate cash flow.

2. With a single piece of equipment there is usually a very definite and limited life span, but not so with a company.

3. In straightforward project appraisal, a very pragmatic approach to the selection of a discount factor is common. But what discount factor should be applied to the cash flows of a company overall? This is a very important consideration because the factor chosen will have a major bearing on the assessment.

4. Companies can be funded in many different ways. Various mixtures of equity and loan capital are used. How can these differences be accommodated?

It is these issues that will be explored in the following pages. We will use the SVA Sample Company shown in figure 17.1 to illustrate the discussion.

SVA Sample Company Inc.

Balance sheet ($000s)

Fixed assets		Owners' funds	
		Issued capital	1,440
Net FA		Capital reserves	540
	2,500	Revenue reserves	2,226
			4,206
Current assets			
Inventory	4,000		
Accounts		Long-term loans	1,000
receivable	2,820	Short-term loans	1,544
Cash	170		**2,544**
Miscellanious	510		
		Current liabilities	
		Accounts payable	2,750
		Miscellaneous	500
	7,500		**3,250**
	10,000		**10,000**

Note:
Short-term loans
moved from
current liabilities

Profit/loss account ($000s)

Sales	12,500
Operating costs	11,500
EBIT (Earnings before interest and tax)	1,000
Interest	192
EBT (Earnings before tax)	808
Tax	202
EAT (Earnings after tax)	606
Dividend	0
RE (Retained earnings)	606

Fig. 17.1 SVA Sample Company Inc.

Operating assets

Our first exercise is to re-arrange the balance sheet to separate out the net operating assets i.e. those assets that are fundamental to the operation of the business.* Figure 17.2 illustrates this.

There may be assets in the balance sheet that are not essential to the existing operations, e.g. surplus cash holdings. This matter will be dealt with later.

There are three separate components:

1. Fixed assets $2,500
2. Current assets $7,500
3. Current liabilities * $3,250

* Observant readers will have noted that there are no short-term loans included in current liabilities. These loans are treated as part of the funding of the business for reasons to be seen shortly.

'Current assets' and 'current liabilities' are netted off to yield a figure for 'net working capital' (NWC) of $4,250. Accordingly, the net operating assets are:

1. Fixed assets $2,500
2. Net working capital $4,250

The funds in the balance sheet that match these operating assets we refer to as 'invested capital' (IC).

For this exercise we will assume that all of the items included in operating assets will respond spontaneously to changes in sales volume.

This assumption is reasonable for items in the 'net working capital' category. There is a direct linear relationship between 'Accounts receivable' and the level of sales. So also with inventory, even though the link is not so close. The same may be said of 'Accounts payable' on the liabilities side of the balance sheet. These are the three principal items in the NWC category.

In the case of 'Cash' we distinguish between the basic amount required for operating requirements and surpluses held for other purposes. This basic operating amount is a very small percentage of total assets and it can be losely linked to volume of activity.

For a comment on the relationship between 'fixed assets' and sales see the following section.

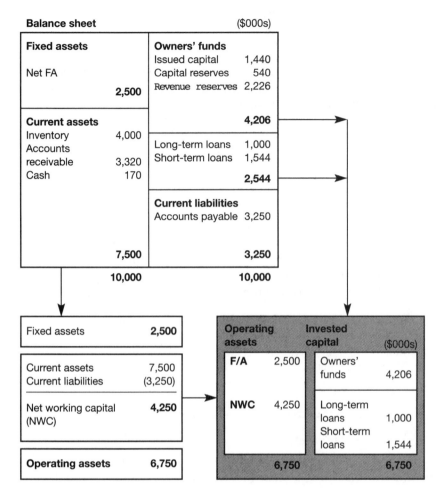

Balance sheet ($000s)

Fixed assets		Owners' funds	
Net FA		Issued capital	1,440
		Capital reserves	540
	2,500	Revenue reserves	2,226
			4,206
Current assets		Long-term loans	1,000
Inventory	4,000	Short-term loans	1,544
Accounts receivable	3,320		**2,544**
Cash	170	**Current liabilities**	
		Accounts payable	3,250
	7,500		**3,250**
	10,000		**10,000**

Fixed assets	**2,500**

Current assets	7,500
Current liabilities	(3,250)
Net working capital (NWC)	**4,250**

Operating assets	**6,750**

Operating assets		Invested capital	($000s)
F/A	2,500	Owners' funds	4,206
NWC	4,250	Long-term loans	1,000
		Short-term loans	1,544
	6,750		**6,750**

Fig. 17.2 Identify operating assets/funds

Approach to valuation (1)

Forecast assumptions

Having identified the net operating assets, we will set about estimating the value of this company as determined by its expected future cash flows and the discount factor to be applied to these.

We will illustrate this for our example company using some very simple assumptions, such as a constant growth in sales of 10 percent.

There will be two main components to the cash flow:

1. Operating profits after tax

2. Cash flows arising from movements in assets.

The first of these is normally positive (cash in-flow) and the second negative (cash out-flow). We have seen in chapter 10 that an increase in assets gives rise to a cash out-flow. If assets are currently fully utilized, the extra volume of sales will probably require extra assets in support.

We must make some assumptions about the future operations. These are:

1. Growth in future sales	10 percent p.a.
2. Period of forecast	four years
3. Margin on sales	8 percent
4. Tax rate	25 percent
5. Fixed assets required	Linear to sales
6. Net working capital required	Linear to sales

Figure 17.3 shows expected Sales, Fixed assets and Net working capital amounts forecast for the next four years on an assumed growth rate of 10 percent.

Note: *We have suggested that there is strong justification for assuming a linear relationship between 'net working capital' and sales. But it is not realistic to assume that fixed assets will move exactly in line with sales in any one year. However, over longer periods this assumption may hold true. We are using a simplified example here. In a practical application much thought would be given to assessing fixed asset and working capital requirements.*

Forecast values

	Historic period	Forecast period – years			
	0	1	2	3	4
Sales **Growth 10%**	$ 12,500	$ 13,750	$ 15,125	$ 16,638	$ 18,301
Fixed **assets** **Linear relationship** **to sales**	2,500	2,750	3,025	3,328	3,660
Net working **capital** **Linear relationship** **to sales**	4,250	4,675	5,143	5,657	6,222

Fig. 17.3 SVA Example Company Inc. forecast sales, fixed assets and net working capital

Approach to valuation (2)

Forecast net cash flow

Figure 17.4 shows cash flow forecasts for the SVA Sample Company Inc. We take each of the three items forecast in the previous section and derive its corresponding cash flow :

Section A: Sales: (growth rate 10 percent per annum)

A.2 We apply the sales margin percentage (8 percent) to derive operating profit.

A.3 Tax is calculated at 25 percent and deducted.

A.4 Net operating profit after tax (NOPAT). This is the figure we take for the positive operating cash flows per annum that arise from trading.

Two questions immediately come to mind :

a What about the depreciation charged in the accounts? Should the forecast cash flows not be increased by a corresponding amount? and

b Why has tax been charged to profits before interest has been deducted?

Both of these questions will be dealt with below.

Section B: Fixed assets:

■ B.2 The negative cash flow reflects the increase in value in FA each year

Section C: Net working capital:

■ C.2 The negative cash flow reflects the increase in value of NWC each year

Section D: Overall cash flow:

D.1 Cash flows from A, B, and C above are netted off to give values for expected net cash flows for each of the next four years.

Depreciation and cash flow

We know that that cash flow from a trading operation can be defined as net profit plus depreciation. Should we not therefore add back depreciation to our cash flows? Strictly speaking, the answer is 'yes.'

However in our simple illustration, we ignore this adjustment both in the income statement and again when we come to look at investment in fixed

A Cash flow forecasts

Operations	Historic period	Forecast period – years			
	0	1	2	3	4
A.1 **Sales**	$ 12,500	$ 13,750	$ 15,125	$ 16,638	$ 18,301
A.2 **Margin 8%**	1,000	1,100	1,210	1,331	1,464
A.3 **Tax 25%**		275	303	333	366
A.4 **NOPAT** (Net operating profit after tax)		825	907	998	1,098

B Investment – fixed assets

	0	1	2	3	4
B.1 Closing balance	$ 2,500	$ 2,750	$ 3,025	$ 3,328	$ 3,660
B.2 Cash flow		(250)	(275)	(303)	(332)

C Investment – net working capital

	0	1	2	3	4
C.1 Closing balance	$ 4,250	$ 4,675	$ 5,143	$ 5,657	$ 6,222
C.2 Cash flow		(425)	(468)	(514)	(565)

D Net cash flow

	0	1	2	3	4
D.1 Net cash flow A.4 + B.2 + C.2		$ 150	$ 164	$ 181	$ 201

Fig. 17.4 Cash flow forecasts

assets. In the latter case by taking only the net increase we ignore the investment required to maintain a constant level of assets. This could be equated to the depreciation charge. Consequently these two items cancel out.

Tax: We have charged tax at the full rate on operating profit. Would this not be shielded by our interest charge which would be deducted prior to the tax charge? The reason for the treatment used here is that the question of funding is ignored. We can say that for the moment we are assuming that funding is entirely from equity.

Total present value

In figure 17.5 we perform three exercises:

- We adopt a discount rate of 9.64 percent
- We discount the four-year cash flow back to period zero
- We decide on a 'terminal value' at year 4 and discount it back.

Likewise three important questions spring to mind at this stage:

- Why use four years in preference to some other time period?
- How do we decide on value remaining in the company at the end of whatever time period we chose?
- Why use 9.64 percent as our discount factor?

These crucial questions will all be addressed in detail in due course.

The present value of the first four years of operation amounts to $550.

Terminal Value

This is perhaps the most important number in the whole equation.

There are many approaches and formulae used to estimate it, but in this simple illustration we will assume that the company will have a market value equal to ten times its 'net operating profit after tax' (NOPAT).

i.e., NOPAT (year 4)   =$1,098
       Value at end of year 4 =$10,980 (NOPAT × 10)

This is the amount we could sell the company for at the end of year 4. We can therefore treat this figure as if it were a cash in-flow in that year. We apply our discount rate of 9.64 percent to give a present value of $7,598, but see figure 17.13 for the revised method.

Present value

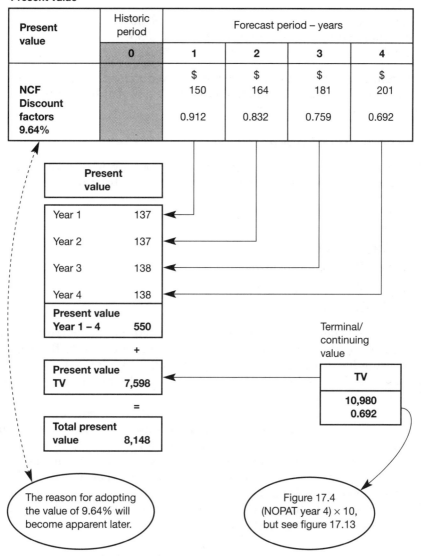

Present value	Historic period	Forecast period – years			
	0	**1**	**2**	**3**	**4**
NCF **Discount** **factors** **9.64%**		$ 150 0.912	$ 164 0.832	$ 181 0.759	$ 201 0.692

Present value	
Year 1	137
Year 2	137
Year 3	138
Year 4	138
Present value **Year 1 – 4**	**550**

+

Present value **TV**	**7,598**

=

Total present **value**	**8,148**

Terminal/
continuing
value

TV
10,980 **0.692**

The reason for adopting
the value of 9.64% will
become apparent later.

Figure 17.4
(NOPAT year 4) × 10,
but see figure 17.13

Fig. 17.5 Calculating present value

The total present value for the company can now be stated as follows:

First four years	$550
Indefinite period beyond four years	$7,598
Total	$8,148

This sum of $8,148 is the value we have arrived at for the 'operating business.' In due course we will translate this amount into a value for the equity shareholders (see figure 17.7).

Interpretation of present value

The illustration so far has shown how we can put a value on a company's operations by considering a small number of **value drivers**:

1. Sales growth
2. Margin percentage
3. Tax percentage on profits
4. New Fixed asset investment
5. New Working capital investment
6. The discount factor.

Note that neither the existing assets employed nor the corresponding investment by the shareholders and others have entered into the calculation. Value lies solely in the future profitability of planned operations, the tax position, and the investment that will be required to support these operations.

While we do not utilize any balance sheet figures in our calculation of value, we are very interested in the relationship that exists between our calculated value and the underlying investment in the business.

If our newly determined value is greater than the investment shown in the balance sheet, then value has been created. In other words, the business today, valued in terms of its future propects, has more than justified the investment that has gone into creating that business. If the result is less, then value has been destroyed.

Figure 17.6 shows the results of this comparison for the Example Company.

- The operating assets and the corresponding funds are $6,750
- The value derived for the operations is $8,148
- There is a surplus of (**value added**) $1,398

This surplus is a measure of management's performance. It is a quantification of the planning, decision-making, and operating skills they have employed to bring the present business into being.

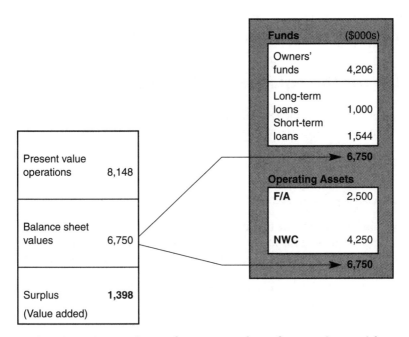

Fig. 17.6 Comparison of present value of operations with balance sheet values

We can see what a powerful tool we have not only for decision-making, but for assessing and rewarding managerial performance.

Value for the equity shareholders

The calculated value of $8,148 relates to the operating business. We must now translate this into a value for the equity shareholders.

Two adjustments are required:

1. Non-operating assets

There may be assets in the balance sheet that are not essential to the existing business. The most obvious case is where a company, for one reason or another, holds a large cash balance. It may be that the company is planning future acquisitions.

The value of such assets must be added to that of the operations to arrive at the company value.

2. Non-equity funds

The equity shareholder stands at the end of the queue of those who provide funds to a business. The claims of those who provide loan and preference share capital have precedence.

All such prior claims must be deducted from the company value to arrive at the value for the equity shareholders.

SVA Example Company
In figure 17.7 these calculations have been performed for the example company. Note that:

- there are no non-operating assets in this case
- the total non-equity funds amount to $2,544
- the resulting equity value is $5,604.

The equity investment in the balance sheet amounts to $4,206, so the surplus is again $1,398. The total amount of the value added as a result of good management has accrued to the equity shareholders. Hence the term 'SVA' (shareholder value added) that is given to this technique.

SVA Example Company		($000s)
Value of operations		8,148
Add non-operating assets*		0
Total		**8,148**
Less non-equity funds		
Long loans	(1,000)	
Short loans	(1,544)	**2,544**
Value remaining for equity		**5,604**
Balance sheet value of equity		**4,206**
Value added for equity		**1,398**

* This item relates to any assets, such as surplus cash, in the balance sheet that are not essential to the operations that are being assessed. This method of treatment assumes that they could be seperated out and realised in cash, without affecting the operations.

Fig. 17.7 Value of equity

We use the technique not only to calculate a value for a particular operating business, but also to compare and decide between alternative strategies for a particular operation. Furthermore its particular strength may not even be to look at an overall business, but rather to identify which of its component parts are adding value and which are destroying value.

In arriving at a value for the company we have skirted around some very important matters:

- **The appropriate discount factor to be applied to the cash flows.**
- **The terminal value of the business, i.e. its continuing value at the end of the forecast period.**

Discount factor

All the funds used to support the business have a cost. This cost is obvious in the case of loan funds. They carry a precise (but maybe varying) interest rate and their cost has always been charged against the profits of an operation.

In the case of common stock (equity) the cost is just as real but it has not always been so obvious. Indeed it is one of the main criticisms of more traditional methods of assessment that this cost has not been made more explicit and charged against operations. In the SVA method of assessment the cost of equity is fully assessed and charged. The method employed is to use a discount factor based on the weighted average cost of capital.

Weighted average cost of capital (WACC)

Figure 17.8 shows the calculation.

- We identify each source of funds and its corresponding cost. Some costs, such as interest on loans, are tax deductible, other are not. We must therefore express all charges in constant after-tax terms. For instance if a loan carries a 10 percent coupon and the tax rate is 25 percent, the after-tax cost is 8 percent.
- We calculate for each source of funds its weighting, i.e. its percentage of the total. For instance if total funds are $200 and we have a loan of $50, we apply a weighting of 25 percent to that loan.
- We multiply the cost of each source by its weighting to obtain its weighted cost. The sum of all the weighted costs is WACC.

See important note (to figure 17.8) on the correct weights to use for calculating WACC.

Funds ($000s)

Owners' funds		Book weights	After-tax costs	Weighted costs
	4,206	62%	12%	7.44%
Long-term loans	1,000	15%	7%	1.05%
Short-term loans	1,544	23%	5%	1.15%
	6,750	**100%**		**9.64%**

These costs are assumed for this example but see p. 278

Weighted average cost of capital WACC

Important note:

An issue arises in respect of the correct weights to use for sources of funds. The choice lies between book weights and market weights. If we choose book weights we use balance sheet values. For market weights we must weigh in proportion to the current market value of the different types of funds. This issue is most important is the case of equity funds that generally have a market value considerably in excess of book value.

It is more correct to use market values where they are available, but for simplicity the examples here use book values.

Fig. 17.8 Weighted average cost of capital

The cost of equity capital

The cost of loan capital is simply the after-tax interest cost. The cost of common equity is not so easy to establish. It is an issue that has exercised many eminent minds over a number of decades.

The problem is that the cost of equity is not based on a contract but on the expectations.

When the equity shareholder invests he/she does so on the basis of two estimates:

■ What return can I expect?

■ What degree of confidence can I have in this expectation?

The assessment of expected return will be based on the investors view of the following benefits (see figure 17.9):

■ The stream of annual dividends

■ The growth in the share market price.

The degree of confidence will be a function of the perceived risk of the investment. The investor knows that risk is inherent in business. He/she does not like to take risks and he/she will have to be rewarded for doing so. The higher the perceived risk the greater the return he/she will require.

The investor has a wide range of opportunities for investment. These can be classified into low-risk investments yielding relatively low returns, e.g., government securities, and higher risk investments that must offer the promise of higher returns. Equity shares fall into this latter category.

The cost of equity to the company is the overall rate of return it must promise to deliver to the investor to persuade him/her to invest. It can also be expressed as the amount an extra unit of equity brought into the company must earn in order not to dilute the return to the existing shareholders.

In order to ascertain this cost of equity the two great imponderables are:

■ growth from an existing position

■ risk.

Because we are dealing with estimates that exist in the minds of thousands of investors it is very difficult to quantify these factors. All we can do is to observe behavior in the market-place and try to construct models to explain that behavior.

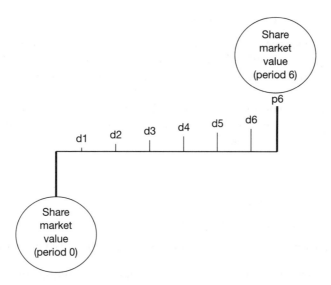

Fig. 17.9 The cost of equity capital

The capital asset pricing model

Models of considerable complexity have been derived for the purpose of estimating the cost of equity capital for a specific company. The most durable of these is that known as 'the capital asset pricing model' (CAPM).

It is based on the premise that investors require a minimum rate of return even when no risk is involved, and this required rate increases as the apparent risk increases.

The input values required by the model are:

1. The risk-free rate
2. The average return to equity shares across the total market
4. A measure of the riskiness of the specific share (its beta value).

1. **Risk-free rate:** This is taken to be the rate available on government bonds. In section A of figure 17.10 we assume a rate of 8 percent and we plot it on the left-hand vertical of the chart

2. **The average rate of return that has been achieved by the total equity market over a specific time period:** The returns on a sample of shares representative of the total market is plotted over a time period that is considered normal, i.e. when values were not artifically high or low. In section B of figure 17.10 we assume this rate to be 12.5 percent. We assign it a risk coefficient of 1.0 and we plot it midway along the horizontal axis.
   The Market Premium is simply the value in (2) above less the value in (1) above, i.e., 4.5 percent. (See section C of figure 17.10.)

3. **Beta value:** A measure of the specific firm's risk profile compared to that of the total equity market. It measures the degree to which returns on the specific share have moved in unison with the overall market. Its normal range is from 0.5 (low risk) to 1.5 (high risk), with the value one 1.0 indicating that its risk profile is identical to that of the total market. For our example we have chosen a high-risk value of 1.25.

These four values are used to derive an appropriate cost of equity for a specific company. See section D of figure 17.10. The formula is:

Cost of equity (company k) = Risk-free rate + [Market premium × beta-k]
13.6 % = 8 % + [4.5 % × 1.25]

It is not the purpose of this book to go into further detail of this complex subject.

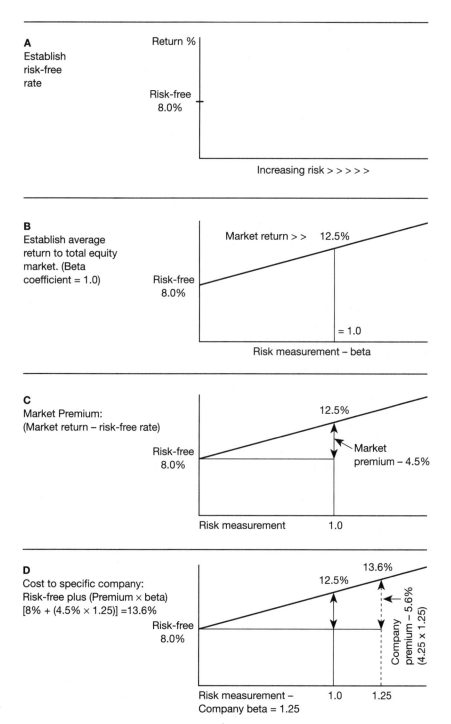

A
Establish
risk-free
rate

Return %

Risk-free
8.0%

Increasing risk > > > >

B
Establish average
return to total equity
market. (Beta
coefficient = 1.0)

Market return > >   12.5%

Risk-free
8.0%

= 1.0

Risk measurement – beta

C
Market Premium:
(Market return – risk-free rate)

12.5%

Risk-free
8.0%

Market
premium – 4.5%

Risk measurement   1.0

D
Cost to specific company:
Risk-free plus (Premium × beta)
[8% + (4.5% × 1.25)] =13.6%

13.6%

12.5%

Risk-free
8.0%

Company
premium – 5.6%
(4.25 x 1.25)

Risk measurement –
Company beta = 1.25

1.0   1.25

Fig. 17.10 Capital asset pricing model

How added value is created

The cost of equity as calculated above is, as we have seen, combined with the cost of non-equity funds to give an overall weighted cost of capital. This WACC figure is of crucial importance. It represent the long-term hurdle rate that a company must exceed for sustainable achievement.

We will here introduce the term ROIC (return on invested capital). (For a full description refer to appendix 1.)

This is another means of measuring performance that is similiar to ROTA. We use a new measure here because we must adopt a definition of assets that corresponds to the funds base used for calculating the cost of capital.

The relationship between a company's ROIC and its WACC is the key variable that determines its success measured in SVA terms (see figure 17.12).

If we were to look at a company that had a WACC of 10 percent and an ROIC of 12 percent we would know that value is being created. This excess value should be reflected in the company's market capitalization.

With a zero growth expectation we could expect to see the market value of the company at 20 percent above its book value. However if we add growth to the equation this value increases rapidly (see figure 17.11).

The reason for the upward curve is as follows. Where there is zero growth, earnings are constant and each year they can be paid out in full. So the return is similiar to that of a high-yielding fixed interest bond. The price of such a bond is determined by its return relative to its required yield. There is a premium of 20 percent in this situation.

However where some of the earnings are not paid out but in order to achieve growth are re-invested at the premium rate the effect on value is compounded. The funds that are re-invested earn a higher rate of return than they would if they had been paid out. The higher the rate of retention and re-investment the greater will be the effect on value.

But all this assumes that the company can re-invest at the premium ROIC. For these conditions to apply, the company must have a strong strategic position in a high-growth market.

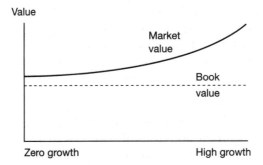

Market v book values
relative to growth of a
company where
ROIC is greater than WACC

Value

Market
value

Book
value

Zero growth   High growth

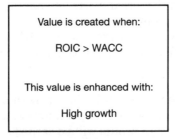

Value is created when:

ROIC > WACC

This value is enhanced with:

High growth

Fig. 17.11 How value is affected when return on invested capital (ROIC) is greater than weighted average cost of capital (WACC)

Alternative growth/value scenarios

In figure 17.12 three scenarios are depicted.

In **section A** the chart, repeated from figure 17.11, shows the interaction of growth with a high rate of return. We can see that the really successful company is one of high growth and an ROIC in excess of WACC.

A relatively small number of companies occupy this position for more than a short period of time. Such companies attract strong competition which almost invariably erodes their competitive advantage. There are economic laws that tend to push companies into a position where ROIC almost exactly equals WACC.

In **section B** we see the dramatic negative impact that growth has on the value of low profit companies. There are not many companies that persist with overall high growth and with low profitability, but within individual companies there are nearly always divisions, business units or single products have these characteristics. They reduce value of the total company. Very often this factor is not easily seen from the figures presented to management. The real worth of shareholder value analysis lies in the light that it throws on these situations.

In **section C** we have a situation where ROIC is exactly equal to WACC. Here growth has no effect on value. Intuitively it can be difficult to accept this concept.

The reason for this phenomenon is that growth almost always requires extra investment. The funds for this extra investment will have to be paid for at the WACC rate. Extra profits will be earned at the ROIC rate. Where these are exactly equal, they cancel one another out. Therefore no extra benefit accrues to the existing shareholders. Growth has not added value.

In economics we are taught that extra increments of investment will continue to be made so long as the extra returns exceed the extra costs, but the return will be less with each increment. Equilibrium is reached only when the extra returns and costs are equal. We will use this concept to put a value on a company at a specific future time.

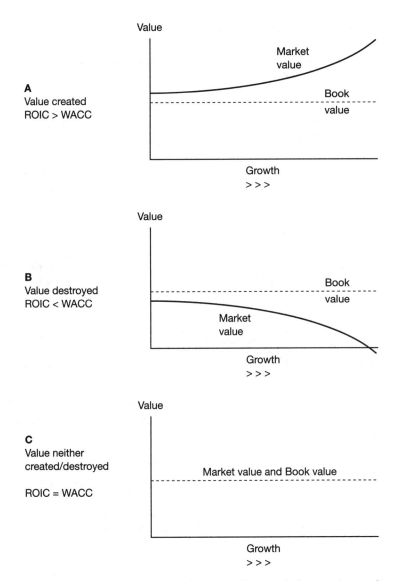

A
Value created
ROIC > WACC

B
Value destroyed
ROIC < WACC

C
Value neither
created/destroyed

ROIC = WACC

Fig. 17.12 Alternative scenarios: creating and destroying value

Terminal (continuing) value

The second important issue we did not fully deal with is the question of terminal value. We simply assumed this to be ten times the amount of profit in the final year.

 We need a more soundly based approach than this. We will use the ROIC – WACC relationship to direct us towards a logical solution.

Management's objective is to implement strategies that will give their company a competitive advantage that will allow it to earn a return greater than WACC. Where they achieve this premium return they add value for the shareholders.

However this premium return will inevitably attract competition that will whittle away its advantage over time. Without some competitive advantage a company will not continue to earn premium profits, so its ROIC will fall back to the level of WACC. Of course, good management will continuously seek to put in place new strategies that will restore the advantage.

> The valuation approach we use here is one that measures the value of the company as it now stands with its existing strategies.

In shareholder value analysis we assess the number of years forward for which current strategies will continue to add value. At the end of that 'horizon period' there will be equality between ROIC and WACC. Further growth beyond that date will not add value. We make this the point where we assess the continuing or terminal value of the company.

To calculate the terminal value we simply take the cash flow in that final year and assess it as we would value an annuity. That is we divide the cash flow by the cost of capital. When we use this more logically sound approach in our example we produce a value somewhat in excess of the earlier shortcut approach. See figure 17.13.

See appendix 1 for futher discussion of terminal value calculations.

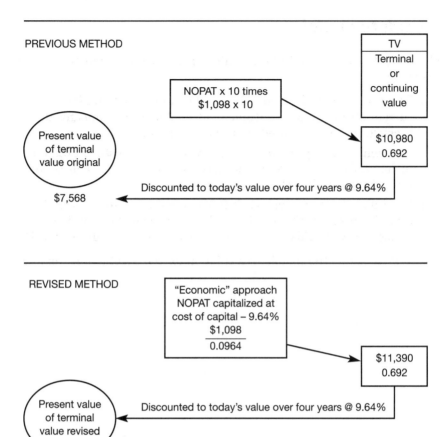

PREVIOUS METHOD

NOPAT x 10 times
$1,098 x 10

TV
Terminal
or
continuing
value

$10,980
0.692

Present value
of terminal
value original

$7,568

Discounted to today's value over four years @ 9.64%

REVISED METHOD

"Economic" approach
NOPAT capitalized at
cost of capital – 9.64%
$1,098
―――――
0.0964

$11,390
0.692

Present value
of terminal
value revised

$7,882

Discounted to today's value over four years @ 9.64%

Fig. 17.13 Calculating terminal value

Complete model

Therefore, to carry out a full total value appraisal on a company, it is necessary to:

- Decide on the 'horizon period', i.e., the number of years for which current strategies will continue to add value to the company. In practice this number tends to be between six and ten years.
- For each of these years forecast operating and investment cash flows in detail. Discount each year back to the present using a discount factor based on WACC.
- Capitalize the final year's cash flow using the long-term cost of capital. This gives the terminal value at the end of the horizon period. Discount this value back to the present again using WACC.

Figure 17.14 shows the complete calculation for the SVA Sample Company.

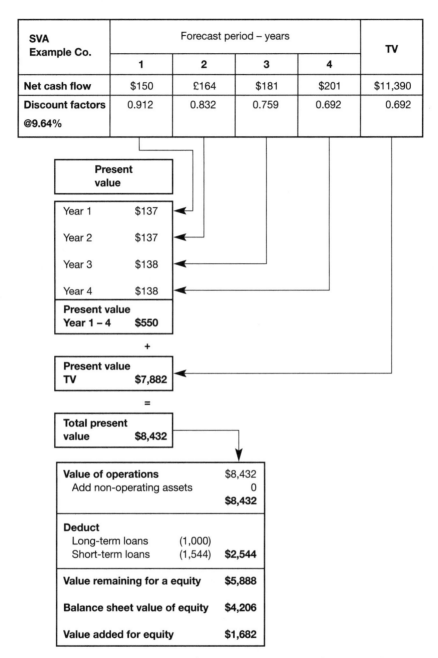

SVA Example Co.	Forecast period – years				TV
	1	2	3	4	
Net cash flow	$150	£164	$181	$201	$11,390
Discount factors @9.64%	0.912	0.832	0.759	0.692	0.692

Present value

Year 1	$137
Year 2	$137
Year 3	$138
Year 4	$138
Present value Year 1 – 4	**$550**

+

| **Present value TV** | **$7,882** |

=

| **Total present value** | **$8,432** |

Value of operations	$8,432
Add non-operating assets	0
	$8,432
Deduct	
Long-term loans (1,000)	
Short-term loans (1,544)	**$2,544**
Value remaining for a equity	**$5,888**
Balance sheet value of equity	**$4,206**
Value added for equity	**$1,682**

Fig. 17.14 SVA Example Company Inc. total appraisal

Acquisition analysis

*Those who can win a war well can rarely
make a good peace and those who could make
a good peace would never have won the war.*
SIR WINSTON CHURCHILL (1930)

Introduction

The acquisition/takeover scene has many similarities with a military campaign and it is where all aspects of financial analysis and company valuation come into their own.

In this chapter we will illustrate the steps needed for the financial analysis of one company acquiring another. We will examine the effects on both sets of shareholders and we will consider the financial viability of the two companies separately as stand-alone entities. From this we will derive an offer that should meet the needs of both sets of shareholders.

The two companies we will use in the illustration are called Alpha Inc. and Beta Inc., and their financial accounts are shown in figures 18.1 and 18.3. Both companies manufacture components for the residential construction industry.

Alpha is a longstanding successful company with a large customer base. The main product that it supplies is high-quality aluminium and steel guttering. However, sales growth has been less than buoyant in recent years.

Beta is a newer company that supplies a largely similar product manufactured from a specialized polymer material originally developed for the automotive industry. For a number of years now it has shown good growth and has made considerable inroads into this general market segment.

The management of Alpha has made preliminary approaches to the Beta team regarding a possible link-up and these have not been rebuffed. Both parties agree that for a merger to be successfully negotiated it would have to be shown that both sets of shareholders would benefit.

Financial profile of Alpha Inc.

The accounts for Alpha Inc. are shown in figure 18.1, and a number of important measures have been calculated in order to get an overall profile of the company. We will look at this profile in terms of profitability, liquidity, growth and valuation.

Profitability

The two main measures are ROE and ROTA:

- ROE   15 percent
- ROTA   13 percent

Both are more than satisfactory. We are looking at a very profitable operation.

Liquidity

The measures are:

- Current ratio   1.3 times
- Interest cover   6.0 times
- Leverage   56 percent

The current ratio is a little weak. We would like to see long-term trends here, but in isolation these values do not give cause for concern.

Growth

From a single set of accounts we cannot ascertain any values for growth, but we are told that historically sales have grown at approximately 6 percent p.a. and that this trend is likely to continue.

Valuation – Price earnings ratio

These measures are:

- PE ratio   17.5 times
- Market/book ratio   2.6 times

These valuation numbers are very good when measured against any set of standards.

Summary profile

Figure 18.2 gives a visual overview of the strengths and weaknesses of Alpha Inc. under each of the four headings already listed. The value '0' means an adequate result, '+1' and '+2' mean good to excellent, '–1' and '–2' mean fair to poor.

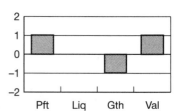

Fig. 18.2 *Company profile – Alpha Inc.*

We read that Alpha Inc. has good profitability, adequate liquidity, poor growth, and relatively high market value.

Alpha Inc.

Balance sheet $m

Long investment	$	$	Owners' funds	$	$
Intangibles	0		Issued capital	126	
Net fixed assets	193		Reserves	54	
					180
		193	**Long loans**	58	
					58
Current assets			**Current liabilities**		
Inventories	92		Short-term loans	63	
Accounts receivable	113		Accounts payable	104	
Cash	7				
		212			**167**
		405			**405**

Profit and loss account

	$	$
Sales		603
EBIT (Earnings before interest and tax)		54
Interest	9	
EBT (Earnings before tax)		45
Tax	18	
EAT (Earnings after tax)		27
Dividend	9	
RE (Retained earnings)		18

Issues shares (million)		**12.6**
Share market price	$	**37.5**
Market capitalization	$	**472.5**

Profitability			
ROE	EAT/Owners' funds	$27/$180	15%
ROTA	EBIT/TA	$54/$405	13%

Liquidity			
Current ratio	CA/CL	$212/$167	1.3
Interest cover	EBIT/Interest	$54/$9	6
Leverage	(LTL+CL)/TA	(58+167)/405	56%

Valuation			
PE ratio		**Market/book ratio**	
EPS	EAT/Issued shares	$2.14	Market capitalization/Owners' funds
PE	Share price/EPS	17.5	$472.5/$180	2.6

Fig. 18.1 Financial accounts 2001 – Alpha Inc.

Financial profile of Beta Inc.

The accounts for Beta Inc. are shown in figure 18.3.

Profitability

The two main measures are:

- ROE   12.4 percent
- ROTA   10.3 percent

While this company is showing an adequate performance, it is much less profitable then Alpha Inc.

Liquidity

The measures are:

- Current ratio   1.5 times
- Interest cover   3.5 times
- Leverage   62 percent

These figures indicate a company that is getting close to financial difficulty. Again, compared with Alpha Inc. the balance sheet is weak.

Growth

We are told that sales have an actual and anticipated growth rate of approximately 12 percent p.a.

Valuation – Price earnings ratio

These measures are:

- PE ratio   11.4 times
- Market/book ratio   1.4 times

Both the price earnings and market/book ratios show mediocre values. The investing community has identified this company as being fairly weak. The actual and expected high growth rates do not compensate for the other weaknesses shown above.

Summary profile

Figure 18.4 gives a visual overview of the strengths and weaknesses of Beta Inc. under each of the four headings already listed. The value '0' means an adequate result, '+1' and '+2' mean good to excellent, '–1' and –'2' mean fair to poor.

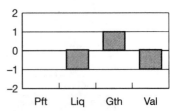

Fig. 18.4 *Company profile – Beta Inc.*

We read that Beta Inc. has adequate profitability, poor liquidity, high growth and relatively low market value.

Beta Inc.

Balance sheet $m

Long investment	$	$	Owners' funds	$	$
Intangibles	0		Issued capital	68	
Net fixed assets	148		Reserves	77	
					145
		148	Long loans	80	
					80
Current assets					
Inventories	122		**Current liabilities**		
Accounts receivable	104		Short-term loans	58	
Cash	4		Accounts payable	95	
		230			**153**
		378			**378**

Profit and loss account

		$	$
Sales			**495**
EBIT (Earnings before interest and tax)			39
	Interest	11	
EBT (Earnings before tax)			28
	Tax	10	
EAT (Earnings after tax)			18
	Dividend	5	
RE (Retained earnings)			13

Issues shares (million)		**13.6**
Share market price	$	**15**
Market capitalization	$	**204**

Profitability			
ROE	EAT/Owners' funds	$18/$145	12.4%
ROTA	EBIT/TA	$39/$378	10.3%

Liquidity			
Current ratio	CA/CL	$230/$153	1.5
Interest cover	EBIT/Interest	$39/$11	3.5
Leverage	(LTL+CL)/TA	(80+153)/378	62%

Valuation			
PE ratio		**Market/book ratio**	
EPS EAT/Issued shares	$1.32	Market capitalization/Owners' funds	
PE Share price/EPS	11.4	$204/$145	1.4

Fig. 18.3 Financial accounts 2001 – Beta Inc.

Acquisition – first offer

Alpha's shares have a market value of $37.5 while those of Beta have a market value of $15. So as a first attempt at formulating a bid we say: 'Alpha will give one of its shares in exchange for 2.5 Beta shares'. (1 Alpha share @ $37.5 = 2.5 Beta shares @ $15.)

Beta has 13.6 million shares on issue. Therefore, Alpha will have to issue (13.6/2.5) 5.44 million shares in exchange. Alpha shares have a value of $37.5 each, so the price offered for Beta Inc. amounts to (5.44 * $37.5) $204m, which is exactly equal to its current market capitalization.

Even though this offer may have little chance of success, we can use it to establish certain facts that will have a bearing on any subsequent offer.

In figure 18.5 the profit and loss accounts for both companies are laid out side by side and aggregated. We ignore for the moment any possible synergies, so we simply assume that the profits of the combined operation will be the aggregate of the two separate companies. We will use these tables to establish earnings per share for the combined company.

The number of issued shares in the new company will be:

- The original shares in Alpha   12.6m
- Plus the new shares issued for the acquisition of Beta   5.44m

Thus:

- Total shares in new company   18.04m
- EAT in new company $45m
- EPS of combined company ($45/18.04) $2.49

This figure of $2.49 highlights the first major effect that the acquisition can have, i.e. a significant increase in EPS for the acquiring company. Alpha shareholders earned $2.14 per share prior to the merger but they would earn $2.49 per share if this proposal were to be implemented. If all other things were equal, this jump of 16 percent in EPS would drive up the market price of Alpha shares.

We will now explore the reasons behind this phenomenon.

Profit and loss accounts

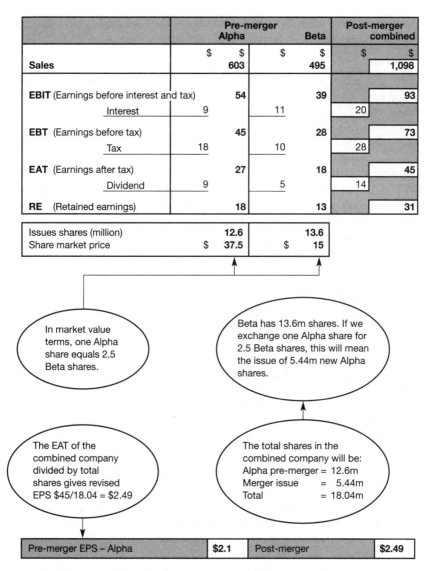

	Pre-merger Alpha		Beta	Post-merger combined	
	$	$	$	$	$	$
Sales		603		495		1,098
EBIT (Earnings before interest and tax)		54		39		93
Interest	9		11		20	
EBT (Earnings before tax)		45		28		73
Tax	18		10		28	
EAT (Earnings after tax)		27		18		45
Dividend	9		5		14	
RE (Retained earnings)		18		13		31

Issues shares (million)		12.6		13.6	
Share market price	$	37.5	$	15	

In market value terms, one Alpha share equals 2.5 Beta shares.

Beta has 13.6m shares. If we exchange one Alpha share for 2.5 Beta shares, this will mean the issue of 5.44m new Alpha shares.

The EAT of the combined company divided by total shares gives revised EPS $45/18.04 = $2.49

The total shares in the combined company will be:
Alpha pre-merger = 12.6m
Merger issue   = 5.44m
Total   = 18.04m

Pre-merger EPS – Alpha	$2.1	Post-merger	$2.49

Fig. 18.5 Profit and loss accounts for Alpha Inc. and Beta Inc.

Acquisition impact on EPS

It is the relative price to earnings ratios of the two shares that are the key to understanding the increase in EPS of Alpha Inc.

When company A acquires company B by means of a straight exchange of shares and when that exchange is made exactly at the market prices of the two shares, then if company A has a higher price to earnings ratio than company B, company A gains an automatic increase in EPS.

The reasons are easy to explain. Prior to the acquisition, Alpha Inc. had EAT of $27m. Post-acquisition, these profits have risen to $45m, i.e. an increase of 66 percent. However, the increase in the number of shares has only been 5.44 million on the 12.6 million original issued shares in Alpha Inc., i.e. an increase of 43 percent.

We see in figures 18.1 and 18.3 that, whereas the Alpha Inc. PE was 17.5 times, the corresponding number for Beta Inc. was 11.4 times, and it this difference in PE values that has enabled Alpha Inc. to acquire 66 percent extra profit for an increase of only 43 percent in the number of shares (see figure 18.6).

Thus a company on a high PE has a great advantage in the acquisition process.

But we must also consider what has been the impact on Beta Inc. These shareholders have exchanged 2.5 old Beta shares for one new Alpha share.

We see in figure 18.3 that prior to the acquisition each Beta share commanded an EPS of $1.33. Accordingly for 2.5 shares they should expect to receive $3.3 (2.5 * $1.32) from each new Alpha share. In fact they receive only $2.49. This number translates back to $0.99 for each share that they have surrendered, which represents a loss of 24 percent.

Therefore, in terms of the important measure of EPS, Alpha shareholders have benefited to the extent of 16 percent, while Beta shareholders have suffered a loss of 24 percent.

There are other variables of interest to both sets of shareholders that are also affected by the merger, and these will now be explored.

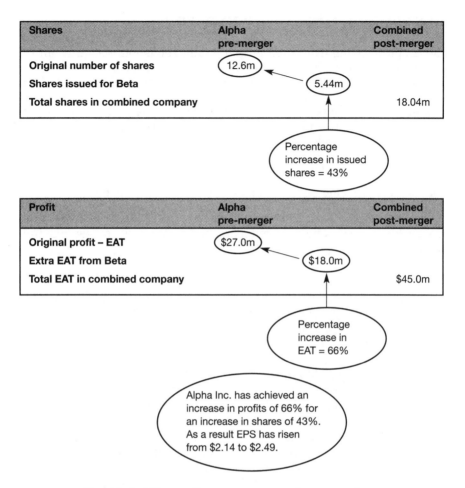

Fig. 18.6 Effects of merger on earnings per share

Shareholder effects – generalized

The proposal being examined is that Alpha Inc. should acquire all the issued shares in Beta Inc. in exchange for 5.44 million Alpha shares.

If that proposal were implemented the existing Alpha shareholders would continue to own their current 12.6 million shares in the enlarged company and the Beta shareholders would own 5.44 million shares. The total number of shares in the new company is 18.04 million.

The percentages held by each set of shareholders are:

- Alpha shareholders   [12.6/18.04]   70 percent
- Beta shareholder   [5.44/18.04]   30 percent

These relative values are important, as they will help us to understand why each set of shareholders gains or loses under various headings from the proposed merger.

In the combined company the Alpha shareholders will get 70 percent and the Beta shareholders will get 30 percent of everything, irrespective of how much each contributes.

In terms of earnings Alpha Inc. contributes an EAT value of $27m and Beta Inc. contributes $18m, to give a combined value of $45m (see figure 18.5). The Alpha contribution to the total is 60 percent ($27/$45) and the Beta contribution is 40 percent ($18/$45).

Alpha brings in 60 percent of the total profit of the combined company, but in the post-merger situation it will own 70 percent of the combined profit. This feature again explains the increase in EPS for Alpha shareholders.

On the other hand, Beta Inc. brings in 40 percent of the profits of the new company, but receives only 30 percent after the event. Accordingly, these shareholders lose out in EPS terms. Beta shares commanded an EPS of $1.30 before the merger, but they would have only $0.99 afterwards.

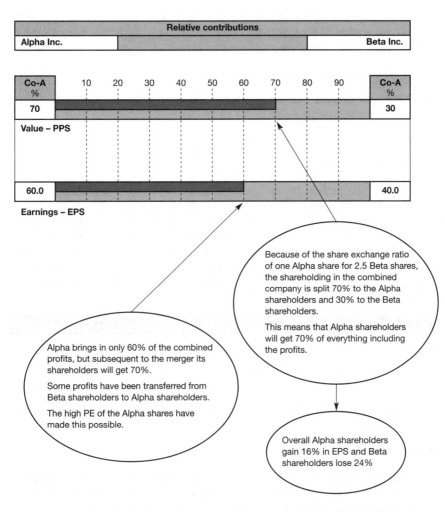

Fig. 18.7 Market value and earnings – relative contributions

We have examined the effect that the proposed merger would have on both sets of shareholders in terms of EPS. We will now use figure 18.8 to consider each company's contribution in terms of:

- APS (assets per share)
- DPS (dividend per share)
- PPS (price per share)

APS (assets per share)

The owners' funds box in the balance sheet shows the net assets in the company that are owned by the shareholders. When we divide this value by the number of issued shares we establish the asset value per share.

In an acquisition situation we are interested in the total net assets that each company brings into the combined operation, and from the individual shareholder's point of view we are of course interested in the assets per share.

We get the owners' fund values and the share issued numbers from the accounts in figures 18.1 and 18.3.

	OF	%	No/shares	APS
Alpha Inc.	$180m	55%	12.6m	$14.3
Beta Inc.	$145m	45%	13.6m	$10.6

The relative contributions in terms of owners' funds are 55 percent for Alpha and 45 percent for Beta.

DPS (dividend per share)

We can see in figure 18.5 that the two dividend payments are $9.0 million and $5.0 million for Alpha and Beta respectively. Therefore the relative contributions are 64 percent for Alpha Inc and 36 percent for Beta Inc.

PPS (price per share)

When we talk of price per share we are also talking about the total market capitalization of the company. The two market capitalization amounts are given in figures 18.1 and 18.3. We see that in terms of this variable Alpha Inc. contributes $472.5 million, 70 percent of the total and Beta Inc. contributes $204 million, 30 percent of the total.

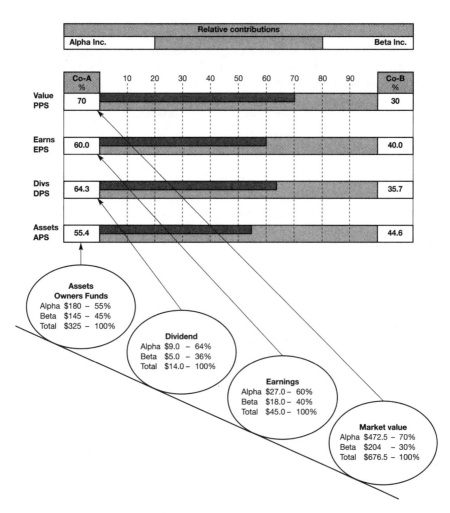

Fig. 18.8 Relative contributions in terms of assets per share, dividend per share and price per share

The before and after situation for each variable is shown in figure 18.9.

As we move down the chart through EPS, DPS and APS we note that Alpha Inc. has brought in less than 70 percent in each case and so the Alpha shareholders have gained and the Beta shareholders have lost under each of these headings.

Market value	Alpha Inc.	Beta Inc.
Pre-merger	$472.5m	$204m
Percentage	*70%*	*30%*
Post-merger *	$472.5m	$204m
Percentage	*70%*	*30%*
Gain/(Loss)	*nil*	*nil*

Earnings	Alpha Inc.	Beta Inc.
Pre-merger	$27m	$18m
Percentage	*60%*	*40%*
Post-merger	$31.5m	$13.5m
Percentage	*70%*	*30%*
Gain/(Loss)	*$4.5m*	*($4.5m)*

Dividend	Alpha Inc.	Beta Inc.
Pre-merger	$9.0m	$5.0m
Percentage	*64%*	*36%*
Post-merger **	$9.8m	$4.2m
Percentage	*70%*	*30%*
Gain/(Loss)	*$0.8m*	*($0.8m)*

Assets–Owners' funds	Alpha Inc.	Beta Inc.
Pre-merger	$180m	$145m
Percentage	*55%*	*45%*
Post-merger	$227m	$98m
Percentage	*70%*	*30%*
Gain/(Loss)	*$47m*	*($47m)*

*For this simple exercise we have so far simply aggregated the two market capitalizations, but the issue of the future capitalization of the combined company is more complex than this and it will be addressed later.

**The approach we have used for calculating post-merger dividends is simplistic. The post-merger dividend will be a matter of company policy and we will return later to this subject.

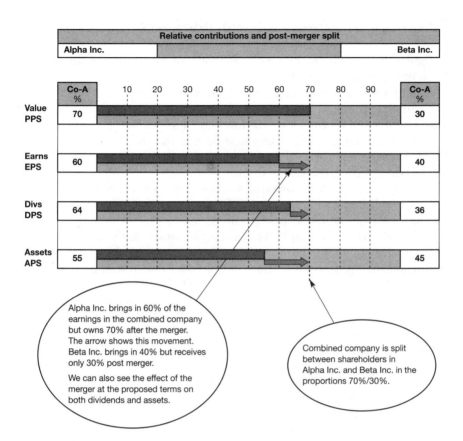

Fig. 18.9 *Relative contributions and post-merger split*

Summary of effects on shareholders

In figure 18.10 we show the results for the two sets of shareholders under the four separate headings.

Apart from the prices per share which remain unchanged for both parties, all the financial gains from the acquisition accrue to the Alpha shareholders and all the losses to the Beta shareholders.

The sole reason for this outcome is that Alpha Inc. has a much higher PE (price earnings ratio) than Beta Inc. and the shares were exchanged on the basis of their relative market prices.

So a high PE is a very powerful weapon in a takeover contest. In fact it is pretty well impossible for a low PE company to acquire another using shares for all or part of the consideration.

But to return to our Alpha/Beta example, while all the gains go to the Alpha shareholders it is not likely that the Beta shareholders will buy into the proposal. First because there is a 20 per cent loss in dividend. The losses in the areas of earnings and assets (EPS and APS) may be of more interest to management, but to the investor the total market value of the shares and the annual dividend paid are the crucial issues.

So if Alpha Inc. really desires to acquire Beta Inc. an increased offer will be necessary. This new offer could be a mixture of shares and cash, all cash, or simply a greater number of shares.

The possible combinations are endless, but overleaf we have put together an increased offer of 6.5 million shares and an increase in the dividend that appears to give Beta shareholders what they would require, i.e. increased market value and no loss of dividend. At the same time, it gives to Alpha Inc. a very desirable increase in earnings per share.

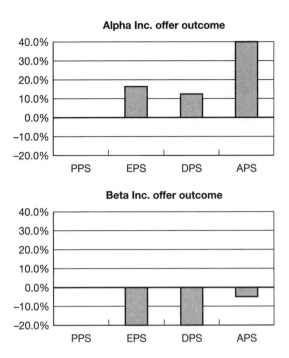

Fig. 18.10 Outcome to shareholders of original offer

Revised offer

Alpha has got a considerable advantage in share price and in order to reap the benefits of a merger it can afford to pass some gains in market value to the acquired company.

We have not yet gone into any detail about what the new share price will be. It will be determined by the investing community, who will decide on a new price to earnings ratio depending on how they view such matters as 'goodness of fit,' etc.

We could consider four possible outcomes for this new PE:

1. Equal to Alpha Inc.

2. Equal to Beta Inc.

3. Average of Alpha and Beta

4. Any number, probably falling between Alpha and Beta.

For this exercise we conservatively assume the average as in outcome 3 above.

This states that the post-merger market value of the combined company will simply equal the aggregate of the two separate companies prior to the merger. Our calculations below are based on this assumption.

The new offer proposed has the following two elements:

- Number of shares 6.5 million instead of 5.44 million

- Increase in dividend payout of 17.5 percent

The effect of this new offer is shown in figure 18.9.

Shareholders in Alpha Inc. would now own 66 percent of the combined company and Beta Inc. shareholders would have the remaining 34 percent. This new split is shown in the upper part of figure 18.11 and the results for the shareholders in the lower part.

The main changes from the original offer are that Beta shareholders gain over 10 percent in share market values and their dividend losses have been more than wiped out.

Theoretically Alpha shareholders lose something on share price (based on the assumptions we made about the PE ratio). However, Alpha Inc. has gained significantly in terms of EPS and this growth should be reflected in a stronger PE.

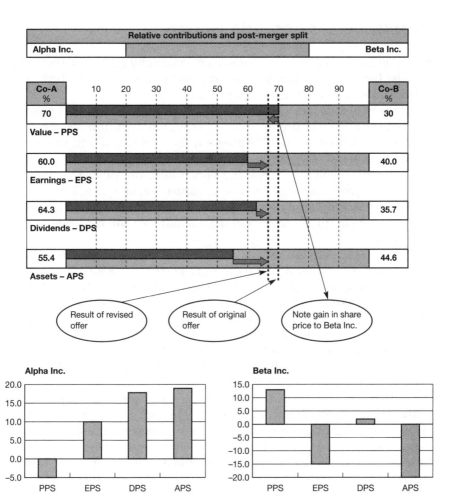

Fig. 18.11 Effects of new offer

Relative versus absolute values

In our deliberations so far we have been examining at the relative values of Alpha Inc. and Beta Inc. We have considered the question: 'How much is Beta Inc. worth in terms of Alpha shares:'

But we now must try to estimate absolute values for both companies, and to do this we will use an SVA – discounted cash flow approach. We will come up with estimated future cash flows which we will discount to derive estimates of absolute value for both companies.

The model we will use is basic but very useful. We will use the information we have from the accounts of both companies, and we will make some simplifying assumptions about the future. For instance, we will assume that existing margin on sales and tax percentages will continue at their current levels.

We will use the growth rates that have been indicated for the two companies, i.e. 6 percent for Alpha Inc. and 12 percent for Beta Inc.

We will make one other important assumption, i.e. that both fixed assets and working capital will grow linearly with sales. For example, if sales were to grow by 10 percent then we assume that both groups of assets would grow by the same percentage.

This assumption is probably justified in the case of working capital, because the levels of inventory, accounts receivable and accounts payable tend to move closely in line with sales.

However, this is not true for fixed assets. A company that grows significantly over a period will at some time have to increase its fixed asset base, but this investment will probably not take place in small annual increments. Rather it will take the form of major investments every two or three years, and when looking at a potential acquisition it would be most important to establish the amounts and timing of these investments.

However, for our simplified exercise we will assume the annual incremental approach.

In figure 18.12 we repeat the basic accounts for Alpha Inc. and we derive certain values that are needed for our later calculations.

Alpha Inc.

Balance sheet

$m

Long investment	$	$	Owners' funds	$	$
Intangibles	0		Issued capital	126	
Net fixed assets	193		Reserves	54	
					180
		193	**Long-term loans**	58	
					58
Current assets					
Inventories	92		**Current liabilities**		
Accounts receivable	113		Short-term loans	63	
Cash	7		Accounts payable	104	
		212			**167**
		405			**405**

Profit and loss account

			$	$
Sales				**603**
EBIT	(Earnings before interest and tax)			**54**
		Interest	9	
EBT	(Earnings before tax)			**45**
		Tax	18	
EAT	(Earnings after tax)			**27**
		Dividend	9	
RE	(Retained earnings)			**18**

Values for use in SVA model

Margin on sales%	EBIT/Sales	$54/$603	9%
Tax%	Tax/EBT	$18/$45	40%
FA/Sales%		$193/$603	32%
Working capital			
Inventory		$92	
Ac-Rec		$113	
(Ac-Pay)		($104)	
Net W/C		$101	
Working capital/Sales%		$101/$603	17%

Fig. 18.12 Financial accounts 2001 and values for use in SVA model –
Alpha Inc.

Value drivers

In figure 18.13 we show the accounts for Beta Inc. and as with Alpha Inc. a number of ratios have been extracted. These are the main inputs to the shareholder value model that will give us estimated absolute values for the equity in both companies. We call these inputs 'Value Drivers'.

Margin on sales
Alpha	9%	Beta	8%

Tax
Alpha	40%	Beta	36%

Fixed assets/Sales
Alpha	32%	Beta	30%

Working capital/Sales
Alpha	17%	Beta	26%

Growth in sales
Alpha	6%	Beta	12%

Weighted average cost of capital (WACC)

We would need more data to do a thorough assessment of the absolute and relative costs of capital of these two companies. We can say that significant public companies typically have costs of between 7 percent and 9 percent. Beta Inc. is showing a balance sheet that is somewhat weaker than Alpha Inc. Accordingly a WACC at the high end of the range has been estimated for Beta Inc. and at the lower end of the range for Alpha Inc.

WACC
Alpha	7.5%	Beta	8.5%

Non-equity funds

The valuation exercise is carried out in two steps. The first step is to calculate the value of operating business irrespective of the method of funding. To arrive at this value we discount the future cash flows from operations using WACC as the discount factor. Then in order to arrive at the equity value, we add on any non-operating assets and deduct all non-equity funds.

There are no non-operating assets in either company. The non-equity amounts that include both the long- and short-term loans are shown below.

Non-equity funds
Alpha	$121m	Beta	$138m

These are the values input to the SVA models for both companies shown overleaf.

Beta Inc.

Balance sheet $m

Long investment	$	$	Owners' funds	$	$
Intangibles	0.0		Issued capital	68.0	
Net fixed assets	148.0		Reserves	77.0	
				145.0	
			Long-term loans	80.0	
		148.0			
				80.0	
Current assets			**Current liabilities**		
Inventories	122.0		Short-term loans	58.0	
Accounts receivable	104.0		Accounts payable	95.0	
Cash	4.0				
		230.0		**153.0**	
		378.0		**378.0**	

Profit and loss account

		$	$
Sales			**495.0**
EBIT (Earnings before interest and tax)			**39.0**
	Interest	11.0	
EBT (Earnings before tax)			**28.0**
	Tax	10.0	
EAT (Earnings after tax)			**18.0**
	Dividend	5.0	
RE (Retained earnings)			**13.0**

Values for use in SVA model

Margin on sales%	EBIT/Sales	$39/$495	8%
Tax%	Tax/EBT	$39/$11	36%
FA/Sales%		$148/$495	30%
Working capital			
Inventory		122	
Ac-Rec		104	
(Ac-Pay)		(95)	
Net W/C		131	
Working capital/Sales%		$131/$495	26%

Fig. 18.13 Financial accounts 2001 and values for use in SVA Model –
Beta Inc.

SVA models – Alpha Inc. and Beta Inc.

In figure 18.14 opposite we show ten-year valuation models for the two companies. Because of space constraints, values for only the first and last two years are shown here. The 'base' column on the left shows values that have been estimated or derived from the published accounts.*

The important output numbers from the model are:

	Alpha Inc.	Beta Inc.
Operating value	$547m	$407m
Equity value	$426m	$269m

Note how these calculated equity values compare with the current stockmarket valuations:

	Alpha Inc.	Beta Inc.
Stockmarket value	$472m	$204m
Calculated equity value	$426m	$269m

Our estimates would suggest that the market is giving these companies high and low values as follows:

	Alpha Inc.	Beta Inc.
Stockmarket value less calculated value	$46m	($65m)
	High value	Low value
	amount	amount

Implication for acquisition exercise

The calculated values for equity show these proportions:

Alpha Inc.	$426m	61%
Beta Inc.	$269m	39%
Total	$695m	100%

These figures suggest that Alpha Inc. can afford in its share exchange with Beta Inc. to give up to 39 percent in the combined company. The initial offer to Beta Inc was 30 percent, and the revised offer brought this up to approximately 34 percent. This second offer is still well within the range that would be beneficial to Alpha Inc.

*At the end of the chapter there is an addendum giving a line by line explanation of the model.

Alpha Inc.

Base		Line No.	1	2	~~~	9	10	TV
$603	Sales	1	639	678	~~~	1,019	1,080	Note-16
6%	Change	2	36	38	~~~	58	61	
9%	Operating profit %	3	58	61	~~~	92	97	
40%	After-tax pft	4	35	37	~~~	55	58	
32%	Investment FA%	5	12	12	~~~	18	20	
17%	WC%	6	6	7	~~~	10	10	
	TOTAL	7	18	19	~~~	28	30	
	Net cash flow	8	17	18	~~~	27	28	824
7.5%	WACC – ftr	9	0.930	0.865	~~~	0.552	0.485	0.485
	Annual PV	10	16	15	~~~	14	14	400

Value of operations	11	$547
Deduct non-eqy	12	$121
Equity value	13	$426
No/shares (m)	14	12.6
Share value ($)	15	$34

Beta Inc.

Base		Line No.	1	2	~~~	9	10	TV
$495	Sales	1	554	621	~~~	1,373	1,537	Note-16
12%	Change	2	59	67	~~~	147	165	
8%	Operating profit %	3	44	50	~~~	110	123	
36%	After-tax pft	4	28	32	~~~	70	79	
30%	Investment FA%	5	18	20	~~~	44	49	
26%	WC%	6	15	17	~~~	38	43	
	TOTAL	7	33	37	~~~	82	92	
	Net cash flow	8	–5	–5	~~~	–12	–14	1037
8.5%	WACC – ftr	9	0.922	0.849	~~~	0.480	0.442	0.485
	Annual PV	10	–4	–5	~~~	–6	–6	459

Value of operations	11	$407
Deduct non-eqy	12	$138
Equity value	13	$269
No/shares (m)	14	13.6
Share value ($)	15	$19.8

Fig. 18.14 Equity values for Alpha Inc. and Beta Inc.

Addendum

The model shown in figure 18.14 uses the methodology covered in chapter 17. We will go through it line by line using Alpha Inc.

1 Sales
In the 'base' column we have sales from the most recent set of accounts. Over the ten-year forecast we see the sales growing by 6 percent p.a. which is the growth percentage we have assumed for the company.

2 Change
The growth percentage of 6 percent in the base column determines the change in sales each year. We will later use this row to establish the amount of new investment required for each of the ten years.

3 Operating profit
Using the 9 percent margin from the base column we derive operating profit values from the sales values in line-1.

4 After-tax profit
We have a 40 percent tax percentage and we use this tax rate to derive the after-tax profit from line-3. The short name we use here is **NOPAT** (net operating profit after tax).

5 Investment in fixed assets
We have established in figure 18.12 that fixed assets show a ratio of 32 percent to sales. In line-2 we have established the annual growth in sales. So we take 32 percent of line-2 as our estimate of the annual investment in fixed assets.

6 Investment in working capital
The procedure here is similar to the previous calculation and we use the working capital percentage. (See figure 18.12)

7 Total investment
Here we show the total annual investment as the sum of line-5 and line-6.

8 Net cash flow
In line-4 we have established the cash in-flow from trading (NOPAT). In line-7 we have the cash out-flow that will result from investment. The net cash flow is derived from line-4 less line-7. It can, of course, be positive or negative.

9 WACC – discount factor

We have used values of 7.5 percent and 8.5 percent as costs of capital for Alpha Inc. and Beta Inc. respectively, and we use these rates to generate discount factors for the ten years.

10 Present value (PV)

The discount factor in line-9 is applied to the cash flow values in line-8 to give the present values for each year.

11 Value of operations

This is simply the sum of line-10.

12 Non-equity

In line-11 we got the value of the total operation. In order to get to the value for the equity shareholders we must deduct prior claims, i.e. long- and short-term loans ($58 + $63 = $121).

13 Equity value

Deduct line-12 from line 11 to obtain the net value for the equity share-holders.

14 Number of equity shares

We get this value from figures 18.1 and 18.3.

15 Value per share

Line-13 divided by line-15 gives us the estimated value per share in Alpha Inc. based on our assumptions about the next ten years.

16 Terminal value

We have used the simple annuity formula. We have taken NOPAT (line-4), and added one year's growth of 6 percent ($58 + $3.48 = $61.48). We then divide by WACC to get the capitalised value of the company at end of year 10, which sum then forms part of the net cash flow in line-8.

Appendix 1: Special Items

Introduction

Values taken from company accounts are used to analyse business performance. For the vast bulk of these values there are no quibbles about their accuracy or realism. However, there are some items that are subject to a number of different interpretations. Whether one interpretation is preferred over another will affect the results of the analysis. A multitude of rules laid down by the accounting bodies, the statutory authorities, the Stock Exchange and others have a bearing in these interpretations. Some understanding of the more important of these rules provides a useful background to analysis.

The principle underlying the rules may be even more important. The overriding principle is the 'true and fair view' that accounts should present. This said, it is often difficult to draw up rules for specific items that will always reflect a true and fair view. It is for this reason that different interpretations can arise to give different answers to our analysis.

As external conditions change, the emphasis moves to different aspects of the accounts – from the profit and loss account to the balance sheet to the cash flow. New problems, such as fluctuating currencies, give rise to the need for new rules and so on. This appendix will address some of the more important 'live' issues in accounting at the present time. It will explain why they are live, what the current state of play is and how different methods of treatment would affect the analysis.

These issues are:

- goodwill
- foreign currencies
- pensions
- deferred tax
- leases
- revaluation of fixed assets
- scrip issues
- miscellaneous long funds
- EBITDA
- terminal value – SVA.

Goodwill on acquisition

When one company acquires another for a price (consideration) in excess of the fair value of its net assets, goodwill is created. This goodwill amount will appear not in the accounts of either the buyer or vendor, but in the consolidated, or, combined accounts of the two companies. Goodwill is called an intangible asset, that is an asset of no physical substance. In many ratios, calculations are based on tangible assets only, thus totally ignoring goodwill. Nevertheless, it has important effects on a company's reported position and so an understanding of its origins and treatment is important.

 First we will look at a non-goodwill situation called Scenario 1 in Figure A1.1. It will serve as a base position from which to work towards a goodwill example.

Company A has paid $100 for Company B, the balance sheet for which is shown with a net worth of $100. The entries that appear in Company A's balance sheet are 'Investment $100' and the investment is balanced by an equivalent long term loan.

When we look at the consolidated balance sheet for Scenario 1 the item 'Investment $100' has disappeared. The values in the following boxes are combined:

- fixed assets
- current assets
- current liabilities
- long-term loans.

The ordinary funds of Company A are unchanged in the consolidated balance sheet. Also' before consolidation, the total assets were $1000 for A and $400 for B. The combined statement is in balance with its total assets being equal to the sum of the two separate companies less the Company A $100 investment and Company B ordinary funds deducted from each side.

When we consider what has happened, we see that the investment of $100 in Company A's balance sheet has simply been replaced by net assets of $100 ($400 assets – $300 liabilities) from Company B.

In practice, the question of 'fair value' of both assets acquired and consideration given would arise. It has been assumed that this is not an issue here.

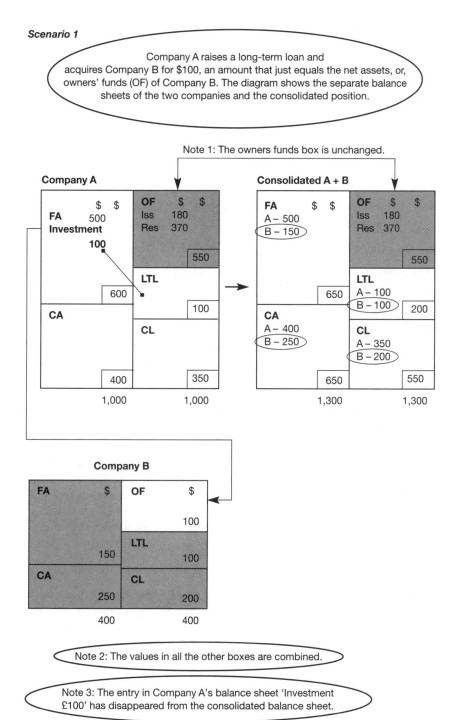

Scenario 1

Company A raises a long-term loan and acquires Company B for $100, an amount that just equals the net assets, or, owners' funds (OF) of Company B. The diagram shows the separate balance sheets of the two companies and the consolidated position.

Note 1: The owners funds box is unchanged.

Company A

	$	$	OF	$	$
FA	500		Iss	180	
Investment			Res	370	
	100				
					550
			LTL		
		600			
					100
CA			CL		
		400			350
	1,000			1,000	

Consolidated A + B

FA	$	$	OF	$	$
A – 500			Iss	180	
B – 150			Res	370	
					550
		650	LTL		
			A – 100		
			B – 100		200
CA					
A – 400			CL		
B – 250			A – 350		
			B – 200		
	650			550	
	1,300			1,300	

Company B

FA	$	OF	$
			100
	150	LTL	
			100
CA		CL	
	250		200
	400		400

Note 2: The values in all the other boxes are combined.

Note 3: The entry in Company A's balance sheet 'Investment £100' has disappeared from the consolidated balance sheet.

Fig. A1.1 Non-goodwill on acquisition

A goodwill acquisition

In Scenario 2 in Figure A1.2, the amount paid by Company A for Company B is $125. Company B is the same firm as in Scenario 1, whose net assets are $100. On consolidation' the extra consideration of $25 is not balanced by physical assets so an intangible asset of this amount must be created. The name we give to this intangible asset is goodwill. (The justification for a high acquisition price and, therefore, the goodwill element, exists in the mind of the buyer, but, logically, it has to be the expectation of extra future profit.)

Once consideration in cash or other assets is given for goodwill a number of questions then arise:

- 'How is it treated in the accounts?'
- 'How will different ways of treating it affect our analysis?'

Three ways of treating goodwill are:

- **by annual charges to the profit and loss account** – it can be depreciated in just the same way as any fixed assets and it will, in time, disappear from the accounts (this way out is not favoured by business people because its effect is to reduce declared profit, which will be reflected in the earnings per share figure and other measures of performance).

- **by an immediate charge against reserves** – assets may be reduced by the amount of goodwill and reserves by the same amount so, at a single stroke, goodwill simply disappears, totally (in the consolidated balance sheet shown in Figure A1.2, reserves of $370 would be reduced by $25 to $345, reported ordinary funds would fall by $25 to $525 and balance sheet totals go down to $1300).

- **by write-off of any impairmant of value** – as reflected in current forecasts of operations.

The effect of the second treatment is that profits are not affected and various balance sheet totals are reduced. Because of higher profits and lower assets the profitability ratios of return on total assets and return on equity will look better. The debt/equity ratio, though, will look worse because equity funds are artificially reduced. It is likely that the high return on total assets, return on equity, and market to book ratios in the sample companies are partly attributable to this treatment of goodwill.

Scenario 2

Company A raises a long-term loan and acquires
Company B for $125, an amount that exceeds the 'net assets', or,
owners' funds (OF) of Company B by $25. The diagram shows the separate
balance sheet of the two companies and
the consolidated position.

Note 1: The owners funds box is unchanged.

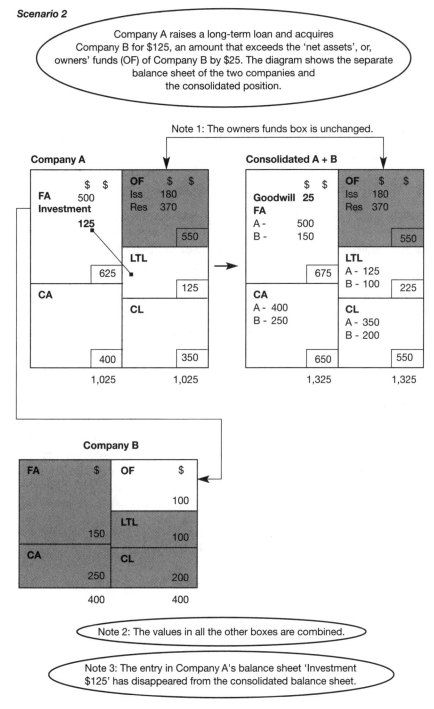

Note 2: The values in all the other boxes are combined.

Note 3: The entry in Company A's balance sheet 'Investment
$125' has disappeared from the consolidated balance sheet.

Fig. A1.2 Goodwill on consolidation

Foreign currency

Movements in exchange rates affect company performance in various ways, principally by way of transactions in the profit and loss account and holdings of overseas assets and liabilities in the balance sheet. We often note that an increase in the value of sterling will cause a weakening in the share price of companies with substantial foreign interests, and vice versa.

In general, gains and losses arising from foreign currency exchange rate movements are treated as follows:

- profit and loss transactions are translated at average currency values for the year
- assets and liabilities in the closing balance sheet are translated at rates that applied at the date of the final accounts.
- net assets of the opening balance sheet are restated at the closing rates the difference from the previous year being taken to reserves
- exchange differences on foreign currency borrowings directly raised for, or to provide a hedge against, overseas fixed assets are taken to reserves and offset against the exchange differences on the assets.
- all other gains and losses are passed through the profit and loss account.

Pensions

Capital sums invested in pension funds and annual contributions have grown so large that they can have a bearing on company performance. The pension funds themselves should not directly impinge on a company's accounts because they are separate funds totally independent of company finances. However, the liability of a company to provide for employees, pensions means that a shortfall in the fund has to be filled by increased annual contributions. Likewise, a surplus can allow the company to take a holiday from contributions, thereby improving its cash flow and profit results. The surplus or deficit on the fund is, therefore, of supreme importance to the value of the company.

Deferred tax

The amount of tax charged in company accounts is often considerably different from the actual tax paid. This arises from 'timing differences that are likely to reverse in the foreseeable future'. Behind this phrase lies government legislation. To encourage investment in fixed assets' many governments give accelerated capital allowances on new plant. They allow a higher charge against profits for the writing down of the fixed assets than would be justified on the basis of a straightforward depreciation calculation.

The result to the company is a lower tax charge in the early years of an investment. However, if excess amounts are taken for depreciation early in the life of plant, there is none left for later years. The result will be heavier tax charges in these latter years. It is accepted that, for business purposes, this artificial distortion of reported profits is better avoided. Accordingly, in the early years, the full tax charge is made in the accounts and the amount not paid is put to the deferred tax account. It will be drawn down in later years. However, this said, a certain amount is left to the discretion of management to determine how much of a charge is 'likely to crystallize in the foreseeable future'.

Finance leases

Assets in the balance sheet include only items that are owned by the company. At least, this was the fundamental rule until quite recently when a considerable amount of off-balance sheet financing came into use. By this phrase is meant that assets were being acquired which were funded by loans, but neither the asset nor the loan appeared in the accounts. In legal terms, these assets were leased, but all the risks and rewards of ownership accrued to the company. The term finance lease is now used in this situation to distinguish it from the ordinary operating lease. With a finance lease, both the asset and the funding must appear in the accounts.

Revaluation of fixed assets

High rates of inflation over two decades had resulted in a situation where the values for property in company accounts were far removed from reality. It was accepted that it was necessary to remove this anomaly and fixed assets were allowed to be shown at valuation rather than at cost.

Our interest here is to consider the effect of revaluation on the various business ratios. First we will look at the accounting treatment that is illustrated in Figure A1.3. The increase in value of the fixed assets is matched by an increase in reserves.

Balance sheet values for fixed assets, total assets and ordinary funds are increased. The impact on business ratios is exactly the opposite to that which resulted from the writing off of goodwill shown earlier in this appendix.

The debt/equity ratio improves, as does the asset backing per share. However, return on total assets and return on equity will worsen. For an analysis of accounts for a series of years, spurious movements in ratios can arise simply from revaluation.

The best way to eliminate these is to back-date the revaluation to the start of the analysis period.

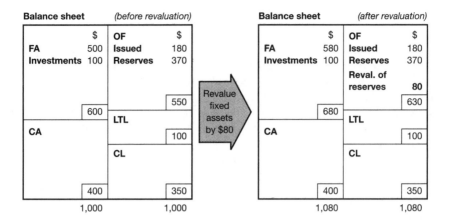

Fig. A1.3 Revaluation of fixed assets

Scrip issue

A scrip, or, bonus issue takes place when shareholders in a company are given extra free shares in proportion to their existing holdings. For instance in a one-for-two scrip, all shareholders will have their number of shares increased by 50 percent. From a ratio point of view, this has an effect on EPS, DPS, assets per share and, normally, market price per share. The historic values must all be moved down in proportion to the increase in number of shares.

In figure A1.4 we show an example of a company that made a one-for-two scrip issue. From a base of 180 shares, it issued 90 extra shares free to its existing shareholders. It also transferred $90 from reserves to issued capital. The pre-scrip market price was $4.80. What is likely post-scrip market price?

Does a scrip bring real benefit to the shareholder? The logic is that there should be no change in their overall position: they own the same fraction of the company after the scrip as before and the total value of the company has not increased. However, in practice, a scrip is a buoyant signal to the market that may improve a share's value. The accounting entry is simply a transfer from reserves to issued capital, as shown in Figure A1.4.

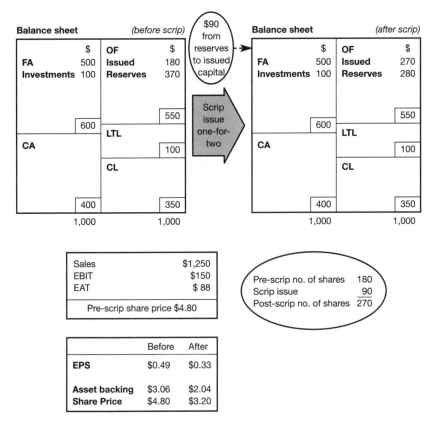

Fig. A1.4 Effects of a scrip issue on the accounts

Miscellaneous long-term funds

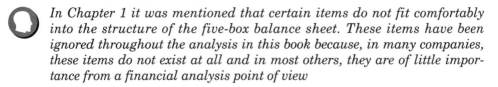

In Chapter 1 it was mentioned that certain items do not fit comfortably into the structure of the five-box balance sheet. These items have been ignored throughout the analysis in this book because, in many companies, these items do not exist at all and in most others, they are of little importance from a financial analysis point of view

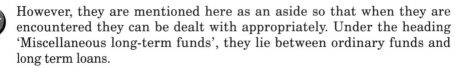

However, they are mentioned here as an aside so that when they are encountered they can be dealt with appropriately. Under the heading 'Miscellaneous long-term funds', they lie between ordinary funds and long term loans.

Preference shares

Preference shareholders paradoxically, have very limited rights. They are part-owners and receive a dividend at a fixed percent before the ordinary shareholder. At one time this was a popular form of funding, but it is now used in very limited and special circumstances. It may be for tax planning or voting control purposes for example. Preference shares will often have conversion rights into ordinary shares and, if so, they can be included with that category. For debt/equity ratio purposes, they can be treated as equity.

Minority interests

This entry occurs when the consolidated group includes subsidiaries that are less than 100 percent owned. They are equity funds but not part of the group's equity. Usually the amount is insignificant, but, for calculating the debt/equity ratio, they could, again, be included with equity.

Deferred tax, grants and miscellaneous provisions

Deferred tax has been discussed above. It is probably best treated as an 'interest-free loan' from the government and, therefore, included as debt. Grants will, in due course, move up into equity. Miscellaneous provisions could be pension funds not fully covered; they are neither debt nor equity. Both items can be ignored in the balance sheet ratios unless the amounts are significant.

EBITDA

EBITDA (earnings before interest, tax, depreciation and amortization) is the newest financial term to come into common use over recent years. It identifies cash flow measured at one particular point in the overall cash-flow cycle.

In order to identify its component parts we will first look at EBIT – earnings before interest and tax. We have seen in chapter 4 that EBIT is the first important measure of profit that we identify in a published and loss account.

It is largely the operating or trading profit of the business (there may be minor adjustments for non-operating income, etc.). Therefore EBIT captures the total operating income and total operating cost of the business.

It is a number of enormous significance because it is from EBIT that a company generates resources to pay interest to bankers, tax to the government, dividends to shareholders, and, maybe even repay loans, etc. And in most companies it represents an ongoing, continuous source of renewable energy.

However, it is a number that is produced according to certain accounting rules, one of these rules relates to the charge that we make for depreciation. We have seen in chapter 8 the role that depreciation plays in linking profit from trading with cash flow from the same source. Depreciation, which is a non-cash cost, must be excluded from the cash flow calculation.

Amortization is the term we use in relation to the writing down of goodwill. For the moment we can consider it as simply depreciation under another name, i.e. a non-cash charge in the profit and loss account.

We add back both depreciation and amortization to EBIT to get EBITDA. It represents the cash that is thrown off from the normal trading activities of the business (before any provision has been made for reinvestment in fixed assets, working capital, etc.). It may also be adjusted for certain non-recurring, non-operating items that have been charged prior to EBIT.

After we separate out any discontinued operations, we can say that EBITDA identifies the sustainable and hopefully growing stream of cash that will flow from the trading activities of the business over the coming years, and it is a number that is largely free from some distortions that can arise from accounting policies. Operating managers and analysts like it for this reason.

We have said that amortization can be considered as another form of depreciation, but there is a significant difference between these two charges. Depreciation is a true cost related to the passage of time, even though it is not a cash cost in the current period. The fact that machines do wear out over time and have to be replaced has to be recognized in the accounts.

Amortization of goodwill, however, is a far more contentious issue. It is difficult to support the theory that it gradually wears out over time.

We can say that goodwill is the premium that one company will pay to acquire the assets of another that appears to have the capacity to earn above normal profits. The inherent value of this goodwill can change as a result of many factors, it can remain constant, it can even grow. It can disappear overnight as we have seen in the cases of telecom companies that have been taken over at extraordinary high premiums.

Therefore, if we decide to write it down by an annual charge over a fixed period of time, just as if we were writing off a regular depreciating fixed asset, we should recognize that this is an artificial charge and allow for that fact in our financial reporting.

Terminal value calculation in the SVA model

The revised method (shown in chapter 17, page 289) for calculating the terminal value of a company some years ahead illustrated one particular approach which we call the 'annuity' method. In this approach we take a particular cash flow, i.e. NOPAT, and we capitalize it simply by dividing by the cost of capital, WACC.

It is logical and correct to do this when we know or can assume that this is a constant cash flow that will persist for a long, indefinite period into the future.

Provided certain conditions are met, this approach to valuation is correct even if the cash flow is not constant but growing. The most important condition here is that the return generated by the company, i.e. ROIC, is exactly equal to its cost of funds, i.e. WACC.

When this condition applies then the benefits of growth in the cash flow will be entirely absorbed by the extra capital required to support the growing business. Because all the benefits of this growth are cancelled out we can ignore it and use a method of valuation that is based on a constant cash flow.

There are strong economic arguments in favour of this approach, but there are also many who argue cogently that growth into the long-term future does have an impact on value and must be allowed for.

In favour of the former position is the economic case that a company that earns profits in excess of the cost of capital will attract competition from new entrants to the market who wish to share in those excess profits. This competition will reduce profitability in the market sector. New entrants will continue to be attracted until overall profitability falls to the exact level of the cost of funds, at which stage the equilibrium is reached.

Proponents of the latter position argue that a large, well-established, well-managed company has a competitive advantage over any new entrants, and such companies can sustain indefinitely a rate of profit considerably in excess of the cost of capital. If this latter proposition is accepted, the annuity approach that we have used in chapter 17 understates the continuing value of the company, and we have to use a new formula which is difficult but more accurate. See opposite.

Formula to establish the terminal value of a company with growth in a competitive advantage situation.

$$[NOPAT(t+1 * (1 - g/r)]/(WACC - g)$$

What this formula says is that we start with final year NOPAT, and we move it forward one year at the expected growth rate, i.e. NOPAT(t+1).

We multiply this value $(1 - g/r)$. The symbol 'g' stands for expected growth rate, and 'r' stands for the company's rate of return.

Let us say that $g = 8\%$ and $r = 12\%$. We multiply by $(1 - 8/12)$ which reduces NOPAT to 33% of its original value.

We then divide this number by $(WACC - g)$. Growth has already been fixed at 8%. Let us say that WACC equals 10%. The values within brackets are therefore $(10\% - 8\%)$ which gives us 2%.

We will work out the values by the two different methods for a hypothetical company with a NOPAT of $100.

Annuity approach

$$
\begin{aligned}
TV \quad &= NOPAT/WACC \\
&= \$100/.10 \\
&= \$1000
\end{aligned}
$$

Long-term growth approach

$$
\begin{aligned}
TV \quad &= [NOPAT(t+1) * (1 - g/r)]/(WACC - g) \\
&= [(\$100 * 1.08) * (1 - 8/12)]/(.10-.08) \\
&= \$1782
\end{aligned}
$$

This second approach has resulted in a much higher value. This value is heavily influenced by the growth rate. The reader may like to check that an assumed growth rate of 4% would give a value much closer to the annuity value, i.e. $1,144.

Appendix 2: Companies used in the sample

United States

Abbot Laboratories
Albertson's Inc.
Amgen Incorporated
Baxter International, Inc.
Bristol-Myers Squibb Co.
Campbell Soup Company
Caterpillar, Inc.
Colgate-Palmolive Co.
Conagra Foods Incorporated
Cvs Corporation
Dover Corporation
Eli Lilly And Company
General Mills, Inc.
Gillette Company (The)
H.J. Heinz Company
Hershey Foods Corporation
Home Depot Inc.
Ingersoll-Rand Company
Johnson & Johnson

Kellogg Co.
Lexmark International, Inc.
Lowe's Companies, Inc.
May Department Stores Co. (The)
Medtronic, Inc.
Merck & Co, Inc.
Parker-Hannifin Corporation
Pfizer Inc.
Pharmacia Corporation
Pitney Bowes Inc.
Quaker Oats Company (The)
Ralston Purina Group
Sara Lee Corporation
Schering-Plough Corporation
Stanley Works
Target Corporation
Walgreen Co.
Wal-Mart Stores Inc.
William Wrigley Jr. Company

United Kingdom

Alvis plc
Arriva plc
Astrazeneca plc
Boots Company plc (The)
Brake Bros plc
Cadbury Schweppes plc
Dfs Furniture Company plc

Dixons Group plc
Domnick Hunter Group plc
Galen Holdings plc
Geest plc
Glaxosmithkline plc
Great Universal Stores plc (The)
Greggs plc

Halma plc
Huntleigh Technology plc
Iceland Group plc
Jjb Sports plc
N Brown Group plc
Northern Foods plc
Nycomed Amersham plc
Richmond Foods plc

Shire Pharmaceuticals Group plc
Signet & Nephew plc
Spirax-Sarco Engineering plc
Tesco plc
Thorntons plc
Unilever plc
Weir Group plc (The)
Wyevale Garden Centres plc

European Union

Altana Ag
Art'E' Spa
Beiersdorf Ag
Boiron Sa
Bongrain Societe Anonyme
Brioche Pasquier
Carraro Spa
Carrefour
Casino, Guichard-Perrachon Et Cie
Clarins Sa
Danone
Finatis
Fresensius Ag
Fromageries Bel
Guyenne Et Gascogne Sa
Heidelberger Druckmaschinen Ag
Industria Macchine Automatiche Spa
Ingenico – Compagnie Industrielle

Interpump Group Spa
Karstadt Quelle Ag
L.D.C. Societe Anonyme
L'Oreal
Manitou Bf Sa
Merck Kgaa
Monoprix Sa
Nestle Deutschland Ag
Parmalat Finanziaria Spa
Pinault-Printemps-La Redoute
Recordati Spa
Roncadin Spa
Royal Canin Sa
Schering Canin sa
Achering Aktiengesellschaft
Sidel Sa
Societa Per la Bonifica Dei Terren
Societe Anonyme Des Galaries Lafay
Unibel

Japan

Arrk Corporation
Banyu Pharmaceutical Co Ltd
Canon Aptex Inc.
Circle K Japan Co., Ltd
Disco Corporation
Ezaki Glico Co., Ltd
Familymart Co., Ltd
Fast Retailing Co., Ltd
Hisamitsu Pharmaceutical Co., Inc.
Hitachi Tool Engineering, Ltd
Hogy Medical Co., Ltd
Homac Corp.
House Foods Corporation
Ishikawa Seisakusho, Ltd
Itoham Foods Inc.

Japan Cash Machine Co., Ltd
Kao Corporation
Katokichi Co., Ltd
Kawasumi Laboratories, Incorporate
Kikkoman Corporation
Kohnan Shoji Co., Ltd
Kojima Co., Ltd
Komeri Co., Ltd
Matsumotokiyoshi Co., Ltd
Meji Milk Products Co., Ltd
Meji Seika Kaisha Ltd
Ministop Co., Ltd
Mitsukoshi, Ltd
Morinaga Milk Industry Co., Ltd
Mutow Co., Ltd

Mycal Hokkaido Corporation
Nichirei Coporation
Nippon Meat Packers, Inc.
Nippon Suisan Kaisha Ltd
Nisshin Flour Milling Co., Ltd
Nissin Food Products Co., Ltd
Ono Pharmaceutical Co., Ltd
Pc Depot Corporation
Q.P. Corporation
Ricoh Company, Ltd
Santen Pharmaceutical Company Ltd
Seiyu Ltd (The)
Shimamuru Co., Ltd

Smc Corporation
Sunkus & Associates Inc.
Takeda Chemical Industries, Ltd
Tokyo Kikai Seisakusho, Ltd
Torii Pharmaceutical Co., Ltd
Toyo Suisan Kaisha, Ltd
Union Tool Co.
Welfide Corp
Yakult Honsha Co., Ltd
Yamanouchi Pharmaceutical Co., Ltd
Yamazaki Baking Co., Ltd
York-Benimaru Co., Ltd
Zeria Pharmaceutical Co., Ltd

Appendix 3: Full set of ratio charts from sample companies

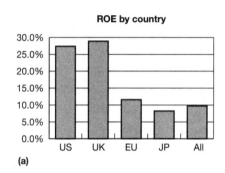

ROE by country

(a)

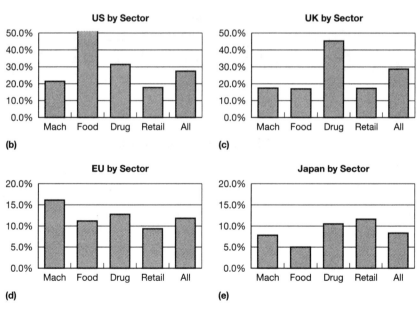

US by Sector

(b)

UK by Sector

(c)

EU by Sector

(d)

Japan by Sector

(e)

Fig. A3.1 Return on equity

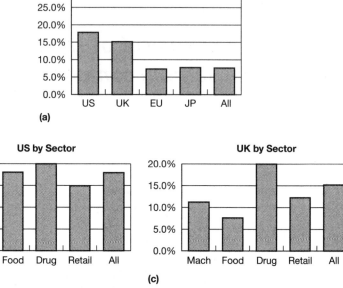

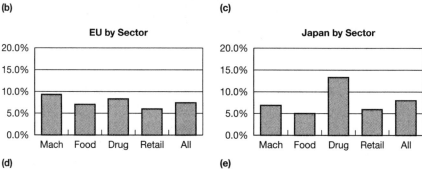

Fig. A3.2 Return on total assets

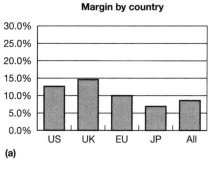

(a)

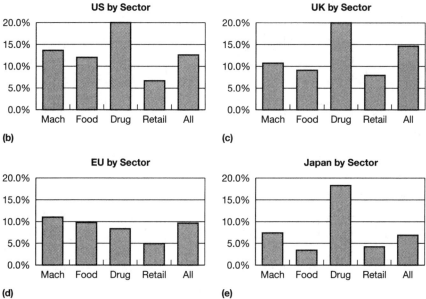

(b)   **(c)**

(d)   **(e)**

Fig. A3.3 Margin on sales

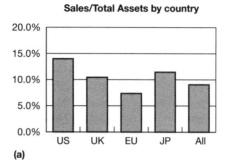

(a)

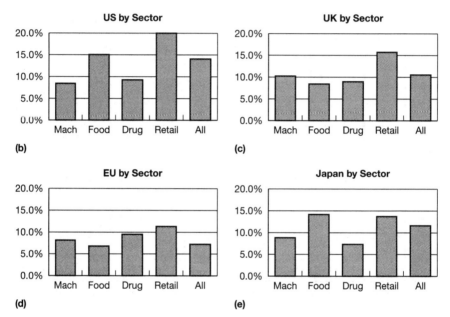

(b)

(c)

(d)

(e)

Fig. A3.4 Sales/TA

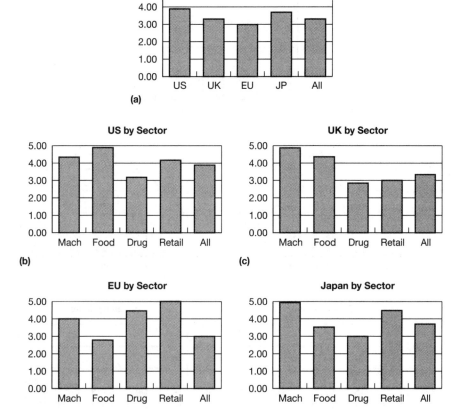

Fig. A3.5 Sales/FA

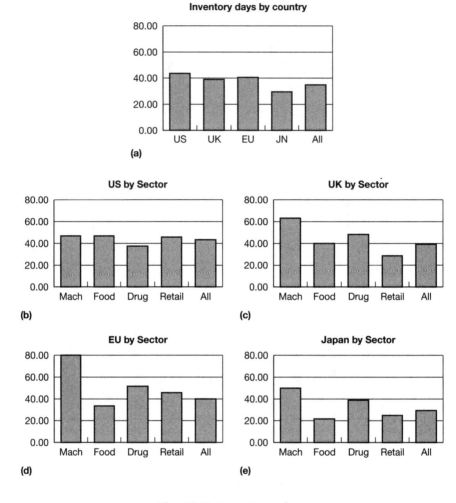

Fig. A3.6 Inventory days

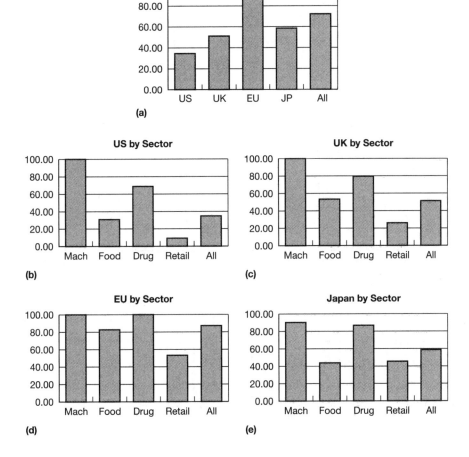

Fig. A3.7 Accounts receivable days

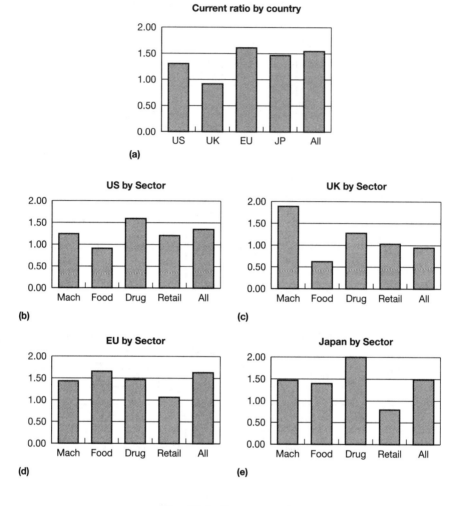

Fig. A3.8 Current ratio

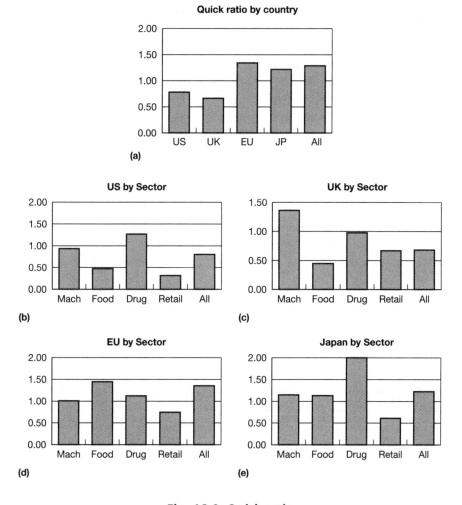

Fig. A3.9 Quick ratio

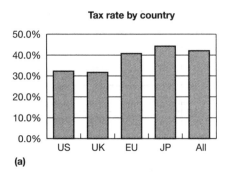

(a)

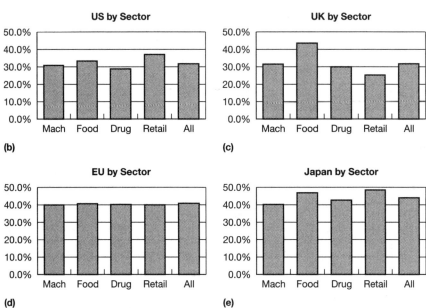

(b)   **(c)**

(d)   **(e)**

Fig. A3.10 Corporate tax

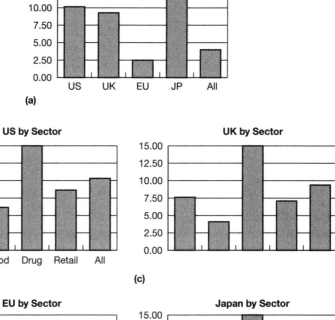

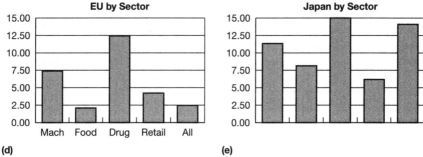

Fig. A3.11 Interest cover

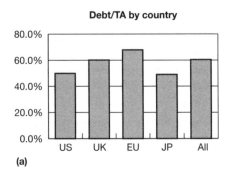

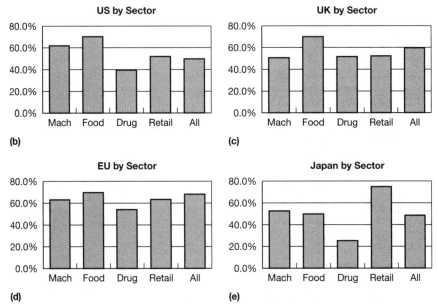

Fig. A3.12 Debt/total assets

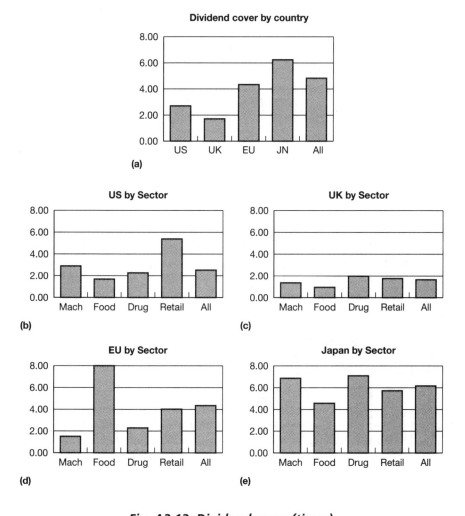

Fig. A3.13 Dividend cover (times)

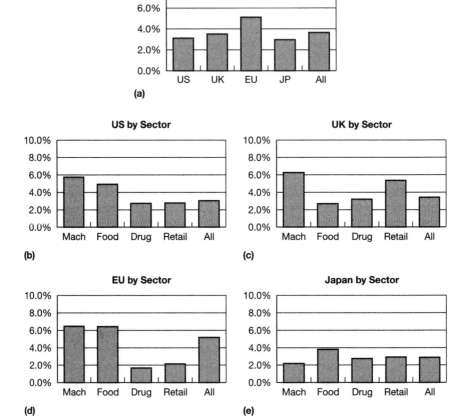

Fig. A3.14 Earnings yield

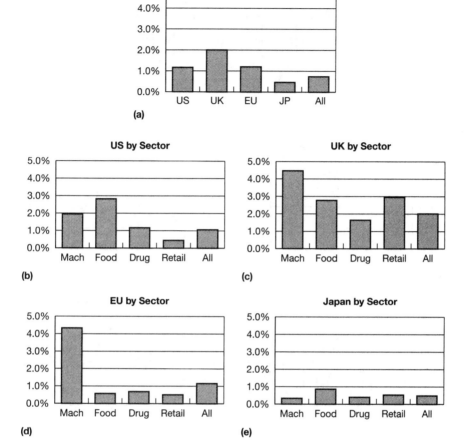

Fig. A3.15 Dividend yield

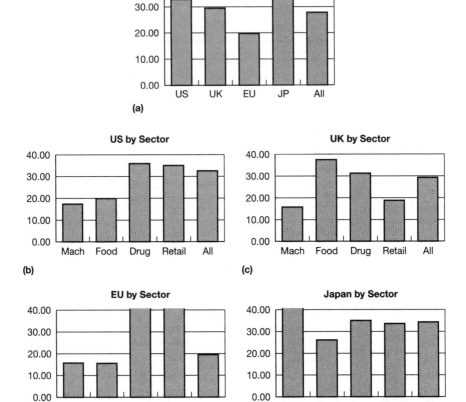

Fig. A3.16 Price/earnings ratio

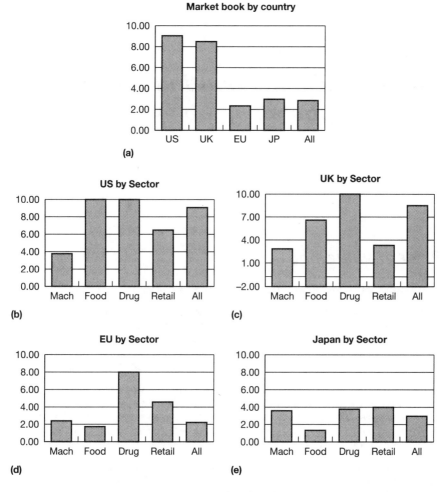

Fig. A3.17 Market/book ratio

Appendix 4: Discounting and compounding tables

Present value of $1

Years	1%	2%	3%	4%	5%	6%	7%	8%	9%	10%	11%	12%
1	0.990	0.980	0.971	0.962	0.952	0.943	0.935	0.926	0.917	0.909	0.901	0.893
2	0.980	0.961	0.943	0.925	0.907	0.890	0.873	0.857	0.842	0.826	0.812	0.797
3	0.971	0.942	0.915	0.889	0.864	0.840	0.816	0.794	0.772	0.751	0.731	0.712
4	0.961	0.924	0.888	0.855	0.823	0.792	0.763	0.735	0.708	0.683	0.659	0.636
5	0.951	0.906	0.863	0.822	0.784	0.747	0.713	0.681	0.650	0.621	0.593	0.567
6	0.942	0.888	0.837	0.790	0.746	0.705	0.666	0.630	0.596	0.564	0.535	0.507
7	0.933	0.871	0.813	0.760	0.711	0.665	0.623	0.583	0.547	0.513	0.482	0.452
8	0.923	0.853	0.789	0.731	0.677	0.627	0.582	0.540	0.502	0.467	0.434	0.404
9	0.914	0.837	0.766	0.703	0.645	0.592	0.544	0.500	0.460	0.424	0.391	0.361
10	0.905	0.820	0.744	0.676	0.614	0.558	0.508	0.463	0.422	0.386	0.352	0.322
11	0.896	0.804	0.722	0.650	0.585	0.527	0.475	0.429	0.388	0.350	0.317	0.287
12	0.887	0.788	0.701	0.625	0.557	0.497	0.444	0.397	0.356	0.319	0.286	0.257
13	0.879	0.773	0.681	0.601	0.530	0.469	0.415	0.368	0.326	0.290	0.258	0.229
14	0.870	0.758	0.661	0.577	0.505	0.442	0.388	0.340	0.299	0.263	0.232	0.205
15	0.861	0.743	0.642	0.555	0.481	0.417	0.362	0.315	0.275	0.239	0.209	0.183
16	0.853	0.728	0.623	0.534	0.458	0.394	0.339	0.292	0.252	0.218	0.188	0.163
17	0.844	0.714	0.605	0.513	0.436	0.371	0.317	0.270	0.231	0.198	0.170	0.146
18	0.836	0.700	0.587	0.494	0.416	0.350	0.296	0.250	0.212	0.180	0.153	0.130
19	0.828	0.686	0.570	0.475	0.396	0.331	0.277	0.232	0.194	0.164	0.138	0.116
20	0.820	0.673	0.554	0.456	0.377	0.312	0.258	0.215	0.178	0.149	0.124	0.104
21	0.811	0.660	0.538	0.439	0.359	0.294	0.242	0.199	0.164	0.135	0.112	0.093
22	0.803	0.647	0.522	0.422	0.342	0.278	0.226	0.184	0.150	0.123	0.101	0.083
23	0.795	0.634	0.507	0.406	0.326	0.262	0.211	0.170	0.138	0.112	0.091	0.074
24	0.788	0.622	0.492	0.390	0.310	0.247	0.197	0.158	0.126	0.102	0.082	0.066
25	0.780	0.610	0.478	0.375	0.295	0.233	0.184	0.146	0.116	0.092	0.074	0.059
26	0.772	0.598	0.464	0.361	0.281	0.220	0.172	0.135	0.106	0.084	0.066	0.053
27	0.764	0.586	0.450	0.347	0.268	0.207	0.161	0.125	0.098	0.076	0.060	0.047
28	0.757	0.574	0.437	0.333	0.255	0.196	0.150	0.116	0.090	0.069	0.054	0.042
29	0.749	0.563	0.424	0.321	0.243	0.185	0.141	0.107	0.082	0.063	0.048	0.037
30	0.742	0.552	0.412	0.308	0.231	0.174	0.131	0.099	0.075	0.057	0.044	0.033

Present value of $1

Years	13%	14%	15%	16%	17%	18%	19%	20%	21%	22%	23%	24%
1	0.885	0.877	0.870	0.862	0.855	0.847	0.840	0.833	0.826	0.820	0.813	0.806
2	0.783	0.769	0.756	0.743	0.731	0.718	0.706	0.694	0.683	0.672	0.661	0.650
3	0.693	0.675	0.658	0.641	0.624	0.609	0.593	0.579	0.564	0.551	0.537	0.524
4	0.613	0.592	0.572	0.552	0.534	0.516	0.499	0.482	0.467	0.451	0.437	0.423
5	0.543	0.519	0.497	0.476	0.456	0.437	0.419	0.402	0.386	0.370	0.355	0.341
6	0.480	0.456	0.432	0.410	0.390	0.370	0.352	0.335	0.319	0.303	0.289	0.275
7	0.425	0.400	0.376	0.354	0.333	0.314	0.296	0.279	0.263	0.249	0.235	0.222
8	0.376	0.351	0.327	0.305	0.285	0.266	0.249	0.233	0.218	0.204	0.191	0.179
9	0.333	0.308	0.284	0.263	0.243	0.225	0.209	0.194	0.180	0.167	0.155	0.144
10	0.295	0.270	0.247	0.227	0.208	0.191	0.176	0.162	0.149	0.137	0.126	0.116
11	0.261	0.237	0.215	0.195	0.178	0.162	0.148	0.135	0.123	0.112	0.103	0.094
12	0.231	0.208	0.187	0.168	0.152	0.137	0.124	0.112	0.102	0.092	0.083	0.076
13	0.204	0.182	0.163	0.145	0.130	0.116	0.104	0.093	0.084	0.075	0.068	0.061
14	0.181	0.160	0.141	0.125	0.111	0.099	0.088	0.078	0.069	0.062	0.055	0.049
15	0.160	0.140	0.123	0.108	0.095	0.084	0.074	0.065	0.057	0.051	0.045	0.040
16	0.141	0.123	0.107	0.093	0.081	0.071	0.062	0.054	0.047	0.042	0.036	0.032
17	0.125	0.108	0.093	0.080	0.069	0.060	0.052	0.045	0.039	0.034	0.030	0.026
18	0.111	0.095	0.081	0.069	0.059	0.051	0.044	0.038	0.032	0.028	0.024	0.021
19	0.098	0.083	0.070	0.060	0.051	0.043	0.037	0.031	0.027	0.023	0.020	0.017
20	0.087	0.073	0.061	0.051	0.043	0.037	0.031	0.026	0.022	0.019	0.016	0.014
21	0.077	0.064	0.053	0.044	0.037	0.031	0.026	0.022	0.018	0.015	0.013	0.011
22	0.068	0.056	0.046	0.038	0.032	0.026	0.022	0.018	0.015	0.013	0.011	0.009
23	0.060	0.049	0.040	0.033	0.027	0.022	0.018	0.015	0.012	0.010	0.009	0.007
24	0.053	0.043	0.035	0.028	0.023	0.019	0.015	0.013	0.010	0.008	0.007	0.006
25	0.047	0.038	0.030	0.024	0.020	0.016	0.013	0.010	0.009	0.007	0.006	0.005
26	0.042	0.033	0.026	0.021	0.017	0.014	0.011	0.009	0.007	0.006	0.005	0.004
27	0.037	0.029	0.023	0.018	0.014	0.011	0.009	0.007	0.006	0.005	0.004	0.003
28	0.033	0.026	0.020	0.016	0.012	0.010	0.008	0.006	0.005	0.004	0.003	0.002
29	0.029	0.022	0.017	0.014	0.011	0.008	0.006	0.005	0.004	0.003	0.002	0.002
30	0.026	0.020	0.015	0.012	0.009	0.007	0.005	0.004	0.003	0.003	0.002	0.002

Note: To convert $1 in the future into a present value apply the factor that matches both the number of years and the interest rate, for example, 6 years, 4 per cent = $0.790.

Present value of annuity of $1

Years	1%	2%	3%	4%	5%	6%	7%	8%	9%	10%	11%	12%
1	0.990	0.980	0.971	0.962	0.952	0.943	0.935	0.926	0.917	0.909	0.901	0.893
2	1.970	1.942	1.913	1.886	1.859	1.833	1.808	1.783	1.759	1.736	1.713	1.690
3	2.941	2.884	2.829	2.775	2.723	2.673	2.624	2.577	2.531	2.487	2.444	2.402
4	3.092	3.808	3.717	3.630	3.546	3.465	3.387	3.312	3.240	3.170	3.102	3.037
5	4.853	4.713	4.580	4.452	4.329	4.212	4.100	3.993	3.890	3.791	3.696	3.605
6	5.795	5.601	5.417	5.242	5.076	4.917	4.767	4.623	4.486	4.355	4.321	4.111
7	6.728	6.472	6.230	6.002	5.786	5.582	5.389	5.206	5.033	4.868	4.712	4.564
8	7.652	7.325	7.020	6.733	6.463	6.210	5.971	5.747	5.535	5.335	5.146	4.968
9	8.566	8.162	7.786	7.435	7.108	6.802	6.515	6.247	5.995	5.759	5.537	5.328
10	9.471	8.983	8.530	8.111	7.722	7.360	7.024	6.710	6.418	6.145	5.889	5.650
11	10.37	9.787	9.253	8.760	8.306	7.887	7.499	7.139	6.805	6.495	6.207	5.938
12	11.26	10.58	9.954	9.385	8.863	8.384	7.943	7.536	7.161	6.814	6.492	6.194
13	12.13	11.35	10.63	9.986	9.394	8.853	8.358	7.904	7.487	7.103	6.750	6.424
14	13.00	12.11	11.30	10.56	9.899	9.295	8.745	8.244	7.786	7.367	6.982	6.628
15	13.87	12.85	11.94	11.12	10.38	9.712	9.108	8.559	8.061	7.606	7.191	6.811
16	14.72	13.58	12.56	11.65	10.84	10.11	9.447	8.851	8.313	7.824	7.379	6.974
17	15.56	14.29	13.17	12.17	11.27	10.48	9.763	9.122	8.544	8.022	7.549	7.120
18	16.40	14.99	13.75	12.66	11.69	10.83	10.06	9.372	8.756	8.201	7.702	7.250
19	17.23	15.68	14.32	13.13	12.09	11.16	10.34	9.604	8.950	8.365	7.839	7.366
20	18.05	16.35	14.88	13.59	12.46	11.47	10.59	9.818	9.129	8.514	7.963	7.469
21	18.86	17.01	15.42	14.03	12.82	11.76	10.84	10.02	9.292	8.649	8.075	7.562
22	19.66	17.66	15.94	14.45	13.16	12.04	11.06	10.20	9.442	8.772	8.176	7.645
23	20.46	18.29	16.44	14.86	13.49	12.30	11.27	10.37	9.580	8.883	8.266	7.718
24	21.24	18.91	16.94	15.25	13.80	12.55	11.47	10.53	9.707	8.985	8.348	7.784
25	22.02	19.52	17.41	15.62	14.09	12.78	11.65	10.67	9.823	9.077	8.422	7.843
26	22.80	20.12	17.88	15.98	14.38	13.00	11.83	10.81	9.929	9.161	8.488	7.896
27	23.56	20.71	18.33	16.33	14.64	13.21	11.99	10.94	10.03	9.237	8.548	7.943
28	24.32	21.28	18.76	16.66	14.90	13.41	12.14	11.05	10.12	9.307	8.602	7.984
29	25.07	21.84	19.19	16.98	15.14	13.59	12.28	11.16	10.20	9.370	8.650	8.022
30	25.81	22.40	19.60	17.29	15.37	13.76	12.41	11.26	10.27	9.427	8.694	8.055

Present value of annuity of $1

Years	13%	14%	15%	16%	17%	18%	19%	20%	21%	22%	23%	24%
1	0.885	0.877	0.870	0.862	0.855	0.847	0.840	0.833	0.826	0.820	0.813	0.806
2	1.668	1.647	1.626	1.605	1.585	1.566	1.547	1.528	1.509	1.492	1.474	1.457
3	2.361	2.322	2.283	2.246	2.210	2.174	2.140	2.106	2.074	2.042	2.011	1.981
4	2.974	2.914	2.855	2.798	2.743	2.690	2.639	2.589	2.540	2.494	2.448	2.404
5	3.517	3.433	3.352	3.274	3.199	3.127	3.058	2.991	2.926	2.864	2.803	2.745
6	3.998	3.889	3.784	3.685	3.589	3.498	3.410	3.326	3.245	3.167	3.092	3.020
7	4.423	4.288	4.160	4.039	3.922	3.812	3.706	3.605	3.508	3.416	3.327	3.242
8	4.799	4.639	4.487	4.344	4.207	4.078	3.954	3.837	3.726	3.619	3.518	3.421
9	5.132	4.946	4.772	4.607	4.451	4.303	4.163	4.031	3.905	3.786	3.673	3.566
10	5.426	5.216	5.019	4.833	4.659	4.494	4.339	4.192	4.054	3.923	3.799	3.682
11	5.687	5.453	5.234	5.029	4.836	4.656	4.486	4.327	4.177	4.035	3.092	3.776
12	5.918	5.660	5.421	5.197	4.988	4.793	4.611	4.439	4.278	4.127	3.985	3.851
13	6.122	5.842	5.583	5.342	5.118	4.910	4.715	4.533	4.362	4.203	4.053	3.912
14	6.302	6.002	5.724	5.468	5.229	5.008	4.802	4.611	4.432	4.265	4.108	3.962
15	6.462	6.142	5.847	5.575	5.324	5.092	4.876	4.675	4.489	4.315	4.153	4.001
16	6.604	6.265	5.954	5.668	5.405	5.162	4.938	4.730	4.536	4.357	4.189	4.033
17	6.729	6.373	6.047	5.749	5.475	5.222	4.990	4.775	4.576	4.391	4.219	4.059
18	6.840	6.467	6.128	5.818	5.534	5.273	5.033	4.812	4.608	4.419	4.243	4.080
19	6.938	6.550	6.198	5.877	5.584	5.316	5.070	4.843	4.635	4.442	4.263	4.097
20	7.025	6.623	6.259	5.929	5.628	5.353	5.101	4.870	4.657	4.460	4.279	4.110
21	7.102	6.687	6.312	5.973	5.665	5.384	5.127	4.891	4.675	4.476	4.292	4.121
22	7.170	6.743	6.359	6.011	5.696	5.410	5.149	4.909	4.690	4.488	4.302	4.130
23	7.230	6.792	6.399	6.044	5.723	5.432	5.167	4.925	4.703	4.499	4.311	4.137
24	7.283	6.835	6.434	6.073	5.746	5.451	5.182	4.937	4.713	4.507	4.318	4.143
25	7.330	6.873	6.464	6.097	5.766	5.467	5.195	4.948	4.721	4.514	4.323	4.147
26	7.372	6.906	6.491	6.118	5.783	5.480	5.206	4.956	4.728	4.520	4.328	4.151
27	7.409	6.935	6.514	6.136	5.798	5.492	5.215	4.964	4.734	4.524	4.332	4.154
28	7.441	6961	6.534	6.152	5.810	5.502	5.223	4.970	4.739	4.528	4.335	4.157
29	7.470	6.983	6.551	6.166	5.820	5.510	5.229	4.975	4.743	4.531	4.337	4.159
30	7.496	7.003	6.566	6.177	5.829	5.517	5.235	4.979	4.746	4.534	4.339	4.160

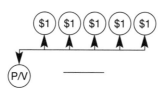

Note: To convert a future cash flow of $1 per period into a present value, apply the factor that matches both the number of years and the interest rate, for example, 6 years, 4 per cent = $5.242

Future value of $1

Years	1%	2%	3%	4%	5%	6%	7%	8%	9%	10%	11%	12%
1	1.010	1.020	1.030	1.040	1.050	1.060	1.070	1.080	1.090	1.100	1.110	1.120
2	1.020	1.040	1.061	1.082	1.103	1.124	1.145	1.166	1.188	1.210	1.232	1.254
3	1.030	1.061	1.093	1.125	1.158	1.191	1.225	1.260	1.295	1.331	1.368	1.405
4	1.041	1.082	1.126	1.170	1.216	1.262	1.311	1.360	1.412	1.464	1.518	1.574
5	1.051	1.104	1.159	1.217	1.276	1.338	1.403	1.469	1.539	1.611	1.685	1.762
6	1.062	1.126	1.194	1.265	1.340	1.419	1.501	1.587	1.677	1.772	1.870	1.974
7	1.072	1.149	1.230	1.316	1.407	1.504	1.606	1.714	1.828	1.949	2.076	2.211
8	1.083	1.172	1.267	1.369	1.477	1.594	1.718	1.851	1.993	2.144	2.305	2.476
9	1.094	1.195	1.305	1.423	1.551	1.689	1.838	1.999	2.172	2.358	2.558	2.773
10	1.105	1.219	1.344	1.480	1.629	1.791	1.967	2.159	2.367	2.594	2.839	3.106
11	1.116	1.243	1.384	1.539	1.710	1.898	2.105	2.332	2.580	2.853	3.152	3.479
12	1.127	1.268	1.426	1.601	1.796	2.012	2.252	2.518	2.813	3.138	3.498	3.896
13	1.138	1.294	1.469	1.665	1.886	2.133	2.410	2.720	3.066	3.452	3.883	4.363
14	1.149	1.319	1.513	1.732	1.980	2.261	2.579	2.937	3.342	3.797	4.310	4.887
15	1.161	1.346	1.558	1.801	2.079	2.397	2.759	3.172	3.642	4.177	4.785	5.474
16	1.173	1.373	1.605	1.873	2.183	2.540	2.952	3.426	3.970	4.595	5.311	6.130
17	1.184	1.400	1.653	1.948	2.292	2.693	3.159	3.700	4.328	5.054	5.895	6.866
18	1.196	1.428	1.702	2.026	2.407	2.854	3.380	3.996	4.717	5.560	6.544	7.690
19	1.208	1.457	1.754	2.107	2.527	3.026	3.617	4.316	5.142	6.116	7.263	8.613
20	1.220	1.486	1.806	2.191	2.653	3.207	3.870	4.661	5.604	6.727	8.062	9.646
21	1.232	1.516	1.860	2.279	2.786	3.400	4.141	5.034	6.109	7.400	8.949	10.80
22	1.245	1.546	1.916	2.370	2.925	3.604	4.430	5.437	6.659	8.140	9.934	12.10
23	1.257	1.577	1.974	2.465	3.072	3.820	4.741	5.871	7.258	8.954	11.03	13.55
24	1.270	1.608	2.033	2.563	3.225	4.049	5.072	6.341	7.911	9.850	12.24	15.18
25	1.282	1.641	2.094	2.666	3.386	4.292	5.427	6.848	8.623	10.83	13.59	17.00
26	1.295	1.673	2.157	2.772	3.556	4.549	5.807	7.396	9.399	11.92	15.08	19.04
27	1.308	1.707	2.221	2.883	3.733	4.822	6.214	7.988	10.25	13.11	16.74	21.32
28	1.321	1.741	2.288	2.999	3.920	5.112	6.649	8.627	11.17	14.42	18.58	23.88
29	1.335	1.776	2.357	3.119	4.116	5.418	7.114	9.317	12.17	15.86	20.62	26.72
30	1.348	1.811	2.427	3.243	4.322	5.743	7.612	10.06	13.27	17.45	22.89	29.96

Future value of $1

Years	13%	14%	15%	16%	17%	18%	19%	20%	21%	22%	23%	24%
1	1.130	1.140	1.150	1.160	1.170	1.180	1.190	1.200	1.210	1.220	1.230	1.240
2	1.277	1.300	1.322	1.346	1.369	1.392	1.416	1.440	1.464	1.488	1.513	1.538
3	1.443	1.482	1.521	1.561	1.602	1.643	1.685	1.728	1.772	1.816	1.861	1.907
4	1.63	1.689	1.749	1.811	1.874	1.939	2.005	2.074	2.144	2.215	2.289	2.364
5	1.842	1.925	2.011	2.100	2.192	2.288	2.386	2.488	2.594	2.703	2.815	2.932
6	2.082	2.195	2.313	2.436	2.565	2.700	2.840	2.986	3.138	3.297	3.463	3.635
7	2.353	2.502	2.660	2.826	3.001	3.185	3.379	3.583	3.797	4.023	4.259	4.508
8	2.658	2.853	3.059	3.278	3.511	3.759	4.021	4.300	4.595	4.908	5.239	5.590
9	3.004	3.252	3.518	3.803	4.108	4.435	4.785	5.160	5.560	5.987	6.444	6.931
10	3.395	3.707	4.046	4.411	4.807	5.234	5.695	6.192	6.727	7.305	7.926	8.594
11	3.836	4.226	4.652	5.117	5.624	6.176	6.777	7.430	8.140	8.912	9.749	10.66
12	4.335	4.818	5.350	5.936	6.580	7.288	8.064	8.916	9.850	10.87	11.99	13.21
13	4.898	5.492	6.153	6.886	7.699	8.599	9.596	10.70	11.92	13.26	14.75	16.39
14	5.535	6.261	7.076	7.988	9.007	10.15	11.42	12.84	14.42	16.18	18.14	20.32
15	6.254	7.138	8.137	9.266	10.54	11.97	13.59	15.41	17.45	19.74	22.31	25.20
16	7.067	8.137	9.358	10.75	12.33	14.13	16.17	18.49	21.11	24.09	27.45	31.24
17	7.986	9.276	10.76	12.47	14.43	16.67	19.24	22.19	25.55	29.38	33.76	38.74
18	9.024	10.58	12.38	14.46	16.88	19.67	22.90	26.62	30.91	35.85	41.52	48.04
19	10.20	12.06	14.23	16.78	19.75	23.21	27.25	31.95	37.40	43.74	51.07	59.57
20	11.52	13.74	16.37	19.46	23.11	27.39	32.43	38.34	45.26	53.36	62.82	73.86
21	13.02	15.67	18.82	22.57	27.03	32.32	38.59	46.01	54.76	65.10	77.27	91.59
22	14.71	17.86	21.64	26.19	31.63	38.14	45.92	55.21	66.26	79.42	95.04	113.6
23	16.63	20.36	24.89	30.38	37.01	45.01	54.65	66.25	80.18	96.89	116.9	140.8
24	18.79	23.21	28.63	35.24	43.30	53.11	65.03	79.50	97.02	118.2	143.8	174.6
25	21.23	26.46	32.92	40.87	50.66	62.67	77.39	95.40	117.4	144.2	176.9	216.5
26	23.99	30.17	37.86	47.41	59.27	73.95	92.09	114.5	142.0	175.9	217.5	268.5
27	27.11	34.39	43.54	55.00	69.35	87.26	109.6	137.4	171.9	214.6	267.6	333.0
28	30.63	39.20	50.07	63.80	81.13	103.0	130.4	164.8	208.0	261.9	329.1	412.9
29	34.62	44.69	57.58	74.01	94.93	121.5	155.2	197.8	251.6	319.5	404.8	512.0
30	39.12	50.95	66.21	85.85	111.1	143.4	184.7	237.4	304.5	389.8	497.9	634.8

Note: To convert $1 today into a future value apply the factor that matches both the number of years and the interest rate, for example, 6 years, 4 per cent = $1.265.

Future value of annuity of $1

Years	1%	2%	3%	4%	5%	6%	7%	8%	9%	10%	11%	12%
1	1.000	1.000	1.000	1.000	1.000	1.000	1.000	1.000	1.000	1.000	1.000	1.000
2	2.010	2.020	2.030	2.040	2.050	2.060	2.070	2.080	2.090	2.100	2.110	2.120
3	3.030	3.060	3.091	3.122	3.152	3.184	3.215	3.246	3.278	3.310	3.342	3.374
4	4.060	4.122	4.184	4.246	4.310	4.375	4.440	4.506	4.573	4.641	4.710	4.779
5	5.101	5.204	5.309	5.416	5.526	5.637	5.751	5.867	5.985	6.105	6.228	6.353
6	6.152	6.308	6.468	6.633	6.802	6.975	7.153	7.336	7.523	7.716	7.913	8.115
7	7.214	7.434	7.662	7.898	8.142	8.394	8.654	8.923	9.200	9.487	9.783	10.09
8	8.286	8.583	8.892	9.214	9.549	9.897	10.26	10.64	11.03	11.44	11.86	12.30
9	9.369	9.755	10.16	10.58	11.03	11.49	11.98	12.49	13.02	13.58	14.16	14.78
10	10.46	10.95	11.46	12.01	12.58	13.18	13.82	14.49	15.19	15.94	16.72	17.55
11	11.57	12.17	12.81	13.49	14.21	14.97	15.78	16.65	17.56	18.53	19.56	20.65
12	12.68	13.41	14.19	15.03	15.92	16.87	17.89	18.98	20.14	21.38	22.71	24.13
13	13.81	14.68	15.62	16.63	17.71	18.88	20.14	21.50	22.95	24.52	26.21	28.03
14	14.95	15.97	17.09	18.29	19.60	21.02	22.55	24.21	26.02	27.97	30.09	32.39
15	16.10	17.29	18.60	20.02	21.58	23.28	25.13	27.15	29.36	31.77	34.41	37.28
16	17.26	18.64	20.16	21.82	23.66	25.67	27.89	30.32	33.00	35.95	39.19	42.75
17	18.43	20.01	21.76	23.70	25.84	28.21	30.84	33.75	36.97	40.54	44.50	48.88
18	19.61	21.41	23.41	25.65	28.13	30.91	34.00	37.45	41.30	45.60	50.40	55.75
19	20.81	22.84	25.12	27.67	30.54	33.76	37.38	41.45	46.02	51.16	56.94	63.44
20	22.02	24.30	26.87	29.78	33.07	36.79	41.00	45.76	51.16	57.27	64.20	72.05
21	23.24	25.78	28.68	31.97	35.72	39.99	44.87	50.42	56.76	64.00	72.27	81.70
22	24.47	27.30	30.54	34.25	38.51	43.39	49.01	55.46	62.87	71.40	81.21	92.50
23	25.72	28.84	32.45	36.62	41.43	47.00	53.44	60.89	69.53	79.54	91.15	104.6
24	26.97	30.42	34.43	39.08	44.50	50.82	58.18	66.76	76.79	88.50	102.2	118.2
25	28.24	32.03	36.46	41.65	47.73	54.86	63.25	73.11	84.70	98.35	114.4	133.3
26	29.53	33.67	38.55	44.31	51.11	59.16	68.68	79.95	93.32	109.2	128.0	150.3
27	30.82	35.34	40.71	47.08	54.67	63.71	74.48	87.35	102.7	121.1	143.1	169.4
28	32.13	37.05	42.93	49.97	58.40	68.53	80.70	95.34	113.0	134.2	159.8	190.7
29	33.45	38.79	45.22	52.97	62.32	73.64	87.35	104.0	124.1	148.6	178.4	214.6
30	34.78	40.57	47.58	56.08	66.44	79.06	94.46	113.3	136.3	164.5	199.0	241.3

Future value of annuity of $1

Years	13%	14%	15%	16%	17%	18%	19%	20%	21%	22%	23%	24%
1	1.000	1.000	1.000	1.000	1.000	1.000	1.000	1.000	1.000	1.000	1.000	1.000
2	2.130	2.140	2.150	2.160	2.170	2.180	2.190	2.200	2.210	2.220	2.230	2.240
3	3.407	3.440	3.472	3.506	3.539	3.572	3.606	3.640	3.674	3.708	3.743	3.778
4	4.850	4.921	4.993	5.066	5.141	5.215	5.291	5.368	5.446	5.524	5.604	5.684
5	6.480	6.610	6.742	6.877	7.014	7.154	7.297	7.442	7.589	7.740	7.893	8.048
6	8.323	8.536	8.754	8.977	9.207	9.442	9.683	9.930	10.18	10.44	10.71	10.98
7	10.40	10.73	11.07	11.41	11.77	12.14	12.52	12.92	13.32	13.74	14.17	14.62
8	12.76	13.23	13.73	14.24	14.77	15.33	15.90	16.50	17.12	17.76	18.43	19.12
9	15.42	16.09	16.79	17.52	18.28	19.09	19.92	20.80	21.71	22.67	23.67	24.71
10	18.42	19.34	20.30	21.32	22.39	23.52	24.71	25.96	27.27	28.66	30.11	31.64
11	21.81	23.04	24.35	25.73	27.20	28.76	30.40	32.15	34.00	35.96	38.04	40.24
12	25.65	27.27	29.00	30.85	32.82	34.93	37.18	39.58	42.14	44.87	47.79	50.89
13	29.98	32.09	34.35	36.79	39.40	42.22	45.24	48.50	51.99	55.75	59.78	64.11
14	34.88	37.58	40.50	43.67	47.10	50.82	54.84	59.20	63.91	69.01	74.53	80.50
15	40.42	43.84	47.58	51.66	56.11	60.97	66.26	72.04	78.33	85.19	92.67	100.8
16	46.67	50.98	55.72	60.93	66.65	72.94	79.85	87.44	95.78	104.9	115.0	126.0
17	53.74	59.12	65.08	71.67	78.98	87.07	96.02	105.9	116.9	129.0	142.4	157.3
18	61.73	68.39	75.84	84.14	93.41	103.7	115.3	128.1	142.4	158.4	176.2	196.0
19	70.75	78.97	88.21	98.60	110.3	123.4	138.2	154.7	173.4	194.3	217.7	244.0
20	80.95	91.02	102.4	115.4	130.0	146.6	165.4	186.7	210.8	238.0	268.8	303.6
21	92.47	104.8	118.8	134.8	153.1	174.0	197.8	225.0	256.0	291.3	331.6	377.5
22	105.5	120.4	137.6	157.4	180.2	206.3	236.4	271.0	310.8	356.4	408.9	469.1
23	120.2	138.3	159.3	183.6	211.8	244.5	282.4	326.2	377.0	435.9	503.9	582.9
24	136.8	158.7	184.2	214.0	248.8	289.5	337.0	392.5	457.2	532.8	620.8	723.5
25	155.6	181.9	212.8	249.2	292.1	342.6	402.0	472.0	554.2	651.0	764.6	898.1
26	176.9	208.3	245.7	290.1	342.8	405.3	479.4	567.4	671.6	795.2	941.5	1115
27	200.8	238.5	283.6	337.5	402.0	479.2	571.5	681.9	813.7	971.1	1159	1383
28	227.9	272.9	327.1	392.5	471.4	566.5	681.1	819.2	985.5	1186	1427	1716
29	258.6	312.1	377.2	456.3	552.5	669.4	811.5	984.1	1194	1448	1756	2129
30	293.2	356.8	434.7	530.3	647.4	790.9	966.7	1182	1445	1767	2160	2641

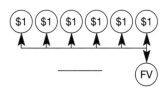

Note: To convert a cash flow of $1 per period into its equivalent 'future value' at the end of the period, apply the factor that matches both the number of years and the interest rate, for example, 6 years, 4 per cent = $6.633.

Glossary

All items in *italics* are defined elsewhere in the glossary

Acid test *See quick ratio.*

Activity ratios These measure the relationship between key assets and sales. They express how well assets are being utilized. For instance, 'accounts receivable days' (*see debtor days*) shows how long cash is tied up in accounts receivable; likewise *inventory days*. We use the *sales to fixed assets ratio* to give a measure of the output being generated by major fixed assets. The term 'asset utilization ratios' is also used in this context.

Amortization of loan The repayment of a loan by equal periodic payments that include both interest on outstanding balance plus some repayment of principal.

Annuity A series of equal payments made at equal intervals of time. Many financial calculations can be treated by the annuity formulae, for example repayment of a term loan, straight line depreciation charges, and so on.

Arbitrage The operation of buying and selling a security simultaneously in two different markets to take advantage of inconsistencies in pricing.

Asset backing Also known as 'asset value per share,' it is calculated by dividing total ordinary funds in the balance sheet by the number of issued ordinary shares.

Asset utilization ratios *See activity ratios.*

Asset value per share *See asset backing.*

Authorized share capital The maximum value of share capital that can be issued. It is specified in the company Articles and can be increased only by permission of the shareholders.

Average collection period *As debtor days.*

Average interest rate paid The apparent rate of interest paid on loans, calculated by expressing the interest charge in the profit and loss account as a percentage of loan funds in the balance sheet. It must be kept in mind that loans at the balance sheet date may not be a true reflection of the average over the year.

Bear Term for an investor who anticipates a falling market in financial securities. This investor may sell securities not owned in order to profit from the expected drop in price. *See also bull.*

Beta value A measure of the risk in a share that cannot be eliminated by diversification. High risk brings the need for a high return. Therefore the beta value is used by analysts to derive an appropriate share value.

Blue chip A first-class commercial security.

Bond US term for medium- to long-term loan. Legally it is the certificate that gives the holder the right to periodic interest payments and repayment of principal.

Bonus issue New equity shares issued from reserves and given free to company shareholders in proportion to their existing share holdings.

Book value per share The value of a share based on the balance sheet values. *See* also *asset backing.*

Borrowing ratio Long-term plus short-term loans expressed as a percentage of ordinary funds plus preference shares less intangibles.

Break-even point The level of activity at which the fixed costs of an operation are just covered by the contribution from sales. At this point neither a profit nor a loss ensues.

Break-even analysis A form of analysis that relates activity to totals of revenue and costs based on the classification of costs into fixed and variable types.

Bull An investor who anticipates a rise in the price level of financial securities. This investor may purchase securities with the intention of resale before the time for settlement is due. *See* also *bear*.

Bullet A single payment of the total amount of a loan at the end of the period (as opposed to periodic payments during its life).

Capital asset pricing model (CAPM) A model that links risk and return for all types of security. Applied to the valuation of equity shares, it uses the risk coefficient (*beta value*) of the share to calculate the required risk premium. This risk premium is added to the risk-free rate (rate on *gilts*) to give the appropriate yield for the share.

Call The amount demanded from shareholders from the balance outstanding on non-paid-up shares.

Call option An option to purchase. *See* also *option*.

Capital employed The total of the long-term funds in the balance sheet. It includes shareholders' funds, long-term loans, preference shares, minority interests and miscellaneous long-term funds. It can also be expressed as total assets less current liabilities.

Capital market The financial market for long-term securities.

Capital project appraisal Evaluation of expenditure on capital assets to establish its rate of return with a view to deciding on whether or not to make the investment.

Capital reserves Shareholders' funds that have originated from sources other than trading or the nominal value of new issues.

Capital structure The mix of financing in a company. It usually refers to the proportions of debt and equity in the balance sheet.

Cash cycle A model of working capital cash flow that identifies the time required for cash paid out for raw materials and expenses to come back in from accounts receivable.

Cash flow, incremental The extra cash in-flow or out-flow that comes from selecting one alternative over another in capital project appraisal.

Cash flow per share Profit after interest, tax, minority and preference dividends plus depreciation divided by the number of shares.

Caveat emptor 'Let the buyer beware' – an expression that emphasizes the duty of a party to a contract to ensure that his interests are protected.

Certificate of deposit (CD) A short-term negotiable certificate issued by a bank as evidence of a deposit that is repayable on a fixed date. It is a highly liquid bearer instrument.

Collateral A physical or financial asset used as security for a loan.

Commercial paper Loan notes issued by high-credit corporations to raise short-term funds direct from the money markets rather than from a lending institution.

Common size financial statements Statements that have been standardized by having each component expressed as a percentage of sales or total assets.

Compensating balance The minimum amount by which a company must stay in credit on a deposit account under the terms of a loan.

Consols UK Government stock secured on the Consolidated Fund. They are effectively non-redeemable loans to the government with a low nominal interest rate.

Constant growth model A valuation model, derived by Professor Gordon, that calculates a share value from its dividend flow to infinity under assumptions of constant growth.

Contingent liability A potential liability that may not arise but which must be mentioned in the notes to the published accounts of a company.

Conversion ratio The number of shares the holder of a convertible security receives for each bond on conversion.

Convertible Loan A loan that gives the lender the option to convert into shares at a fixed price for a period of time.

Cost of capital The weighted average cost of funds to a company, based on the mix of equity and loan capital and their respective costs. A distinction is usually drawn between the average cost of all funds in an existing balance sheet and the marginal cost of raising new funds.

Covenant, restrictive A clause in a loan agreement to restrict the freedom of the borrower to act in a way that would weaken the position of the lender, such as increasing the amount of the dividend.

Credit period The number of days' sales represented by the accounts receivable. It corresponds with the term *debtor days*.

Current assets The sum of inventories, accounts receivable, cash and cash equivalents and miscellaneous short-term assets.

Current liabilities The sum of accounts payable, short-term loans and miscellaneous accruals all due for repayment within one year.

Debenture A legal document that acknowledges a loan. In the US, the term refers to an unsecured loan. In the UK it may be secured by a fixed or floating charge on the assets.

Debtor days, or, accounts receivable days The figure for trade debtors in the balance sheet is divided by the average sales per day to express the average number of days' credit taken by customers.

Debt to equity ratio The principal measure of the mix of funds in a company's balance sheet. It can be expressed in a number of different ways. The most common way is to calculate the percentage that total interest bearing debt bears to ordinary plus preference shareholders' funds.

Debt to total assets ratio One of the debt to equity measures. Long-term loans plus current liabilities are expressed as a percentage of total assets.

Deferred tax A taxation amount that has been charged to the profit and loss account but which has not been paid over to the authorities and is not currently payable. Timing differences between accounting and taxation computations of taxable profit on account of depreciation and so on are the root cause.

Departmental ratios The effectiveness of the major departments can be assessed by using an approach similar to that for the total operation, as illustrated in chapter 7. For each department, costs and assets classified under selected headings are related to sales, cost of sales or standard hours of work produced as appropriate. Suggested ratios for Marketing and Production are shown below:

- Marketing: cost to sales ratios
  salaries and commission
  travel expenses
  advertising costs
  sales office costs

- Marketing: assets to sales ratios
  fixed assets: office
  fixed assets: cars/equipment
  finished goods
  accounts receivable

- Production: cost to cost of sales ratios
  direct material
  direct labor
  overtime
  indirect labor
  maintenance
  production planning
  supervision and so on

- Production: asset to cost of sales ratios
  fixed assets: factory premises
  fixed assets: plant
  fixed assets: vehicles
  raw material
  work in progress.

Dilution The reduction in the *earnings per share* value due to an increase in the number of shares issued or contracted to be issued in the future.

Discounted cash flow (DCF) A method of appraisal for investment projects. The total incremental stream of cash from a project is tested to assess the return it delivers to the investor. If the return exceeds the required, or, *hurdle rate*, the project is recommended on financial terms and vice versa. Two approaches can be used in the assessment: *see net present value (NPV)* and *internal rate of return (IRR)*.

Discounting A technique used to calculate the present value of a cash flow occurring in some future time period. It is used in connection with the sale for immediate cash of a future debt and, more extensively, in translating future cash flow from an investment into present values.

Dividend cover Expresses the number of times that dividends to the ordinary shareholders are covered by earnings. *See* also *payout ratio*.

Dividend per share (DPS) The actual dividend paid on each ordinary share. It can be calculated from the accounts by dividing the total ordinary dividend by the number of ordinary shares.

Dividend yield Actual dividend per share expressed as a percentage of the current share price. In the UK, imputed tax is added to dividends paid and the calculation gives gross dividend yield.

Earnings per share (EPS) The profit earned for the ordinary shareholders as shown in the profit and loss account is divided by the number of issued ordinary shares to give earnings per share. (To be strictly orthodox, the weighted average number of share should be used.)

Earnings yield Earnings per share expressed as a percentage of the current share price. In the UK, imputed tax is added to earnings to give gross yield.

EBITDA Earnings before interest, tax, depreciation and amortization (see appendix 1 for explanation).

Employee ratios To measure the productivity of labor, three major variables – sales, profits and assets – are related back to the number of employees and their remuneration. The principal ratios used are:

- remuneration to employee
- sales to employee
- sales to remuneration
- profit to employee
- profit to remuneration
- fixed assets to employee
- working capital to employee.

Equity gearing Common funds plus preference shares expressed as percentage of long-term loan plus current liabilities.

Eurodollar Deposits denominated in US dollars in a bank outside the US owned by a non-resident of the US.

Extraordinary item A significant transaction outside the normal activities of the business and likely to be non-recurring. An example would be the sale of the corporate head office at a large profit. There is a strong argument that such a transaction should not be allowed to distort the trading results and that it should be isolated from the reported earnings. However, the contrary argument that all such gains and losses should be included in the profit and loss account now prevails.

Factoring A method of raising funds by the selling of trade debtors.

Fixed cost A type of cost where the total expenditure does not vary with the level of activity or output.

Fixed assets Land and buildings, plant and equipment and other long-term physical assets on which the operations of the company depend.

Floating rate note (FRN) Loan on which the interest rate varies with prevailing short-term market rates.

Forward cover The purchase or sale of foreign currency for delivery at a fixed future time. It is used to cover against the risk of an adverse exchange rate movement.

Forward exchange rate A rate fixed to govern the exchange of currencies at a fixed future date.

Free borrowing percentage The percentage of non-equity funds that is made up of 'free' debt, that is accounts payable, accruals and deferred tax.

Futures contract A contract in an organised exchange to trade in a fixed quantity of a security at a fixed price at a future date.

Gearing A relationship between different types of funds in a company, such as loans and equity. The higher the amount of loan funds the higher the amount of fixed interest charge in the profit and loss account. Where interest charges are high, a small change in operating profit will have a much increased result in return to the equity for shareholders.

Gilts The term 'gilt-edged' refers to government longer term borrowing instruments. They are described as 'short' where the maturity is up to five years, 'medium' for periods of five to 15 years and 'long' for over 15 years to infinity.

Hedging A technique for reducing the risk of an exposed position by taking a compensating position in another security.

Hurdle rate The rate of return decided on by a company as the minimum acceptable for capital investment. It will be governed by the firms' cost of capital and it may allow for different levels of risk.

Intangible assets Long-term non-physical assets in the balance sheet such as goodwill and brand values.

Interest cover A liquidity ratio that expresses the number of times the interest charged in the profit and loss account is covered by profit before interest and tax.

Internal rate of return (IRR) The rate of discount that brings the present value of all the cash flows associated with a capital investment to zero. It measures the effective yield on the investment. If this yield is greater than the 'hurdle rate' the investment is deemed to be financially desirable and vice versa.

Inventory days The inventory value in the balance sheet is expressed in terms of days. The divisor is usually the average daily cost of sales. Separate calculations are made for raw materials, work in progress and finished goods.

Investments Investments in subsidiary and associated companies and other long-term financial assets.

Junk bonds High-interest-bearing bonds with little security of assets issued by a company with good cash flow.

LIBOR London Interbank Offered Rate – the rate at which major banks in the short-term money market lend to each other. It is a benchmark for many international loans and floating-rate issues to corporations

Lease – finance A lease under which the lessee assumes all the risks and rewards of ownership. It extends over the estimated economic life of the assets and cannot easily be canceled. Under current accounting rules, such a lease is treated as a loan.

Leverage *See gearing.*

Leveraged buy-out The acquisition of a firm by using large amounts of debt.

Liquidity The ability to provide cash to meet day-to-day needs as they arise.

Long-term loans (LTL) Bank and other loans of more than one year.

Market to book ratio The relationship between the balance sheet value of the ordinary shares and their market value. The expression 'price to book' is also used.

Market capitalization The notional total market value of a company calculated from the latest quoted market price of the share multiplied by the number of shares. The quoted price may not give an accurate value for the total shares, it may refer to only one small block of shares.

Market value weights In cost of capital calculations, the weighted cost can be derived using either the book value or market value weights to determine the overall weighted cost.

Matching principle A rule that a firm should match short-term uses of funds with short-term sources and long-term uses with long-term sources.

Minority interests The book value of shares in a subsidiary that are owned by members who are not shareholders of the parent company.

Miscellaneous current assets Sundry receivables and pre-payments due for realization within one year.

Miscellaneous long-term funds A composite entry in the balance sheet that may include deferred tax, unamortized government grants, provision for pensions and so on.

Money market A term applied to the trading in short-term financial instruments in London.

Mutually exclusive projects In an investment appraisal exercise these are projects that compete with one another so that the acceptance of one means the exclusion of the others.

Net working capital *See working capital.*

Net worth (NW) The sum of common ordinary shares plus all reserves plus preference shares less intangibles assets.

Net present value (NPV) A positive or negative value arrived at by discounting the cash flow from a capital project by the desired rate of return. If the value is positive, it means that the project is financially desirable and vice versa.

NOPAT Net operating profit after tax (see chapter 17 for explanation).

Off-balance sheet A term that refers to borrowing that does not appear on the balance sheet. Sometimes achieved by a finance lease that gives the lessee all the risks and rewards, but not the legal status, of ownership.

Opportunity cost The alternative advantage foregone as a result of the commitment of resources to one particular end.

Optimal capital structure The point at which the cost of capital to a company is reduced to the minimum by the best mix of debt and equity.

Option A financial instrument that gives the holder the right, but not the obligation, to purchase or sell a specified asset at a specified price on or before a set date. *See put option; call option.*

Owners funds (OF) The sum of the issued shares, capital reserves and revenue reserves. The total represents the assets remaining to the shareholders after all prior claims have been satisfied.

Over the counter (OTC) Refers to the market where shares and financial instruments are traded outside the formal exchanges.

Overtrading A company is in an overtrading situation when there is not sufficient *liquidity* to meet comfortably the day-to-day cash needs of the existing level of business. There is constant danger of bankruptcy, even though the company may be trading profitably. Such a situation can come about because of past trading losses, excessive expansion and so on, but can be cured by the injection of long-term funds or, maybe, the sale of fixed assets.

Paid borrowing percentage The percentage of non-equity funds consisting of interest-bearing debt.

Par value A notional value assigned to a share largely for accounting purposes.

Payback period A term used in investment appraisal. It refers to the time required for the non-discounted cash in-flow to accumulate to the initial cash out-flow in the investment.

Payout ratio The percentage of earnings available for distribution that is paid out in dividends. This ratio is the reciprocal of *dividend cover*.

Preference capital Shares that have preferential rights over common shares. These rights normally relate to distribution of dividends and repayment of capital. The shares usually carry a fixed dividend but also carry very little voting power.

Preferred creditors Creditors who, in an insolvency, have a statutory right to be paid in full before any other claims. Employees who have pay due to them would normally be in this category.

Present value (P/V) A sum calculated by discounting the stream of future cash flow from a project using an interest rate equal to the desired rate of return. It differs from *net present value* in that the amount of the investment is not included in the cash flows.

Price to earnings multiple (PE) The value derived by dividing the current share price by the *earnings per share*. Latest reported earnings or prospective earnings for the coming year may be used in the calculation.

Prime rate The rate at which banks lend to corporations with the highest credit ratings.

Profitability index A measure for assessing the relative merit of an investment by expressing the present value of the future cash flows as a percentage of the investment amount.

Profit after tax (PAT) Profit available for the shareholders after interest and tax has been deducted.

Profit before interest, tax and depreciation (PBITD) This value corresponds very closely to cash flow from trading.

Profit before interest and tax (PBIT) Operating profit plus other income.

Profit before tax (PBT) Operating profit plus other income less total interest charged.

Pro forma statements Projected financial statements

Proxy vote Vote cast by an authorized person on behalf of another.

Put option An option to sell. *See also option*.

Quick ratio (acid test) A short-term liquidity ratio calculated by dividing current assets less inventories by current liabilities.

Retained earnings (RE) The final figure from the profit and loss account that is transferred to reserves in the balance sheet.

Repurchase agreement (REPO) A technique for providing short-term cash to a borrower who agrees to sell a security at one price and buy it back at a slightly higher price in the future. The price difference is the effective interest payment to the lender.

Return on capital This is profit before tax but after interest as a percentage of capital employed.

Revenue reserves Increases in shareholders' funds that have arisen from retained profits and are available for distribution as dividends.

Rights issue A new issue of shares made by a company to its existing shareholders at a price below the current market value.

Risk-free rate of interest The yield available on government *gilts*.

Return on assets (ROA) Profit before interest and tax as percentage of total assets. The corresponding term used in this book is return on total assets.

Return on capital employed (ROCE) Capital employed includes all the long-term funds in the balance sheet, that is shareholders' funds plus long-term loan plus miscellaneous long-term funds. Profit before tax is often expressed as a percentage of this to give return on capital employed. However, as the denominator includes long-term loan, the corresponding interest on these loans should be added back into the numerator.

Return on equity (ROE) A measure of the percentage return generated by a company for the equity shareholders. It is calculated by expressing profit after tax as a percentage of shareholders' funds. (Where preference shares exist, they should first be deducted from shareholders' funds and the preference dividends also be deducted from the profit figure.)

Return on invested capital (ROIC) See chapter 17 for explanation.

Return on investment (ROI) A term that is very widely used in connection with the performance of a company or project. It is calculated in many different ways. Usually a pre-tax profit figure is expressed as a percentage of either the long-term funds or the total funds in the balance sheet.

Return on total assets (ROTA) Profit before interest and tax expressed as a percentage of total assets.

Sales and leaseback agreement A method of raising finance whereby a firm sells property to the funding agency and simultaneously signs a long-term lease agreement. The company receives an immediate lump sum in exchange for a series of lease payments in the future.

Sales to fixed assets (times) An activity and performance ratio, calculated by dividing the net fixed assets value in the balance sheet into the sales turnover figure.

Senior debt Debt that ranks ahead of junior, or, subordinated debt in the event of a liquidation. *See subordinated debt.*

Sensitivity analysis Analysis of the change in the output values of an equation from small changes in input values. It is used to assess the risk in an investment project.

Share premium The difference between a share's nominal value and its sale price.

Shareholders' funds Issued ordinary shares plus reserves plus preference shares.

Spontaneous financing Short-term financing that automatically results from the normal operations of the business. Creditors/accounts payable and certain accruals are the main sources.

Short-term loans (STL) The bank overdraft, current portion of long term debt and other interest-bearing liabilities due within one year.

Subordinated debt Debt that ranks for repayment after *senior debt.*

Subsidiaries A company is a subsidiary of another if the other owns more than 50 per cent of the equity or effectively controls the company by means of voting shares or composition of the board of directors.

Sundry accruals An entry in the current liabilities section of the balance sheet that includes sundry accounts payable plus accrued dividends, interest, tax plus other accruals.

SWAP The exchange of debt and/or currency obligations between parties to their mutual benefit. The benefit can arise from their differing needs for currency and/or fixed/floating interest charges.

Tangible assets The total of all assets in the balance sheet less intangibles, such as goodwill.

Tax rate The apparent rate of tax on profit found by expressing tax charged in the accounts as a percentage of profit before tax.

Term loan Usually a medium-term loan (three to seven years) repaid in fixed, periodic instalments that cover both interest and principal over the life of the loan.

Terminal value A notional cash in-flow attributed to a capital project to allow for value remaining in the project at the final year of the assessment.

Total assets The sum of fixed assets plus intangibles plus investments plus current assets.

Treasury stock Ordinary or common shares that have been repurchased by the company.

Ultra vires 'Beyond authorized powers.' An act is deemed to be *ultra vires* if carried out by an agent or director of a company in excess of their authority. The person who so acts may incur personal liability.

Underwriting Banks or other financial institutions guarantee to take up an issue of shares at a specific price in order to ensure the success of the issue. This process in called underwriting.

Variable costs A type of cost where the total expenditure varies in proportion to activity or output.

Weighted average cost of capital (WACC) *See cost of capital.*

Warrant Sometimes attached to loan stock as a sweetener at the time of issue, warrants give an option to the holder to purchase a stated amount of equities at a fixed price for a defined period.

Window dressing The alteration of financial statements at the time of publication to give an artificially improved appearance to the company situation. For instance the temporary sale of inventories to a bank with agreement to repurchase could give an enhanced view of company liquidity.

Working capital The excess of current assets over current liabilities.

Working capital days The length of the working capital cycle is often calculated as inventories plus accounts receivable less accounts payable days.

Working capital to sales A liquidity ratio that is calculated by expressing working capital as a percentage of sales.

Z-growth factor A value that gives an indication of the self-funding growth rate of a company. It is calculated by expressing retained earnings before *extraordinary items* as a percentage of opening owners funds. It is assumed for this calculation that all assets are linearly related to sales, likewise all items in the profit and loss account. It also assumes that existing debt to equity ratios will be maintained.

Zero coupon bond A bond that pays no interest but is issued at a discount on its face value. The redemption of the bond at par ensures the desired yield to the purchaser.

Index

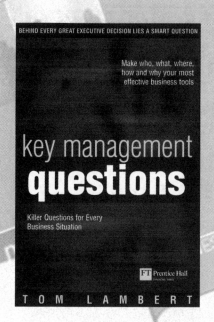

More power to your [business-mind]

Even at the end there's more we can learn. More that *we* can learn from your experience of this book, and more ways to add to *your* learning experience.

For who to read, what to know and where to go in the world of business, visit us at **business-minds.com**.

Here you can find out more about the people and ideas that can make you and your business more innovative and productive. Each month our e-newsletter, *Business-minds Express*, delivers an infusion of thought leadership, guru interviews, new business practice and reviews of key business resources directly to you. Subscribe for free at

▶ **www.business-minds.com/goto/newsletters**

Here you can also connect with ways of putting these ideas to work. Spreading knowledge is a great way to improve performance and enhance business relationships. If you found this book useful, then so might your colleagues or customers. If you would like to explore corporate purchases or custom editions personalised with your brand or message, then just get in touch at

▶ **www.business-minds.com/corporatesales**

We're also keen to learn from your experience of our business books – so tell us what you think of this book and what's on *your* business mind with an online reader report at business-minds.com. Together with our authors, we'd like to hear more from you and explore new ways to help make these ideas work at

▶ **www.business-minds.com/goto/feedback**

[www.business-minds.com
www.financialminds.com]